Tastes of Jewish Tradition

Recipes, Activities & Stories for the Whole Family

Harold & Terry Nash JCC Parenting & Family Center

Jody Hirsh, Idy Goodman, Aggie Goldenholz and Susan Roth

Rabbi Joseph Telushkin

Tastes of Jewish Tradition

Recipes, Activities & Stories for the Whole Family

Proceeds from *Tastes of Jewish Tradition* will be used to support and expand the Family and Jewish education at the Harry & Rose Samson Family Jewish Community Center.

Copyright © 2002

Harry & Rose Samson Family
Jewish Community Center of Milwaukee
6255 N. Santa Monica Boulevard
Milwaukee, WI 53217-4353

Cover Art by Betsy Kaplan

Cover Design by Deb Lessila

Text Design by Julie Rivera

Illustrations by Cindy Cooper

First Printing January 2002

Library of Congress Catalog Card Number 2001096649

ISBN 0-9713461-0-0

Printed in the USA by

WIMMER

C O O K B O O K S

Memphis
1-800-548-2537

Dedication

This book is dedicated to my grandmother, Fannie Brafman Bloom, or "Nannie" as we call her. The author of Milwaukee's first kosher cookbook, my grandmother has always dreamed of publishing a cookbook for children. *Tastes of Jewish Tradition* is that and so much more.

Fannie Brafman Bloom was one of the first kosher caterers in Milwaukee. Whether we are visiting over a corned beef sandwich at Benji's or chicken salad at Heineman's, someone will invariably come over to make conversation: "Your grandmother catered my daughter's wedding (or my son's bar mitzvah)…We go way back, your grandmother and I." They will share a smile or a wink and then Nannie will ask about their lives. She played an integral role in so many people's simchas and they love her for it.

Nannie also dedicated herself to our family's holiday traditions and rituals. I remember the Shabbat dinners she hosted in her 51st Street flat with the long skinny hallway and the deafening front door buzzer. She would gather her sisters' families and anyone who didn't have a place to celebrate the Sabbath. We would talk and laugh over my grandmother's noodle kugel, chicken soup and borscht.

My grandmother worked her magic on our Rosh HaShanah celebrations as well. She served steaming plates of kishke, stuffed cabbage rolls, brisket and potato kugel, and she only had one oven! Her table was the backdrop for lively discussions of our respective rabbis' sermons and sometimes my Uncle Abe would tell stories about his heroic escape from Russia.

After our bellies were full and the last card table chair had been folded, my grandmother would emerge from her bedroom with a white cardboard box from the Boston Store. Rows of mandelbrot, almond cookies and apple strudel resting on pastel wrappers lined the box. On the cover of each package she scrawled "For you to enjoy."

Nannie's Jewish rituals have provided me with a sense of my own Jewish identity and the traditional tastes she introduced in my life linger on my palette. Each Friday I set my table with my grandmother's china, silver, and white lace tablecloth, and family and friends gather in our home to welcome the Sabbath. On behalf of my family, I hope that this book will be a resource for you to create your own Jewish traditions and rituals. So here it is… *Tastes of Jewish Tradition* …"For you to enjoy."

MICHELLE BRAFMAN HELF

About the Authors

Jody Hirsh, a Ph.D. candidate in modern Hebrew literature, an internationally known and highly respected Jewish educator, served as the key consultant as well as a contributing author. Mr. Hirsh has held prominent positions as a Jewish educator in Los Angeles, Houston, and Hong Kong and has taught Jewish studies at UCLA, UC Berkeley, Hebrew Union College and LA's University of Judaism. He currently serves as the Director of Judaic Education at the Jewish Community Center in Milwaukee. As a playwright, Mr. Hirsh is a 1989 OBIE Award winner.

Idy Goodman holds a Master's in Jewish Education from Cleveland College of Jewish Studies and a Master's Degree in Special Education from the University of Wisconsin. As the Jewish Family Educator at the Jewish Community Center of Milwaukee, Idy plans, coordinates and facilitates a wide range of Family Education programs.

Aggie Goldenholz received her Master's in Jewish Studies from the Cleveland College of Jewish Studies. She is Director of Judaic Education at the New Orleans Jewish Day School.

Susan Roth holds a Bachelor's degree in education and social work. She began as an early childhood teacher but upon moving to Milwaukee in 1986, Susan envisioned and developed The Parenting Center at the Milwaukee JCC. Susan is continually creating a myriad of new programming, adding to her already long list of tried and true classes for infants, toddlers, young children, new moms and young families.

About the Artists

Cindy Cooper is a popular Milwaukee illustrator whose work includes children's workshops, puppet shows and Ketubot (elaborate Jewish marriage contracts). She received a Bachelor's in Fine Arts & Teaching Certificate from the University of Wisconsin-Milwaukee. She is currently an artist on staff at the Coalition for Jewish Learning.

Betsy Kaplan, whose artwork graces the cover of *Tastes of Jewish Tradition,* is inspired by her Jewish roots and passion for nature and animals. Her greatest wish is that her art brings fun and enchantment to every space it touches.

Table of Contents

Foreword by Rabbi Joseph Telushkin

Introduction

Shabbat 1

Rosh HaShanah 23

Yom Kippur 41

Sukkot 55

Hanukkah 69

Tu Bishvat 89

Purim 105

Passover 125

Lag B'Omer 149

Yom Ha'Atzmaut 161

Shavuot 177

Recipes 191

   In the Beginning (Appetizers, Breads, Salads & Soups) 192

   Then There Was (Main & Side Dishes) 218

   And in the End (Desserts) 250

Templates 270

Prayers and Blessings 283

Index 289

Foreword

In 1965, *Look* magazine published a cover story on the "Vanishing American Jew," which predicted that by the year 2000, the Jews of the United States would number about two million and be on the road to eventual extinction. More than thirty-five years have passed and, as my friend Michael Medved has noted, "Look at the Jewish people and look at *Look* magazine."

Indeed, one sign that the Jews are not only not becoming extinct, but are actually thriving, is *Tastes of Jewish Tradition,* this exciting new publication of the Harry & Rose Samson Family Jewish Community Center of Milwaukee. Hundreds of people have cooperated and sent in recipes and reminisces, original art and heartfelt reflections, all revolving around the theme of the Jewish holidays. Had someone predicted in 1965, when *Look* published its pessimistic prognosis that such an event, supported by the efforts of so many people, would happen in Milwaukee in 2000, they probably would have been dismissed as hopelessly naïve.

One of the things that so impresses me about this volume is the way in which it invites its readers in, almost like at a Hasidic rebbe's *tisch* (table). First, you learn about the holiday, its origin and meaning, then you are given suggestions on how to experience it and are also offered a selection of texts. There are stories for children and a menu that enables even the greatest Jewish novice to become something of an instant *maven.*

I am confident that many Jews will return to this book year after year, providing their families with holiday experiences that are intellectual, emotional, spiritual, dynamic and very filling. I extend my sincerest congratulations to the Harry & Rose Samson Family Jewish Community Center of Milwaukee, Wisconsin.

There is a popular proverb in Jewish life: "More than the Jews have kept the Sabbath, the Sabbath has kept the Jews." This teaching applies, of course, to all the other holidays as well. And *Tastes of Jewish Tradition* is going to play a wonderful role in keeping and inspiring Jews for a long time to come.

RABBI JOSEPH TELUSHKIN

Introduction

Tastes of Jewish Tradition was created by the Harold and Terry Nash Parenting & Family Center of the Harry & Rose Samson Family Jewish Community Center of Milwaukee. The book was written in the spirit of our mission of encouraging the transmission of Jewish traditions, values, and rituals from parents to children. It represents the collective effort of a Jewish community committed to Jewish education.

What is the Harold and Terry Nash Parenting & Family Center of the Harry & Rose Samson Family Jewish Community Center of Milwaukee?

In spite of our very long name, we began modestly in 1986 with ten Jewish moms who needed companionship, support and a community. We developed a playgroup here, a music class there, but mostly we personally reached out to other mothers one by one. We listened to their needs; we engaged them in developing programs and then we asked them to help us determine how we were doing.

This personal approach of "consumer driven" programming has resulted in our continued growth in numbers and program development, so that today we have over 800 families participating in over 40 classes each week. These include classes in music, art and gym, support groups on a variety of topics, Shabbat and holiday programs, concerts, parent educational seminars and community-wide Judaic family events.

Why was *Tastes of Jewish Tradition* created?

The Parenting Center provides Judaic learning at every turn through song, music, stories and play. Parents' desire to "take it all home" was the impetus for our creating this book.

Originally, the book was conceived as a cookbook. But as most endeavors of the JCC Parenting Center, it quickly evolved into a community project. Parents provided the vision, direction, recipes and decision-making power. Our Jewish educators, rabbis, local artists and JCC staff became the authors.

How Do I Use *Tastes of Jewish Tradition?*

We feel the title to be especially apt as we provide you with a "taste" of Jewish tradition. Judaism is a rich, multi-level, ancient—while contemporary—religion and culture. Our expectations are that you and your children [and grandchildren] will use *Tastes of Jewish Tradition* to deepen your understanding of Judaism and find a place for its rituals and traditions in your homes.

Eleven significant Jewish holidays are highlighted. Each chapter includes explanations of the holiday, its purpose, how to celebrate it and the biblical origin. The book is designed so that people of all ages and people with all levels of Jewish knowledge and background will find the information useful, interesting and fun. In addition to knowledge-based information found in Experiencing the Holiday, Traditions and Text, and Fascinating Food Facts sections, each chapter includes a read-aloud story to tickle the imagination, recipes to create delicious and beautiful holiday meals and creative projects and crafts that will both entice your children and help decorate your home.

This is a resource book. You may pull it out at any time, start at any point, pick a recipe, a craft, teach your children about a holiday or read a bedtime story. Our hope is that this book wets your appetite to further explore Jewish holidays, traditions and Midrash. *Tastes of Jewish Tradition* is a journey that will connect you and your children to our ancestors and to a future of continuing traditions.

A special thank you to the **Stuart and Lotta Brafman Family**, whose strong belief in "L'dor V'dor" and their support, encouragement and generosity, made *Tastes of Jewish Tradition* possible.

Director of Parenting Center:
Susan Roth

Committee Chairs:
Julie Rosenfeld
Cheryl Moser
Sandi Deshur Cayle

Developmental Editor:
Betsy Ellis - Our heartfelt thanks for elevating this book to a higher level.

Editors:
Lisa Aiken
Pnina Goldfarb
Rebecca Guralnick
Michelle Merens
Lisa Atkin Vondra
Sarahn Williams
Susan Pittelman-whose insight and expertise guided us from dream to reality.

Contributing Writers:
Nir Barkin
Pnina Goldfarb
Holly Williamson

Judaic Advisor:
Jody Hirsh

Financial Advisor:
Patricia Goodstein

Culinary Advisor:
Rebecca Guralnick

Desktop Publishers:
Lindsey Booth
Janice Courchaine
Rose Delaney
Deborah Oknin

Proofreaders:
Esther Kahn
Clare Hamilton
Lisa Vondra

A special warm thanks to our wonderful JCC staff, who gave so much of their time and creativity.

Authors of Read-Aloud Stories:
Rabbi David Cohen
Sharon Cohen
Cindy Cooper
Rabbi David Fine
Jody Hirsh
Marty Katz
Liza Wiemer

Title Page Artists:
Cindy Benjamin
Vicki Chiger
Cindy Cooper
Shelly Jubelirer
Barbara Kohl Spiro
Lise Meisner
Karen Mittenthal
Linda Sugarman Mollick
Jeanine Semon
Holly Williamson
Ardis Zarem

Tastes of Jewish Tradition, **Cooking and Tasting Committee:**
Sandi Deshur Cayle
Sharon Cohen
Kathy Davis
Carrie Ellerbrock
Jennifer Friedman
Idy Goodman
Sabina Hack
Jill Katz
Julie Mezrow
Cheryl Moser
Sharyl Paley
Julie Rosenfeld
Susan Roth
Marla Rothenberg
Sheryl Rubin
Shari Sadek
Naomi Sobel
June Wallace

Crafts and Activities Committee:
Sharon Cohen
Aggie Goldenholz
Idy Goodman
Lenny Kass
Marsha Loeb
Cheryl Moser
Sarahn Williams
Mary Yanny

Special thanks to Cindy Cooper and Alice Jacobson from the Coalition for Jewish Learning (CJL), for consultation and use of materials.

Tastes of Jewish Tradition wants to thank everyone who donated their favorite recipes. Unfortunately, due to space limitations, we couldn't include all of the recipes.

Recipe Contributors and Tasters:

Naomi Arbit
Robin Arenzon
Nancy Baime
Cheryl Baraty
Maureen Bard
Elizabeth Beauchamp
Linda Berman
Natanya Blanck
Judy Bluestone
Barb Bodner
Marilyn Bodner
Fannie Brafman Bloom
Sharon Brink
Jill Brodkey
Jayne Butlein
Debbie Callif
Elaine Callif
Linda Cayle
Shari Cayle
Jane Chernof
Sara Cherny
Belle Cohen
Sharon Cohen
Toby Colton
Julie Cooley
Joanne Davidson
Kathy Davis
Rita Degen
Sandi Deshur Cayle
Penny Deshur
Dana Dorf
Eva Dorf
Ellen Dryden
Jill Eder
Marge Eiseman

Jennie Elias
Carrie Ellerbrock
Patty Fedderly
Cheryl Fielkow
Neena Florsheim
Dori Frankel-Steigman
Elaine Friedman
Jennifer Friedman
Heidi Gardipee
Ethel Gill
Donna Glassman
Aggie Goldenholz
Pnina Goldfarb
Julia Goldsmith
Abby Goodman
Bill Goodman
Idy Goodman
Patricia Goodstein
Lisa Gorelick
Dorothy Granof
Rebecca Guralnick
Joyce Gutzke
Sabina Hack
Helen Hamilton
Beryl Harris
Barbara Heilbronner
Sara Hermanoff
Cheryl Himmelhoff
Jody Hirsh
Dorothy Holman
Mayme Isenberg
Betty Jones
Esther Kahn
Sylvia Kahn
Debbie Kasle

Debra Katz
Jill Katz
Marty Katz
Mary Kaufman
Meg Kinney
Judy Kleiner
Shelly Kominsky
Maureen Komisar-
   Schatz
Debbie Lakritz
Rixanne Lefco
Cindy Levy
Sari Luber
Sylvia Luber
Ann Marciano
Marc Mayerhoff
Michael Mazur
Bonnie McLean
Cheryl Mendelson
Barrie Merar
Ruth Messnick
Julie Mezrow
Bea Miller
Cheryl Moser
Jeff Nelson
Meg Nelson
Stacey Nye
Lena Obar
Dorene Paley
Sharyl Paley
Janna Papermaster
Barbara Perchonok
Susan Pittelman
Stephanie Redpath
Lola Rosenblatt

Julie Rosenfeld
Linda Ross
Susan Roth
Marla Rothenberg
Harriet Rothman
Sheryl Rubin
Jane Rublein
Shari Sadek
Alicia Sadoff
Marcia Sadowsky
Marla Satinsky
Meg Schies
Eva Schneiderman
Beverly Schuminsky
Leslie Schwartz
Diane Sehler
Micki Seinfeld
Esther Shaw
Talma Silver
Diane Sobel
Naomi Sobel
Rachel Sprung
Julie Stasiak
Chickie Steinberger
Masha Wagner
June Wallace
Ruth Wallace
Ilene Wasserman
Patty Weigler
Emily Weiss
Sarahn Williams
Kathleen Witkin
Merri Wymann
Gina Yauck
Diane Zall

Cindy Cooper

Shabbat

Imagine a place that you can go to get away from your rushed life. Imagine a place where you are surrounded by friends and family. Smell the aroma of baking challah and the fragrance of fresh flowers. See the world as it is meant to be. Can you feel the wonder and miracles all around you? This is Shabbat.

Experiencing Shabbat

From sunset on Friday until sunset on Saturday, we celebrate the perfection of the world God* created. We celebrate Shabbat.

Making Shabbat with our family is one of the most significant steps in creating a Jewish home and strong Jewish identity. It is the high point of the Jewish week. Some families make an extra effort to sit down together to share a meal. Many bake braided challah for the Shabbat table. Small children can participate by making their own miniature loaves. This is also a wonderful night to invite friends over to join you for dinner, perhaps for a joyous potluck supper.

As the sun sets, we come together to light and bless the candles, and to say the blessings over the wine and challah. In addition to thanking God for helping us through all the ups and downs of the week, parents say a special blessing over their children.

Each family must decide what makes Shabbat meaningful for them. Some families eat dinner and then go to the synagogue for services. Others have a quiet Friday evening, reading together or playing games. Some families attend Shabbat services Saturday morning. Some people choose not to drive, answer the telephone, or conduct business in any way. Others refrain from typical weekend activities such as movies, television, or shopping. You might decide to put away your watch or cell phone for the day. The important thing is to set this day aside from the rest of the week, making it a time for rest, reflection, study, and renewal.

As the sun sets on Saturday night and the first three stars appear in the sky, we are ready to say goodbye to Shabbat with a special service called Havdalah. The word *Havdalah* means "separation" and represents the marker between the holiness of Shabbat and the "busyness" of the weekdays.

At Havdalah we recite blessings, light a braided candle, and pass a small container filled with sweet-smelling spices (such as cloves, nutmeg, orange peel, and allspice) from person to person until all have had a chance to inhale the pungent aroma. We say blessings over the wine, and as we extinguish the flame of the candle in the wine cup, we wish everyone a sweet and peaceful week to come. Shabbat is over.

As a sign of respect and reverence, many Jews are reluctant to write out God's name and write "G-d" instead of "God." We, in keeping with many Jewish texts published in English, and with the understanding that the English word is not actually the name of God, consistently spell "God" fully.

Traditions & Text

The Torah is ambiguous about why we should, in fact, observe Shabbat. The Ten Commandments appear twice in the Torah, and each time give us a different rationale.

In Exodus, Chapter 20, we are told we should observe the Shabbat *"for in six days the Lord made heaven and earth, the sea, and all that is in them, and rested on the seventh day; wherefore the Lord blessed the Sabbath day, and hallowed it."*

Yet in Deuteronomy, Chapter 5, the Torah tells us that *"thou shalt remember that thou wast a servant in the land of Egypt, and the Lord thy God brought thee out from there with a mighty hand and an outstretched arm; therefore, the Lord thy God commanded thee to keep the Sabbath day."*

Shabbat, then, is defined as two things: an imitation of God—we refrain from working on the seventh day just as God did; and a proof of our freedom—unlike slaves, free men can choose to rest from their toil.

How to observe the Sabbath, too, is ambiguous. We are told that *"Thou shalt not do any manner of work,"* but the Torah leaves the definition of "work" to the Rabbis.

OF BRIDES...

Five hundred years ago, in the holy city of Tzfat, in the mountains of northern Israel, the rabbis had a unique ritual. Just as the sun was setting on Friday, they would dress in pure white and go into the fields. There they would welcome the Sabbath Bride, saying: "Come, let us greet the Sabbath Bride!" For the rabbis, the bride was the perfect symbol of the Sabbath. The mystics would tell us today that it was almost as though the whole of Israel was in love with the Sabbath. They loved and took care of her, and she loved and took care of them. This custom has remained with us ever since. During the *Kabbalat Shabbat* service, we still sing a special song to welcome the Sabbath Bride—the *L'cha Dodi*.

...AND ANGELS

Our sages tell us that two angels, a good angel and an evil one, walk along with each Jew coming home from the synagogue on *Erev Shabbat* (Sabbath Eve). When the Jew enters his house and finds the Sabbath candles lit and the table set, the good angel says, "May it be so every other Shabbat," and the evil angel, against his will, says, "Amen!" If the Jew finds no candles lit or table set, the evil angel says, "May it be so every other Shabbat," and the good angel, against his will, says, "Amen!" [Babylonian Talmud, Shabbat 119a]

Fascinating Food Facts

The most recognizable Shabbat food is the Challah—that braided loaf of bread that we bless at the beginning of the meal. The braided loaf is an *Ashkenazic* (Jewish European) tradition that seems to have spread throughout the whole Jewish world.

On Shabbat, the tradition is to say the blessing over two loaves of bread. We are told that because two portions of mana were given to Moses and the Israelites in the desert for Shabbat, there were two sacrifices offered in the Temple on Shabbat. We bless two loaves to remember those two sacrifices. Traditionally, we sprinkle salt on the challah (or dip it in salt) to remind us of the saltiness of the burnt offerings.

Many years ago, people made bread to be used as an offering in the Temple. They would pull off a piece of the uncooked dough and take it to the priests in the Temple. That piece of dough was called "challah." The priests would bake it as an offering and eat it themselves. Only the priests were permitted to eat the challah.

The official way to bake a challah today is to take a part of the dough and let it burn in the oven. This burnt piece is actually the challah . Since we no longer have consecrated priests who make offerings, NO ONE is allowed to eat this extra piece of dough. Today, we call the part of the loaf that we DO eat "challah," even though, in truth, the challah is actually the part that we *don't* eat.

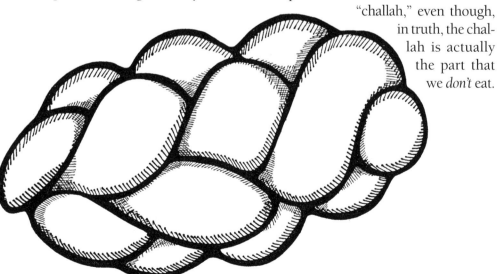

Traditional Shabbat Menu

In a traditional home, blessings are said in a certain order. When beginning your own Shabbat rituals, begin with the blessings you feel comfortable with, gradually adding blessings as you wish. (The letter in parenthesis indicates the appropriate blessing found in "Prayers & Blessings" on p. 283)

The following is a suggested order for the blessings:

The following foods are traditional on most holidays, but feel free to use any of the many delicious recipes in this book.

Blessing over the candles (I)
"Shalom Aleichem"
The husband blesses his wife (K)
The parents bless the children (L)
Blessing over the wine (C)   Wine (or grape juice)
Blessing for hand washing (A)
Blessing over the bread (B)   Challah

Chicken Soup

Salad

Brisket, Chicken or Fish

Potatoes, Rice or Kugel

Yellow, orange or
green vegetable

Dessert

Blessing after the meal
(Birkat HaMazon)(H)

GO TO RECIPE INDEX IN BACK OF BOOK FOR SUGGESTED RECIPES.

Shabbat dinner can be as simple or as involved as you like. Some families treat Shabbat dinner as a formal occasion, but don't let that stop you. No time to prepare? Order a pizza! Try serving pizza on your good china. Or use paper plates. The important thing is not what you eat but that you set aside time to eat together as a family.

Kids in the Kitchen Recipe

My mother-in-law lived in Israel and would spend every Friday morning making challah in her old-fashioned kitchen. Each Shabbat her grandchildren would laugh or giggle while creating their very own miniature challah. The sharing experience between grandparent and grandchild created a special bond and added such sweetness to the Shabbat dinner.

~ Sharon Cohen

CHALLAH SURPRISE

Either use the challah recipe found on page 201 or use a frozen bread dough (to make this more child-friendly)

COOKING EQUIPMENT NEEDED:

Baking sheets or loaf pans

Towel

Pastry brush

Small bowl

Fork

INGREDIENTS:

1 bag of frozen bread dough

1 bar of parve chocolate candy

DIRECTIONS:

1 Following directions on dough package, allow dough to rise.

2 Divide in 3 small loaves.

3 Divide each small loaf into 3 balls. Roll between your hands to make a snake. Repeat with other balls as well.

4 Take your 3 "snakes" and pinch together at the top. Braid until about halfway through—then add the surprise!

5 To each half braided loaf, place a small piece of parve chocolate. Continue braiding until entire loaf is braided and chocolate is hidden.

6 Place each loaf on a greased baking sheet or loaf pan. Cover with towel and allow to rise until double in size (about 2 hours).

7 Bake in a preheated 350 degree oven.

8 Mix 1 raw egg yolk with 1 teaspoon of water. Brush the loaves for a shiny crust. Sprinkle with sesame or poppy seeds if desired.

9 Bake for 15 minutes to brown crust. Then reduce heat to 325 degrees and bake for an additional 15 minutes.

10 Cool and remove from pans.

Read-Aloud Story

The Rabbi and The Emperor

Babylonian Talmud
Retold by Jody Hirsh

Rabbi Judah, the Prince, was good friends with the Roman Emperor Antoninus. One day, the emperor invited the rabbi to eat dinner in his palace. The rabbi ate fruit and pastries the likes of which he had never tasted. The next Friday night, Rabbi Judah invited the emperor to eat at his house. They ate soup, roasted meat, stewed vegetables, pastries, and wines. It was all delicious. It was better than any meal the emperor had ever eaten. "I must eat here again!" said the emperor to the rabbi.

"Come again next Wednesday," the rabbi said.

The next Wednesday, the emperor appeared at the rabbi's house ready for a meal grander than the last. Rabbi Judah served the exact same menu: soup, roasted meat, stewed vegetables, pastries and wines—but somehow the meal wasn't nearly as good as it had been the previous week.

"What's the matter with our food?" asked the emperor. "It's good, of course, but it's not nearly as delicious as it was last week!"

"Ah!" said the rabbi. "That's because I used a special spice last week which made the food taste all the better."

"And what is that special spice?" demanded the emperor. "I must have it!"

"The special spice," said the rabbi, "is Shabbat."

Shabbat Crafts and Activities

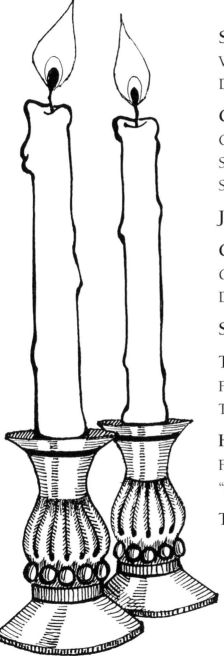

Shabbat Candles
Wax Crystal Candles
Dipped Candles

Candlesticks
Glitter Globe Candlesticks
Soda Bottle Candlesticks
Salt Dough Candlesticks

Jeweled Kiddush Cup

Challah Covers
Collage Challah Cover
Dye-Painted Challah Cover

Shabbat Tablecloths

Tzedakah Boxes
Fimo Clay Tzedakah Box
Tissue Paper Covered Tzedakah Box

Havdalah Spice Boxes
Fruit with Cloves
"Stained-Glass" Spice Bottle

Twisted Havdalah Candles

Shabbat Candles

Because we are commanded first "to observe" and second "to remember" (Exodus 20:8 and Deuteronomy 5:12), at least two candles are lit to welcome the Shabbat. Traditionally, these candles are lit at least eighteen minutes before sunset and are meant to burn throughout dinner. These flickering flames evoke a feeling of wonder and warmth.

Safety hint: Due to Shabbat prohibitions, candlesticks (or anything else to do with fire) should not be moved once they are lit. If you are leaving your home, light the candles in a fire-safe place (like the sink or the stovetop) or cut the candles in half before lighting them, to reduce their burning time.

WAX CRYSTAL CANDLES

MATERIALS:

Wax Crystals – available at craft stores, in many colors, packaged in bags or large containers.

Wax coated wicks – available in craft stores

Disposable container to hold each different color of wax crystals

Plastic spoons or coffee measuring scoops

Straight-sided and cylindrical, clean glass containers such as baby food jars or jelly jars

Toothpicks, thin paintbrush handles, small dowels, or other stick-like tools

DIRECTIONS:

1 Spoon a layer of wax crystals into your glass container.

Hint: Tilt the container so the wax layer is angled. You may or may not want to angle subsequent layers. Each layer can be a different color.

2 Add a second layer. You can slide the toothpick or other tools down along the inside edge of the glass container, pushing the second layer into the first. You can also wait to do this until several layers of wax crystal are added. Experiment.

3 Add several more layers of wax crystal.

4 Stick the waxed wick into the center of the finished candle. It will stand on its own. Trim the wick to about ¾ inch above the top of the last layer of wax.

Hint: Plan on having each child make at least two candles to light on Shabbat.

DIPPED CANDLES

RECOMMENDED FOR OLDER CHILDREN. ADULT SUPERVISION REQUIRED.

MATERIALS:

Tall, wide cans such as coffee cans, with their labels removed

Frying pan or crock pot large enough to hold the cans

Paraffin – CAUTION: Paraffin is highly flammable. Do not overheat or leave unattended.

2 Wicks – each 1½ times the length of the candles (If you want to make 10-inch candles, cut 15-inch wicks.)

Old crayons – with the paper removed and sorted by color

Bucket of cold water

2 Long pencils

DIRECTIONS:

1 Add water to the pan, so that the pan is ⅓ full. Heat the water over a low heat, but do not let boil.

2 Place the cans into the pan of heated water, using one can for each color. Add chunks of paraffin to the cans.

3 Let the wax melt, adding enough paraffin so that the cans are ½ to ⅔ full of melted wax. Caution: Do not let boil. Never leave melting wax unattended. It is flammable.

4 Add crayon stubs to the melted wax— the more crayons used, the deeper the color. Add only one color crayon per can of wax.

5 Turn the heat down. The water in the pan should be kept warm enough to keep the wax liquid.

6 Tie each wick to the middle of a pencil.

7 Dip each wick quickly into the first color of wax.

8 Lift each wick and let it drip into the can of melted wax.

9 Plunge the wax-coated wicks into the bucket of cool water.

10 Repeat the above three steps until the candles are the thickness you desire.

Variation: You can dip the candle into alternative colors and at different depths to create a rainbow effect. Experiment to discover what you like. As candles melt, the different color waxes appear.

Candlesticks

Many Jewish homes display collections of beautiful Judaica, which are handed down from generation to generation or purchased for their special appeal, thus fulfilling the mitzvah of embellishing the Sabbath.

GLITTER GLOBE CANDLESTICKS

MATERIALS:

Clean baby food jars – two for each person (Adults may pre-spray the caps gold or silver.)

Metal nuts with holes the size of your candles – (Bring the candles with you to the hardware store when you go to buy the nuts.)

Liquid mixture: 3 parts corn syrup to 1 part water (For a 4-ounce jar, use 3 ounces of corn syrup to 1 ounce water)

Craft glue

Craft store jewels: sequins, glitter, glitter shapes and other decorative materials

Candles

DIRECTIONS:

1 Fill the jars with the liquid mixture.

2 Drop sequins or glitter into the mixture.

3 Apply the glue in a circle around the inside edge of the lid. Close the jar tightly.

4 Glue one metal nut on top of each lid. Candles should fit securely in the nuts.

5 To focus on the beauty of the Shabbat candles, shake the jars and watch them glitter as the candles are lit.

Variation: Tape short pieces of ribbon or tinsel to the inside bottom of the baby food jar lid. When you close the jar, the streamers will hang down and float in the liquid.

Soda Bottle Candlesticks

CAUTION: SMALL OBJECTS!

MATERIALS:

2 empty and clean 16- or 20-ounce see-through plastic soda bottles

4 bottle caps

2 disposable Shabbat candle holders (available in Jewish gift shops)

Tin foil

Craft glue

Optional: Spoons and a funnel

Containers for the following objects:
Variation 1: Corn kernels, dried peas, black beans, lima beans, kidney beans

Variation 2: Marbles, rocks, pebbles, small seashells

DIRECTIONS:

1 Fill two bottles with layers of objects. Some children like to use their hands, others prefer to use a spoon. Using a funnel is different and fun.

2 Apply the glue in a circle around the inside edge of the bottle cap. Close the bottle tightly.

3 Invert a second bottle cap and glue it on top of the first cap.

4 To use, line the inverted bottle cap with the disposable Shabbat candle holder or tin foil.

Note: You can make different candlesticks each week!

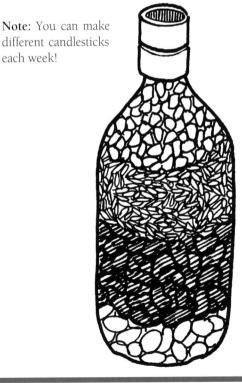

SALT DOUGH CANDLESTICKS

MATERIALS:

Bakers salt dough: (Adult supervised)

  2½ cups all-purpose flour

  1 cup salt

  1 cup water

Food coloring – CAUTION: May stain hands. Rubber gloves can be used

1 small bowl or zip lock baggie for each color used

Sequins, beads, feathers, craft store jewels, stones

Shabbat candle

Metal nuts to hold candles – Bring candle to hardware store to check the correct size.

Waxed paper

DIRECTIONS:

1 Make salt dough by thoroughly combining ingredients in a bowl. Place dough onto a lightly floured surface and knead until smooth. Divide it into several parts, adding a different food coloring to each part. Knead the dough on a piece of waxed paper until the color is thoroughly blended. Keep sections in separate bowls covered with a damp cloth or in closed plastic baggies in the refrigerator until ready to use.

2 Choose the colors of dough you want to work with. Shape into a ball, a cylinder or any desired shape. Each candlestick can be built by stacking two or three separate shapes. Each person should make two candlesticks. **HELPFUL HINT: Make sure the base is wide enough so candlesticks can stand.**

3 To decorate, firmly press sequins, beads, jewels or stones into the dough.

4 Press a nut into the top of the dough. (Make sure the dough doesn't fill up the hole.)

5 Bake the candlesticks at 325 degrees on a lightly greased cookie sheet for about one hour, or until they are a golden brown and feel firm to your touch. The baking time depends on the thickness of the candlesticks. Cool on a wire rack.

Note: Beads or nuts can be glued on if they come loose.

Jeweled Kiddush Cup

The word "kiddush" has the same root as the word "kedusha," to make holy. Pouring wine into a beautiful cup and saying the blessings helps make the Sabbath holy.

MATERIALS:

2 plastic wine cups (Examples: a small plastic tumbler or a disposable wine cup with a detachable base.)

Lightly diluted school glue (Use a small amount of water to dilute.)

Small cups to hold glue

Q-tips or small paint brushes

Tissue paper strips and squares, in many colors

Faux jewels

DIRECTIONS:

1 Pour glue mixture into small cups. Give the child Q-tips or a paint brush to apply glue to the outside of a wine cup.

2 Cover the glue with tissue paper until the cup is totally covered. Apply a second coat of glue over the tissue paper. Let dry.

3 Use a Q-tip to apply a bead of glue to the cup where jewels are to be applied.

4 Carefully place jewels on these beads of glue. Let dry.

5 Place undecorated cup inside decorated cup when drinking wine or grape juice.

Hint: Using a clean baby food jar and lid, make a matching spice box using the above technique. When dry, simply fill the jar with a mixture of spices, including cinnamon, cloves and anise.

Challah Covers

Midrash tells us that as the wine is blessed, the challah may feel ignored. In order to save the challah any embarrassment, there is a tradition to cover it until it is time to say the motzi (the blessing over the bread). If we must consider the feelings of an inanimate object, how much more should we care for each other?

COLLAGE CHALLAH COVER

MATERIALS:

Large, solid color handkerchiefs

Decorative materials such as sticky felt, sticky felt letters, fabric paints, puffy paints, sequins, trim, fringes, adhesive-backed ribbon, rickrack, glitter glue

DIRECTIONS:

1 Cut sticky felt into various shapes (see templates on p. 270 for some ideas) and have the child place them on the handkerchief.

2 "Shabbat" can be spelled out in Hebrew or English on the handkerchief (p. 270).

3 Decorate as desired.

Hints: Sequins will stick to wet puffy paints. Trims can be glued or sewn on. Imagination reigns!!! If you have two children, cover one challah with one cover, the second challah with the second cover.

DYE-PAINTED CHALLAH COVER

For older children – CAUTION: DYE WILL STAIN

MATERIALS:

Rectangular handkerchief or piece of silk or cotton, hemmed or pre-cut with pinking shears

Permanent black magic markers

Dye – Liquid Deka brand silk dyes, non-toxic. They come in many colors and may be diluted with water. **ALTERNATIVE: Food coloring**

Silk wax resist – clear, gold and/or silver (available in art stores)

Small, disposable containers, one for each color of dye

Paint brushes

Newspaper

DIRECTIONS:

1 Cover the work surface with a thick layer of newspaper.

2 Using the black magic marker, make a design on the material. Templates on p. 270 can be used.

3 Trace over the design with wax resist. The gold and silver will keep its color. Let dry thoroughly.

4 Using small paint brushes, fill in the design with dye. The dye will "bleed" into areas not separated by wax resist. That's part of the beauty.

5 Let the challah cover air dry.

6 To set the colors, iron or put in the dryer on appropriate fabric setting.

Variation: Twist and fold sections of the material. Secure the folds with rubber bands and then dip the sections into various colors.

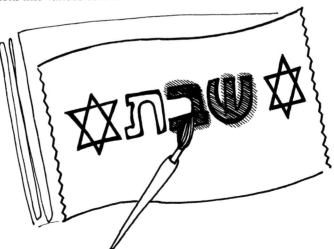

Shabbat Tablecloths

We dress up for Shabbat as one more way to set this special day apart from any other day in the week. We also dress up our Shabbat table, helping to transform the ordinary into the holy.

MATERIALS:

White tablecloth or bed sheet

**Fabric paints and/or markers:
WARNING:** These will stain

Disposable containers for paint (examples: Styrofoam meat trays, paper plates, paper cups)

Paintbrushes

Sponges, cut into squares measuring approximately 2 x 2 inches

Cookie cutters, sponge shapes, cardboard cutouts made from template shapes found on p.270

DIRECTIONS:

1 Cover the table with disposable plastic sheeting. Spread out the tablecloth or bed sheet on the protected surface.

2 Pour paint into individual disposable containers.

3 Dip the cookie cutters and sponges into the paint, tap off the excess, and then press them onto the cloth or lay template shapes on top of the cloth and sponge paint over them.

4 Use the paintbrushes or fabric markers to paint more designs on the cloth.

5 Let the cloth dry 24 hours. If fabric paints are used, you may need to "heat set" the tablecloth for permanency, following the directions on the paint package.

Variations: 1. Have family members press their hands, palm side down, into the tray of paint. Make handprints all over the tablecloth in as many colors as you wish.

2. Family members can paint, draw, or stamp different Shabbat and holiday symbols all over the tablecloth using the cookie cutters, sponges, or conventional rubber stamps. Fabric markers, glitter paint, or sequins can also be used.

3. Use a paper tablecloth, markers and crayons to make a weekly disposable tablecloth. Ideas for decorations include Shabbat symbols, names of guests, Shabbat wishes, praise for children and parents.

Hints: 1. When using your beautiful hand-painted tablecloth, put a clear plastic tablecloth over the top of it to protect it.

2. Adapt this idea for Rosh HaShanah, Hanukkah, Sukkot

Tzedakah Boxes

Tzedakah (justice, righteous actions, charity) is a central value of Judaism. Over and over, the Torah tells us to be fair and just and treat people right. Every Friday, before lighting the Shabbat candles, family members have an additional opportunity to do Tzedakah by contributing a few pennies or food cans to any cause that the family has decided upon together. Performing acts of Tzedakah not only makes the world a better place by helping people in need, it also makes us better people.

Fimo Clay Tzedakah Box

For older children

MATERIALS:

1 metal, china or glass container with lid or bank-like container

Fimo clay – white and other colors of your choice

Small rolling pin

Plastic knife

Small cookie cutters of various shapes, such as a Jewish star

Cardboard cutouts of various shapes made using a reduced version of the templates found on p. 270

Glass cookware, like a pie plate CAUTION: Use only for cooking Fimo

DIRECTIONS:

1 Preheat your oven to 350 degrees.

2 Soften the white Fimo clay and roll out to approximately ⅛ inch thick to fit the outside of your metal, china or glass container. Rub all edges to eliminate any seams. Make sure to leave the lid hinges or the money opening uncovered.

3 Make designs with colored Fimo by forming it into shapes, coils or braids and pressing the shapes onto the white background. The rolled out dough can also be cut into shapes with the plastic knife or cookie cutters using the cardboard template shapes to cut around.

4 Bake the Tzedakah box at 350 degrees for about 20 minutes. Let it cool thoroughly before using.

Tissue Paper-Covered Tzedakah Box

MATERIALS:

Clean, empty containers, boxes, or a cylindrical potato chip container

Tissue paper squares, cut up into small shapes

Diluted glue poured into individual containers

Sponge paint brushes

DIRECTIONS:

1 Cut a rectangular slit large enough to deposit money into the top of the container.

2 Glue tissue paper on the container, avoiding the slit.

3 Coat finished design with more glue to thoroughly seal.

4 Let the Tzedakah box dry thoroughly.

Hint: Write "Tzedakah" on the finished box with permanent markers.

Variation: For younger children, use permanent markers or paint to decorate container. Be careful, these materials also stain.

Havdalah: Spice Boxes

As one of the ritual acts of Havdalah, a spice box filled with a mixture of sweet and fragrant spices, "besamim" is passed around. Their aroma is meant to stay with us throughout the week as a constant reminder of the sweetness of Shabbat.

FRUIT WITH CLOVES

MATERIALS:

1 orange, lemon, lime, or grape-fruit for each child. NOTE: After the holiday of Sukkot, you may use an etrog (a citrus fruit, much like a lemon).

Whole cloves, which can be found in a spice store, grocery store or health food store

DIRECTIONS:

Have children poke many cloves into fruit peel (It may be necessary to make small starter holes in the fruit first.)
ADULTS: you can use a crochet needle, a shish kabob stick, a small knife.

Variation: Fragrant fruits can also be used as an air freshener instead of potpourri baskets by pouching them in scrap fabric and tying them closed with a ribbon.

"STAINED-GLASS" SPICE BOTTLE

MATERIALS:

Clean baby food jars

Thin tipped permanent fabric markers CAUTION: Adult supervision needed for younger children. These will stain.

Cloves, cinnamon sticks, anise

Two 4 x 4 inch squares of different-colored mesh fabric

8-inch length of pretty ribbon

DIRECTIONS:

1 Color the jars with markers. Older children can outline their designs with a black marker and fill in the spaces with other colors. Adults can outline a design that their younger children tell them to make.

2 Place spices in the jar.

3 Cover with the two pieces of mesh fabric.

4 Tie ribbon around the neck of the bottle.

Variation: For Sukkot, make multiple jars and place a floater candle in each, instead of spices. Place around your sukkah. **CAUTION:** Do not cover these jars with mesh. Place jars in spots where they cannot be knocked over.

Twisted Havdalah Candles

Havdalah means "separation." We welcome Shabbat with candles, blessings, song and wine, and we say goodbye to Shabbat with candles, songs and sweet spices. The flickering of the braided Havdalah candle warms our souls and lights the darkness, gently leading us into the coming week.

MATERIALS:

3 thin candles or tapers, at least 12 inches long

Warm water in a rectangular baking pan or a heating pad set on the lowest setting - the candles will not melt

DIRECTIONS:

1 Warm candles in water or fold in heating pad for approximately one minute or until pliable.

2 Braid them together.

Jeanine Semon

Rosh HaShanah

When the weather begins to cool, turning the leaves vibrant shades of red and gold, change is literally "in the air." Nature is in transition and our environment is demonstrating how beautiful change can be.

At Rosh HaShanah God asks us to do the same—to celebrate our beauty and uniqueness, while at the same time preparing to look inward and take stock of how we have lived our lives during the last year.

Experiencing Rosh HaShanah

Rosh HaShanah, literally the "Head of the Year," beckons us to enter a time of honest and humbling introspection. We embark on this journey of emotional and spiritual self-examination to review the choices we have made, the people we have touched and our goals and aspirations. We resolve to improve our relationships and our lifestyles, and reflect on our commitment to our families and the Jewish community.

Rosh HaShanah is a time when the congregation swells. Together in prayer, we ask for peace and tranquility. The eerie sounds of the shofar are heard one hundred times. The blasts stir our souls, renews our dedication to God and community and inspires us to prayer, acts of kindness and *tzedakah* (charity).

Rosh HaShanah is also called *Yom Teru'ah*, the "Day of the Shofar Blast." A ram's horn is chosen most often because of the *parasha* (Torah portion) read on Rosh HaShanah—the binding of Isaac. In this story, God sends Abraham a ram to be sacrificed in place of his son, Isaac.

We are commanded in the Torah to hear the sound of the shofar during Rosh HaShanah and Yom Kippur. When Israel received the Torah on Mount Sinai, great trumpets were sounded. By blowing the shofar, we are renewing our connection to those experiences and our commitment to Torah. Also, the sounds of the shofar represent the soul crying out to God for help in living the life it is intended to live. It is a day when each of us must ask, "Have I been the best 'me' I could be?" Over the course of Rosh HaShanah and Yom Kippur, the rabbi calls out the shofar sound appropriate for that point in the service, and the shofar blower responds. There are four "sounds" made: *Tekiah, Shevarim, Teruah, and Tekiah Gedolah.*

On the eve of Rosh HaShanah, we celebrate the New Year with a festive dinner that traditionally includes sweet foods symbolizing our wishes for a sweet New Year. We serve two round *challot* (plural for *challah*) to represent the cyclical nature of time. After the blessings over the wine and bread, we dip apples.

Greetings on the High Holidays convey our feelings of connection to the community during this special time. The traditional greeting for Rosh HaShanah is *"Shana Tovah!"* which means "Happy New Year" literally, "a good year." The complete version of this greeting is *"L'Shana Tovah Tikatevu"* which means "May you be written for a good year," a reference to your name being recorded in the Book of Life (see page 50).

We remember those who have touched our lives by sending cards with just the right wish for a happy, healthy and prosperous New Year.

Traditions & Text

The section of the Torah that describes Rosh HaShanah does not say what we might expect: *In the seventh month, on the first day of the month, you shall observe complete rest, a sacred occasion commemorated with loud blasts.* (Leviticus 23:32) There is no mention of a "New Year." We're not told much about the significance of the day other than it is celebrated with "loud blasts." Most odd, even though we consider the day the beginning of the New Year, we're told that it is to be celebrated in the seventh month, not the first month. According to the Torah, the first month is Nisan, the month of Passover, and not Tishri, the month of Rosh HaShanah and Yom Kippur. Why, then, did the early Rabbis insist that this holiday of shofar blasts was, in fact, the beginning of the year?

The matter became one of considerable debate 2,000 years ago. Spring was the anniversary of the redemption of the Jews from Egypt. For many, the springtime—the time of Passover—would be the natural time to think about beginnings and the start of a New Year. There's something poetic about things beginning to grow and turning green in the spring. Why start the year in the fall when trees lose their dead leaves and the world of nature grows dormant, seemingly dead?

It is precisely because of the somber nature of autumn that the Rabbis decided that it was appropriate to consider it the beginning of the world. Just as we have faith that the trees will bloom again in the spring, so we have faith that God will not abandon us in a world in which the days are growing constantly shorter. In fact, the Rabbis considered Rosh HaShanah to be the birthday of the world. The blasts of the shofar remind us of the birth of the world and of our faith in the Creator.

AN UNUSUAL SEDER

The Jews of North Africa have celebrated an interesting ceremony. It's kind of a Rosh HaShanah seder. Symbolic foods are eaten preceded by special blessings that point out the symbolism of the food. For example, before eating pomegranate seeds, they say, "May it be Your will, Oh Lord our God and God of our ancestors, that we multiply like the seeds of the pomegranate." Or before eating parts of a fish head (or a lamb's head) they say, "May it be Your will, Oh Lord our God and God of our ancestors, that we be the head and not the tail." Or before eating beets they say, "May it be Your will, Oh Lord our God and God of our ancestors, that our enemies beat it." (This pun, believe it or not, works both in English and in Hebrew.) Try your hand at making up your own Rosh HaShanah food puns!

Fascinating Food Facts

Since we wish each other a good and sweet year on Rosh HaShanah, our tradition is to serve sweet foods: apples and honey, honey cake, and sweet challah with raisins. In San Francisco, they even put colored candy "sprinkles" on their challah. After the Motzi blessing, the challah is dipped in honey rather than the traditional salt. Many people, in fact, are superstitious about eating sour or bitter things - for fear that if you eat something bitter on Rosh HaShanah, you'll have a bitter year. My Aunt Katie would never even consider serving horseradish with her Rosh HaShanah gefilte fish.

Traditional Rosh HaShanah Menu

In a traditional home, blessings are said in a certain order. When beginning your own Rosh HaShanah rituals, begin with the blessings you feel comfortable with, gradually adding blessings as you wish. (The letter in parenthesis indicates the appropriate blessing found in "Prayers and Blessings" on p. 283)

The following is a suggested order for the blessings:	The following foods are traditional on most holidays, but feel free to use any of the many delicious recipes in this book.
Blessing over the candles (J) Blessing over the wine (K) Shehecheyanu (G) Blessing for hand washing (A) Blessing over bread (B)	Wine (or grape juice) Round challah with raisins (Many families dip their challah in honey to guarantee a sweet new year.)
Blessing for fruit of the tree (D) Blessing for a Sweet New Year (P)	Apples dipped in honey Chicken soup with knaidels (matzah balls) Green salad with a sweet or fruity dressing Chicken, Brisket, or Fish Sweet Tzimmes Green Vegetable Honey Cake Apple Crisp Pomegranate (The pomegranate is said to have 613 seeds just as there are 613 mitzvot in the Bible.)
Blessing after the meal (*Birkat HaMazon*) (H)	

GO TO RECIPE INDEX IN BACK OF BOOK FOR SUGGESTED RECIPES.

Kids in the Kitchen

This special recipe uses apples, one of the holiday's most noted symbols. These applesauce cake cones can be used to decorate the table, in addition to being a delicious dessert.

CREATIVE CAKE CONES

COOKING EQUIPMENT NEEDED:

Muffin tin

Measuring cup

Measuring spoons

Large bowl

Wooden stirring spoon

INGREDIENTS:

¼ cup vegetable oil

¾ cup brown sugar

1 cup applesauce

1 teaspoon baking soda

1½ cups flour

1 teaspoon cinnamon

10 flat bottom ice cream cones

DIRECTIONS:

1 Preheat oven to 375 degrees.

2 Mix oil and sugar together.

3 Add applesauce, baking soda, flour and cinnamon.

4 Make sure to stir all the ingredients well.

5 Fill cones ¾ full with batter.

6 Stand cone upright in a muffin tin.

7 Bake on cookie sheet for 20 minutes.

8 When the cones are cool, you can top with peanut butter or cream cheese.

A real treat for kids of all ages!

Rosh HaShanah

Read-Aloud Story

The Hidden Star

Adapted from folk tales by Carolyn Sherwin Bailey
Retold by Sharon Cohen

Once upon a time, a little boy was playing outside while his mother was busy baking the sweet round challot for Rosh HaShanah dinner. The little boy had played with his friends and his toys. He had climbed the trees in the backyard. But now he was bored.

"What else can I do?" he asked his mother.

His mother thought for a moment and then said, "I think you should go on a hike. See if you can find a little red house with no windows or doors, but with a star inside."

The little boy had never heard of a house with no windows or doors, with a star inside, but he liked a challenge. So he set off down the road.

Soon he saw a little girl playing outside. "Do you know where I can find a little red house with no windows or doors, and a star inside?" he asked.

The little girl laughed and laughed.

"You are silly!" she said. "I've never seen a house with no windows or doors, with a star inside. Let's ask my father."

The girl's father was in the barn milking cows. They asked him if he had seen a little red house with no windows or doors, with a star inside. He had never seen such a house, and he suggested that the children ask his neighbor, Safta.

"Go ask Safta," he said. "She is wise. She might know."

The children set off for Safta's house. The smell of chicken soup and matzah balls wafted out of her open windows.

"Safta, Safta," they called. "Where can we find a little red house with no windows or doors, but with a star inside?"

Safta thought and thought. Then, she smiled and said, "Listen to the wind and use your eyes to see the beauty of God's world. Maybe then, you will find your little red house with no windows or doors."

So the children ran outside and called to the wind, "Do you know where we can find a little red house with no windows or doors, but with a star inside?"

The wind answered, "OOOOOHHHHHHHHHHHHHHOOOOOOOOOO...Follow me!" They followed the wind down a path where leaves were blowing about and suddenly found themselves in an apple orchard. Shiny, round, red apples had fallen on the ground. The little boy picked up the prettiest one he could find and took it home to his mother.

Mother was busy setting the holiday table with the warm challot, the wine, candlesticks and a bowl of honey. "Look," he cried. "I have found a little red house, with no windows or doors, but I can't find the star!"

Mother took the beautiful apple from the boy and with a sharp knife she cut the apple right in half, across the middle. And there in the center, formed by five tiny seeds, was a perfect star.

The boy and his mother cut the apple again and dipped it into the sweet bowl of honey.

"L'shanah Tovah, Ima," said the boy.

"L'shanah Tovah to you, my little son," she answered.

Rosh HaShanah Games Corner

ROSH HASHANAH TAG

by Lenny Kass

Learning Objective: To teach children about the Jewish calendar

MATERIALS:

20 or more index cards or stock paper cut into small cards

Red and black markers/pens

Running area (about 20 yards x 10 yards) with boundaries marked

HOW TO PLAY:

1 Mark the 20 cards (or more) with the numbers 0-9. If the numbers in the Jewish Year are 5761 write these numbers in red and the others in black.

2 Create a running area marking the ends (ex: 20 yards long by 10 yards wide) with all kids but one standing at an end which will be considered the start line.

3 Each child should have a card except the one who will be standing in the middle.

4 The child standing in the middle is "it" and yells "Happy New Year." When he yells this, all the kids try running to the other side.

5 If tagged by the child who is "it" and if you have a black number, sit on the sideline. If tagged and you have a red number, you become a helper and try and tag others too. Start!

MAGIC NUMBERS CARD GAME

MATERIALS:

Up to 40 index cards

Red and black marker/pen

Dice and construction paper

HOW TO PLAY:

1 If using the index cards: Make up to 40 cards, all marked with the numbers 0-9, the numbers of the Jewish year in red, all other numbers in black.

2 Deal the cards so that each person has an equal number of cards.

3 Each player flips down one card at the same time.

4 The person who has the highest card showing takes the cards. Cards marked with red have higher values than those marked with black. If the year is 5761, the numbers 1,5,6,7 have higher values than 0,2,3,4,8,9. Ex: if one player flips a 2 and the other flips a 1, 1 wins because it's a number in the Jewish year and marked in red.

TO USE DICE:

1 On a piece of construction paper or cardboard, create a "Road to the New Year."

2 You can use stickers, colors and pictures to decorate.

3 Roll the die and if the number rolled is a number in the year, move the number of spaces indicated on the die.

Rosh HaShanah Crafts and Activities

Shofars
Sewn Paper Plate Shofar
Party Horn Shofar

Stuffed Play Challah

Rosh HaShanah Cards
Apple Print Cards
Sun Catcher Rosh HaShanah Cards

Rosh HaShanah Matching Game

Tashlich Activities
Tashlich Walk
Rosh HaShanah Tactile Board

"Happy Birthday to the World" Banners

Rosh HaShanah Table Setting Box

Shofars

The shofar can be made from the horn of any kosher animal except a cow (which would recall the golden calf built by the Hebrews while waiting for Moses to descend from Mt. Sinai). For most children (and many adults!), the blowing of the shofar is the highlight of the High Holiday service. Children look forward to hearing these loud blasts in the midst of a solemn service and watching the shofar blower hold his or her breath for as long as s/he can on that final note. Having their own shofar to play with makes an even stronger connection to the holiday.

SEWN PAPER PLATE SHOFAR

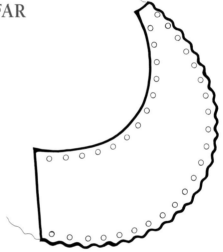

MATERIALS:

2 paper plates cut into shofar shapes—see template page 272

Paper punch

2 pieces of yarn, each knotted at one end and wrapped with tape at the other to make a needle-like "point"

DIRECTIONS:

1 Match up the shofar shapes and punch holes up each side.

2 Give the child yarn to sew the shofar together, making a knot at the beginning and end of each side. Leave the ends of the shofar unsewn.

3 "Puff" out the sides so the child can "blow" the shofar.

Variation: Laminate the shofar shape, punch holes and you now have a lacing shape.

Party Horn Shofar

MATERIALS:

1 store bought party horn for each child

One 8 x 10 inch piece of paper cut from a brown grocery bag

Markers or crayons

Tape

DIRECTIONS:

1 Decorate the piece of paper with markers and/or crayons.

2 Beginning with one corner of the paper, wrap it tightly around the party horn and tape it closed, leaving the mouthpiece uncovered.

3 Bend the outer end upward to form a Shofar shape.

4 Help child try to imitate all the shofar sounds heard in the synagogue during the Rosh HaShanah services: "Tekiah," "Shevarim," "Teruah," "Tekiah Gedolah."

In the synagogue several different sounds are played on the shofar. The Rabbi calls out the name of the sound and the shofar blower responds with the sound that is asked for. Tekiah, the "blast" is one long clear blast of sound. Shevarim, the "broken" sound is 3 short, quick notes. Teruah, the "alarm" is 9 or more short notes played in quick succession. Finally, Tekiah Gedolah, the "great blast" is one single blast sounded as long as possible. The shofar is blown 100 times during the high holidays.

Stuffed Play Challah

Rosh HaShanah is celebrated on the first day of Tishrei (the seventh Hebrew month). As on Shabbat, challah is blessed and served. On Rosh HaShanah, however, the challah is round, symbolizing the cyclical nature of the Jewish year and the roundness of the world, whose birthday falls on Rosh HaShanah.

MATERIALS:

3 clean pantyhose legs (beige colored)

Tissue or poly-fill

1 piece of soft dark material – 4 x 8 inches (an old brown or black sock would work)

DIRECTIONS:

1 Stuff each pantyhose leg with tissue or poly-fil.

2 Take one end of each stuffed leg and tie them together. Braid the three pieces together and knot the other ends together. Coil them tightly into a circle. Take the ends and tuck them in.

3 Cut the dark material into eight strips, 1 inch wide and 4 inches long. Tie each into a knot and trim off their ends. Poke them into the folds of the bread to look like raisins. These knots may also be glued or sewn into place.

Note: Use the challot as table decorations or for children to play house.

Alternative idea: Make a round challah using one stuffed leg. Tie off both ends. Coil it and tuck in the ends.

Rosh HaShanah Cards

Handmade greeting cards can reflect the many themes of Rosh HaShanah: blowing the shofar, apples and honey, The Book of Life, L'Shanah Tovah, etc. Making these cards together with special people in mind makes this a wonderful family activity.

APPLE PRINT CARDS

MATERIALS:

Apples cut in half around the middle (notice the star)

Plastic forks

Styrofoam trays or paper plates

Red, yellow, green paint

White paper, folded in half or quarters

Glitter (optional)

Markers or crayons

DIRECTIONS:

1 Put paint in Styrofoam trays or paper plates.

2 Stab rounded side of apple with plastic fork (to be used as a handle).

3 Dip the flat side of the apple in the paint and scrape off excess against the side of the tray.

4 Stamp the apples onto the front of the white paper.

5 Sprinkle glitter on the wet paint.

6 When the paint is dry, write New Year's greeting.

Sun Catcher Rosh HaShanah Cards

MATERIALS:

Colored construction paper –
9 x 12-inch

2 pieces of clear contact paper –
Each cut to 9 x 12 inch

Scissors

Tissue paper

Jewish confetti shapes
(often found in party stores)

DIRECTIONS:

1 Cut an apple, shofar or book shape out of the center of the 9 x 12 inch construction paper to form a frame.

2 Cut two 9 x 12 inch pieces of clear contact paper.

3 Lay the frame on the sticky side of one piece of the contact paper.

4 Until ready to use, cover with original non-stick backing of the contact paper.

5 Allow the child to creatively arrange cut-up pieces of tissue paper or confetti on exposed sticky contact paper.

6 When the child is finished, carefully seal the finished picture with the second piece of contact paper.

Rosh HaShanah Matching Game

FOR YOUNG CHILDREN

MATERIALS:

12 x 14 inch piece of cardboard

12 x 14 inch piece of black construction paper

School glue or rubber cement

Envelope or large resealable bag

Two shapes each of the following: apples, shofar, honey jar, book, Kiddush cup (see p. 271)

Clear contact paper (The cards can also be laminated.)

DIRECTIONS:

1 Using the glue, cover the cardboard with black paper.

2 Glue one of each shape in a row onto the paper.

3 Laminate or cover with the clear contact paper.

4 Place extra shapes in an unsealed envelope and attach to the back of the cardboard.

5 Play the matching game.

Tashlich Activities

On the first day of Rosh HaShanah (if it doesn't fall on Shabbat), the custom of Tashlich is practiced. This involves going to the banks of any river, lake or stream and literally and symbolically emptying our pockets into the flowing water, an act meant to purify us and wash away our sins. Many people, in addition to turning out their pockets to shake out lint or crumbs, throw additional bread crumbs into the water. This custom comes from a verse from the prophet Micah: "And you [God] shall throw their sins into the depths of the sea" (7:19).

TASHLICH WALK

MATERIALS:

Small baggies with bread crumbs inside

Nearby river, lake, or stream

DIRECTIONS:

1 At Rosh HaShanah lunch, have family members think about how they can make themselves better people. How can you be nicer to other people? What are the one or two things about yourself that you could change? Maybe you could listen better, clean up your toys, or share more.

2 Once you have these ideas, gather up your bread crumbs and go together to a nearby lake, stream or river.

3 As you throw your bread crumbs into the water, say out loud, "Next year, I will listen better." or "Next year, I will share more." Announce whatever it is you have decided to throw away. Everyone in the family can participate.

ROSH HASHANAH TACTILE BOARD

MATERIALS:

Foam core board (available at art supply store)

Wide variety of old pants pockets (with back intact), with a variety of different closures: buttons, Velcro, zippers, snaps, flaps

Textured materials: Cotton balls, sand paper, popsicle sticks, rough scrubby pad, crumbs, felt, velvet

Tacky glue

Bucket or pan of water

DIRECTIONS:

1 Glue the pockets to the foam core board, leaving some slack in each pocket.

2 Let the pockets dry thoroughly.

3 Put a different textured item in each pocket, including crumbs.

4 Let the child find the crumbs from among all the other items in the pockets.

5 Once the crumbs are found, help the child think about what behaviors they want to change.

6 Throw the crumbs into the bucket/pan of water, while talking about what they want to change.

7 Play again by switching around the pocket items.

Variation: Use this board at Passover time to search for the afikoman or at Hanukkah to find matching dreidels. At Purim you can match the characters' pictures.

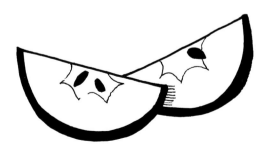

Rosh HaShanah Table Setting Box

It's the New Year and a time to gather together with family members and old friends in our home and in the synagogue. We make our table beautiful for Rosh HaShanah, just like we do for Shabbat. What follows is a very simple and fun idea.

MATERIALS:

Plastic apple

Plastic honey bear

Unbreakable candlesticks covered with tinfoil (to make them look like silver)

Small white paper tablecloth

Napkins

Unbreakable vase

Artificial flowers

Empty box of raisins

Round challah (stuffed pantyhose)

DIRECTIONS:

Open the box and let the children play!

"Happy Birthday to the World" Banners

Midrash tells us that the world was created in the month of Tishrei. That's also when Adam was created, making it the birthday of Adam and Eve.

MATERIALS:

Use a computer-generated banner with apple or honey pot borders, pictures of the world, birthday cards, animals, trees or flowers, but it would be more fun to create your own using:

Long piece of paper for a banner

Magazine pictures

Home-drawn pictures

Rosh HaShanah shapes – (see templates on p. 271) cut out of construction paper

Crayons, markers

Stickers, stamps

Scissors

Tape

Glue

DIRECTIONS:

Use the above materials to create a mixed-media collage, including the words, "Happy Birthday to the World!"

WE ASK FOR FORGIVENESS, HEALTH & HARMONY

Yom Kippur

At some point of every day we find ourselves looking into a mirror. We might turn to examine our profile. We might move in closer to scrutinize our features more closely. Or we might just have a quick look, as if to reassure ourselves that yes, there we are, and everything is okay.

What if we could use that same mirror to look into our souls? A mirror that could show us our thoughts, our feelings, our very essence? Perhaps it could show us an overview of the past year, highlighting our actions and relationships. Would we like what we see? What would we want to change?

And what if this mirror could show us at the very deepest level where we connect with God? Can we see that connection? Can we feel that connection?

So begins the solemn and introspective process of Yom Kippur.

Experiencing Yom Kippur

Yom Kippur, the "Day of Atonement," is the most solemn day of the year. It concludes the Days of Awe, the ten days between Rosh HaShanah and Yom Kippur.

During those ten days we engage in our own spiritual renaissance. We take a complete "inventory" of our weaknesses and shortcomings and make the commitment to work harder to achieve our full potential and purpose in life during the next year. You may even want to set aside time to write in a journal where you can honestly assess your behavior during the past year and how you would like things to be different.

During this time many people approach loved ones, friends, or co-workers and say something like the following, "If I have harmed you or hurt you in any way during the last year, whether intentionally or unintentionally, please forgive me."

As we sit in the synagogue on Yom Kippur, we admit these shortcomings before God and strive to rekindle the spiritual spark within us, empowering it to become the guiding force in our lives. Finally, we are prepared to go forward into the New Year with a clear purpose and a clear conscience. We ask forgiveness for our past mistakes, grant forgiveness to others, and request a year filled with health, prosperity and joy.

To concentrate on the "inner cleansing" that we strive for during this time, most people fast for the twenty-four hours of Yom Kippur, from sundown to sundown. Each person must decide what will constitute his or her fast. Some simply abstain from all food and drink during this time. Others refrain from brushing their teeth. Some parents have their children start fasting when they reach the age of Bat/Bar Mitzvah, although younger children can get used to the practice by fasting for only a small part of the day.

The day spent in prayer and meditation concludes with one long blast of the shofar. Now the mood changes from somber to festive. Families gather to break the fast together (usually a simple meal prepared before sundown the day before), and some begin the task of building their sukkah in order to get ready for Sukkot, which begins just five days after Yom Kippur.

Traditions & Text

A central legend during the observance of Yom Kippur is that of the Book of Life. According to the legend, God judges us during the ten days between Rosh HaShanah and Yom Kippur. Those who truly repent and atone for their sins have their names written in the Book of Life for a good year, and those who have not sufficiently repented are not. We are told repeatedly in the Yom Kippur liturgy that "repentance, prayer, and acts of charity (*teshuvah, tefilah, and tzedakah*) overturn the evil decree."

According to tradition, the only sins that God automatically forgives on Yom Kippur are those committed against God. Sins against other people can only be forgiven if we try to make amends directly to the ones wronged.

Tradition teaches us that it is not enough to regret our mistakes. We must take positive steps to correct them. First, we need to declare that we regret our actions.

Even 2,500 years ago, the prophet Isaiah declared the necessity for this activism. Fasting and religious show aren't enough. His words are read on Yom Kippur:

(The people) long for God to draw near. They say,
"Why should we fast if You never see it?
Why starve our bodies if You never notice?"
(And God answered,)
"Look, you do business on your fast days,
You oppress all your workmen;
Look, you quarrel and squabble when you fast
And strike the poor man with your fist.
Fasting like yours today
Will never make your voice heard on high.
This is the sort of fast that pleases me.
To break unjust fetters
And undo the thongs of the yoke,
To let the oppressed go free,
And shelter the homeless poor.
To clothe the man you see to be naked
And not turn from your own kin."

...Isaiah, Chapter 56

Next, we must make amends, such as apologizing or paying damages. Only then are we free to stand before God and ask for forgiveness.

In Jewish tradition the word that is generally translated to mean, "sin," (חטא) actually means "missing the mark." Judaism permits us to learn lessons through many trials and errors. The point is to have a target, or spiritual direction, to guide you.

Fascinating Food Facts

Although no food is eaten on Yom Kippur, there are lots of traditions that have to do with food. Families have their own traditions about what is eaten before and after the fast. Many families have a full holiday meat meal before the fast — complete with nice tablecloths, dishes and silver. After the holiday, for the "break-fast," most families serve *"milchigs"* a dairy meal with herring, smoked fish and *kugel* (noodle pudding). In Hong Kong, the Kadoorie family invites the entire community to a major buffet dinner, which includes rare roast beef and roasted chicken. Some families traditionally break the fast with a cup of tea, others with a glass of tomato juice. What kind of foods will your "break-fast" include?

Although Yom Kippur is a 25 hour total fast, many people have a formal dinner before the fast (i.e. before sunset). In such a dinner the candles (J) are lit **after** the meal is finished, at the actual beginning of the holiday. Most people feel that salt should be totally avoided since it makes you thirsty.

Traditional Break-the-Fast Menu

The letter in parenthesis indicates the appropriate blessing found in "Prayers and Blessings" on p.283.

The following is a suggested order for the blessings.	Suggested Yom Kippur Break-the-Fast Menu
Blessing for hand washing (A) Blessing over the bread (B)	
	Herring Cheeses Salads Tuna or Egg Salad Fresh Fruit Platter Bagels, lox & cream cheese, sliced red onions, sliced tomatoes, sliced cucumbers Noodle Kugel or Blintzes Lots of Desserts
Blessing after the meal *(Birkat HaMazon)* (H)	

GO TO RECIPE INDEX IN BACK OF BOOK FOR SUGGESTED RECIPES.

Kids in the Kitchen

This recipe will inspire your little cook in the kitchen. Here is a quick snack to have ready when the grownups get home from synagogue.

BREAK-THE-FAST GOODIES

COOKING EQUIPMENT NEEDED:

Large bowl

Measuring cup

Large spoon

Air tight container

INGREDIENTS:

Make a mixture of your favorite cereals. Mix equal portions of sweet cereal (Trix, Honey-nut Cheerios) with non-sweetened ones (Chex, Cheerios).

To add that special taste add:

1 cup chocolate chips

1 cup raisins

1 cup pretzels

DIRECTIONS:

Have your young cook help measure and mix the ingredients. Place in a pretty basket and put it on the "break-fast" table. Store leftovers in an air-tight container.

Read-Aloud Story

Jonah and The Big Fish

The Book of Jonah
Retold by Liza Wiemer

The traditional story of "Jonah and the Big Fish" is always read on Yom Kippur afternoon. It is the perfect story to show us how people can change and to remind us that God is forgiving.

Can you imagine what it would be like to live in the belly of a huge fish? Let me tell you the story about someone who did.

Once upon a time God said to Jonah, "I need your help. Go to the land of Nineveh and tell the people there to stop being selfish and mean and violent." Jonah didn't want to do what God asked. So, Jonah ran away.

He set sail on a big boat with sailors on it of many different religions. Suddenly, a storm came and the roaring sea tossed and turned the boat. The sailors were terrified and prayed to their gods to save them. But no one helped them and the waves grew higher and higher. They decided to look for Jonah and they found him sleeping down below. Awakening him they cried, "Pray to your God to stop the storm!"

Jonah knew in an instant that he was the cause of their misfortune. Instead of doing as God had asked, he had tried to hide from Him. "Listen," he told the sailors, "If you throw me into the sea, it will become calm, for the storm is all my fault." The sailors didn't want to do such a terrible thing but they knew Jonah was right. Finally, they listened to Jonah and threw him into the water and the sea did become calm.

But a big fish appeared before Jonah and swallowed him up. For the next three days and three nights Jonah lived in the belly of the fish. Jonah was sad and lonely and prayed to God for another chance and God heard him.

God made the big fish spit Jonah out on the land and from there Jonah traveled to Nineveh. Jonah spoke to the people and told them that Nineveh would be destroyed. Immediately the people realized that God intended to punish them for being selfish and mean and violent. Everyone from the king, to the people, to the cows were sorry. "We must be kind to one another," they told each other, "God will know…" God did not destroy the Ninevites. They praised God and celebrated in the streets. "God will know that we are sorry when He sees that we have changed."

The people of Nineveh decided to be good friends and neighbors. They prayed to God and said that they were sorry and promised never to be mean again. God heard the words of the people and forgave them.

As for Jonah, he was glad that he didn't have to live in the belly of a big fish. Because of him, the people of Nineveh were saved.

Yom Kippur
Crafts and Activities

Book of Life Scrapbook

Composing Your Own Prayers

Yom Kippur Dress-Up

Decorated Tennis Shoes

Stuffed Torah

Stuffed Torah Cover

Book of Life Scrapbook

There is a legend that tells of God inscribing each of our names in a large book. People whose good deeds outweigh the bad are inscribed in "The Book of Life." Between Rosh HaShanah and Yom Kippur, we greet each other with "G'mar Hatima Tovah," which means "You should finish with a good feeling." After all the praying and doing tzedakah, God will inscribe us in the Book of Life.

A family scrapbook is a great way to record your family's good and happy times.

MATERIALS:

Blank book or photo album

Any combination of the following: sticky backed felt, sticker letters, stickers (moons, stars, "Jewish" stickers), stencils, fancy craft papers

Watercolors, markers, crayons, colored pencils, scissors

Photos, 2-D mementos, magazine pictures

DIRECTIONS:

Book Cover:

1 Decorate with the English or Hebrew year (the Fall of 2002 is 5763) and the words "Book of Life", using sticker or felt letters.

2 Add stickers and decorate with crayons or markers. Add family names, if you like.

Pages:

3 Collect pictures of events during the year. Place them in your book.

4 Children can write or dictate a caption to go under each picture.

5 Children can also draw pictures of what they did.

Composing Your Own Prayers

RECOMMENDED FOR CHILDREN 4 YEARS AND OLDER.

Yom Kippur is a holiday where we try to get especially close to God and express what is in our hearts.

DIRECTIONS:

During a quiet time, sit with your child/children and have them think about what they would say to God to finish these phrases. Younger children may be better able to express themselves through movement, singing or drawing pictures. Several examples of each kind of exercise follows.

I know God is close to me when _____ .

Special gifts God has given me are _____ .

I pray to God when _____ .

When I am sorry about something, I dance to God like this: _____

_____ .

When I want to thank God for everything God has given me, I draw a picture:

_____ .

I sing to God like this: _____ .

Decorated Tennis Shoes

Rabbis and Cantors often wear white robes on Yom Kippur so they can approach God dressed in the color of purity as they lead their congregations in the solemn and fateful prayers which characterize the holiday.

Also on Yom Kippur, traditional Jews are forbidden to wear leather shoes. They think, how can I ask God for forgiveness and mercy when I am wearing shoes made from animal hide?

MATERIALS:

Plain white tennis shoes

Fabric paint, puffy paint

CAUTION: Paint can stain

Gems and sequins (for older children)

Tacky craft glue

Newspaper

DIRECTIONS:

1 Cover the work surface with newspaper.

2 Decorate the tennis shoes to wear to Yom Kippur services

3 Allow 24 hours for the shoes to dry.

4 Sequins and gems should be applied with special tacky craft glue after the paint has dried and set. Allow time for drying before wearing.

Stuffed Torah

MATERIALS:

Torah pattern found on page 273

Muslin – to fit pattern

Scissors

Polyfil

Needle and thread or sewing machine

DIRECTIONS:

Note: Sewing is necessary

1 Cut two Torah shapes out of the muslin.

2 Place them back to back and sew them together, leaving half of one side open.

3 Turn it right side out.

4 Stuff it with poly-fil.

5 Hand-sew it shut

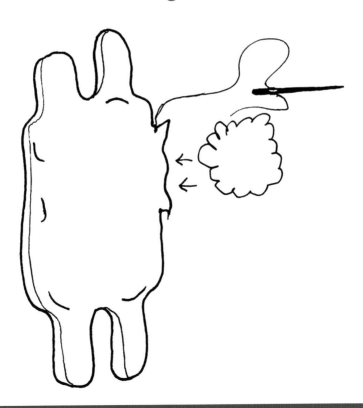

"Stuffed Torah" Cover

Just as the Rabbis and Cantors are dressed in white, so are the Torahs.

MATERIALS:

A **"stuffed Torah"** or small Torah that children receive when they are consecrated or ceremoniously welcomed into years of Jewish education at the synagogue. Consecration usually occurs on Simchat Torah. (These small Torahs can also be purchased at religious supply stores.)

White velvet or felt fabric, cut in a rectangle to fit around and encase the Torah, with 1 inch overlapping

2 sticky-backed Velcro strips, each cut to the height of the piece of fabric

Gold fabric paint or fabric markers

Masking tape

DIRECTIONS:

1 Attach Velcro strips to the center ends of the fabric, one on the top side of one end and one on the bottom side of the other end, so that when the fabric is wrapped around the Torah, it can be closed.

2 Remove fabric from around the Torah to add decorations.

3 Using masking tape, mark off a square or rectangular field on the front of the cover where the decoration will be.

4 Decorate the front of the fabric with fabric markers or fabric paint.

5 Let it dry thoroughly.

6 Remove the tape when Torah cover is dry and wrap the cover around the Torah.

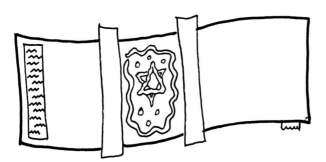

Karen Mittenthal

Sukkot

Count the stars that peek through the branches of your sukkah. Breathe in the aroma of dried autumn leaves, pumpkins, gourds, and cornstalks. Bundle up to share a meal with family and friends as the coolness of a fall evening settles in around you. Feel pride in how your unique sukkah is decorated to reflect your family's traditions and memories. It is time to express gratitude for the abundance of nature and celebrate the gift of family. It is time to celebrate Sukkot.

Experiencing Sukkot

Sukkot, one of the three pilgrimage festivals, comes just five short days after Yom Kippur. This eight-day harvest festival reenacts our ancestors' journey while wandering in the desert, traveling from Egypt to the land known as Israel. Sukkot also recreates the temporary dwellings used during harvest time in the land of Israel.

Tradition tells us that the first task after Yom Kippur is to put up a three-sided booth, or *sukkah*. A sukkah is a temporary structure, built in backyards, on porches or balconies. The roof of the sukkah is made of natural materials (cornstalks, bamboo, branches) known as *"schach,"* thick enough to provide shade, but light enough to enable us to see the stars shining through at night. Decorating the sukkah with strings of popcorn or cranberries is an activity that can really draw on children's energy and creativity. They can hang around its walls, or make paper chains. Some people hang vegetables that represent the fall harvest.

The sukkah is integral in fulfilling one of the three commandments in the Torah specific to Sukkot: "You shall dwell in booths for eight days." This traditionally means eating meals and for some sleeping in the sukkah.

The second commandment related to Sukkot is the mysterious "commandment of the four species": "You shall take...the fruit of goodly trees, branches of palm trees, boughs of thick trees, and willows of the brook." Today, the commandment is fulfilled by using the *lulav* and *etrog*. The *lulav* is a palm branch with three sprigs of myrtle on the right and two sprigs of willow on the left. The *etrog* is an egg-shaped yellow fruit, that looks like a lemon. We shake the lulav and etrog every morning during Sukkot, except on Shabbat.

The lulav is held in your right hand, and the etrog (with its point facing down) is held in your left hand, so they touch. After saying the blessing, the point is turned facing up. Both the lulav and the etrog are then waved in the following sequence: east, south, west, north, up, and down. This ceremony reminds us that God is present everywhere and we are all dependent on God.

"You shall rejoice before the Lord your God eight days" is the third commandment specific to Sukkot. This commandment is probably responsible for making Sukkot the most joyous and popular holiday of ancient Israel.

Today, Sukkot affords families a festive and wonderful time to visit with friends and relatives. Tradition tells us that some of our ancestors, the *Ushpizin*, are guests of the festival and are present in spirit in every sukkah: Abraham, Isaac, Jacob,

Joseph, Moses, Aaron, David, and Solomon. And…why not add the women: Sarah, Rebecca, Rachel, Leah, Miriam, Deborah, and Hannah.

It is customary, as well as a mitzvah (a commandment) to extend hospitality to others, especially the needy, by offering invitations to visit and share meals in the sukkah. "Sukkah hopping," (visiting the sukkahs of neighbors, fellow congregates, family and friends, one after the other) is a popular Sukkot activity.

The hustle and bustle of Sukkot is concluded with the celebration of Simchat Torah. Families gather in the synagogue to complete the reading of the Torah, and immediately start rereading the Torah with the Book of Genesis.

SIMCHAT TORAH

Simchat Torah is a fairly new celebration. It is unclear when and where the practice of reading the entire Torah in a one-year cycle began. In the early middle ages, many communities read the Torah through a cycle that took three years. For the communities that read the Torah through a one year cycle, however, the beginning that is, the reading from the very beginning of Genesis took place after Sukkot, and, therefore ended on the Shabbat during Sukkot. Although there is a certain logic in beginning the year with Rosh HaShanah, communities began their communal year on the Shabbat when the beginning chapters of Genesis were read in the synagogue: communal officers were elected just before that Shabbat, and one volume *machzorim* (prayer books which included all the special prayers for holidays and other observances) began with *Shabbat Breshit* (the first Torah reading in Genesis).

As the name implies, Simchat Torah is a time of great rejoicing. According to Michael Strassfeld in his book, "The Jewish Holidays":

> In the recent past, Simchat Torah has become very much a holiday for children (along with Purim), perhaps because adults have become embarrassed about expressing enthusiastic joy in public. This relegation of Simchat Torah to the children may also reflect our attitude toward Torah—a more distant and ambivalent attitude than that of our ancestors. Yet, even with all of our ambivalences and knowledge of critical biblical scholarship, we should still be able to rejoice in the Torah one day of the year…For those who believe that in some fashion the Torah is "a tree of life to those who grasp it," grasping it on Simchat Torah becomes essential.

Traditions & Text

In Israel, even secular Israelis build a sukkah, those makeshift shacks decorated with fruits. Balconies are full of them. But for many American Jews today, Sukkot is an obscure holiday that is celebrated in the synagogue at best.

In ancient times, however, when the Temple was still standing in Jerusalem, Sukkot was probably the most popular Jewish holiday—so much so that it was called simply "HaChag"—"The Festival." As one of the three pilgrim holidays, it was the one holiday that everyone wanted to celebrate by coming to Jerusalem, even those Jews who lived in Egypt or Babylon. After the seriousness of the high holidays (Sukkot happens five days after Yom Kippur), it was a time of ceremony and Temple sacrifices by day and great frivolity by night. The "Rejoicing at the Place of the Water Drawing" (Simchat Beit HaSho'eva) was a nightly occurrence that is described in the Talmud:

> *Whoever has not seen The Rejoicing at the Place of the Water Drawing has never seen rejoicing in his life. At the end of the first day of "HaChag," the priests and the Levites went down to the court of the women where they had set up a great structure: there were gold lamps with four gold bowls on top of each one and four ladders to each bowl and four youths from priestly families holding jars of oil…which they poured into the bowls. There was not a courtyard in Jerusalem that was not lit by the light of the Place of the Water-Drawing.*

> *Men of piety and good deeds used to dance in front of them juggling lit torches in their hands, singing songs and praises – and Levites without number with harps, lyres, cymbals, and trumpets and other musical instruments. [Babylonian Talmud Sukkah 51a-b]*

Sukkot has Messianic connections as well. According to tradition, the Messiah will come at Sukkot and will usher in a time of peace: "And it shall come to pass that everyone that is left of all the nations that came against Jerusalem shall go up from year to year to worship the King, the Lord of Hosts, and to keep the feast of Sukkot." *[Zechariah 14:16]*

Fascinating Food Facts

The Biblical commandment instructs us to "dwell in booths." What does that mean, exactly? Although there certainly have been people that moved their furniture into their sukkah and literally lived in it for the eight days of Sukkot, the rabbis said that all that is necessary is to *eat* in our sukkah. What holiday would exist without eating (except fast days, of course). The traditional food to eat on Sukkot is any type of stuffed food: stuffed cabbage or peppers, or more exotic fare such as stuffed zucchini, stuffed eggplant, or even stuffed onions. The rabbis caution us that since we're supposed to be happy at Sukkot, we might not want to eat in the rain. "You don't have to eat in the rain," they tell us, "if the rain is hard enough that it will ruin your soup!"

Suggested Sukkot Menu

The lulav is shaken in the morning. The following is a suggested order for the blessings. *(The letter in parenthesis indicates the appropriate blessing found in "Prayers and Blessings" on p. 283)*

Blessing over the candles (J)
(first and last nights only)

Leisheiv ba sukkah (Q)
(blessing for eating in a sukkah)

Blessing over the wine (C)   Wine (or grape juice)
(first two nights and last two nights)

Shehecheyanu (first night only) (G)

Blessing for hand washing (A)

Blessing over the bread (B)   Challah
                                                    Soup
                                                    Salad
                                                    Chili or Stuffed Cabbage
                                                    Potatoes, Rice or Kugel
                                                    Green vegetable
                                                    Desserts - Pumpkin or Zucchini Bread

Blessing after the meal *(Birkat HaMazon)* (H)

GO TO RECIPE INDEX IN BACK OF BOOK FOR SUGGESTED RECIPES.

Kids in the Kitchen

During their escape from Egypt, the Jews sought shelter in temporary huts known as sukkahs, the same structures that farmers slept in to be near their crops during the harvest season. If you can't make a large sit-in sukkah, create this small version as a centerpiece for your dining table.

GRAHAM CRACKER SUKKAH

COOKING EQUIPMENT NEEDED:

Plastic knives

Platter

INGREDIENTS:

3 graham crackers
(1 for each side of sukkah)

1 container of frosting
(white or green)

Fruits, cereal or candies of choice

Pretzels (for twig roof)

DIRECTIONS:

1 Cement the house pieces together with icing. When dry, make the roof with pretzels and small pieces of candies. The icing can also be used to attach the trim.

2 Decorate your sukkah with fruit-shaped cereals or candies of choice.

Note: Use sukkah as a table centerpiece.

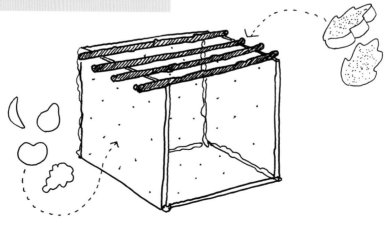

Read-Aloud Story

The Gourd's Journey

by Rabbi David B. Cohen

Once there lived a gourd. He was bumpy and had ridges and valleys all around himself. While he had many colors - yellows, golds, browns, and greens, he was not the prettiest vegetable in the garden.

The gourd lived in a patch of ground he shared with many other vegetables: tomatoes, onions, peppers, zucchini, even horseradishes. But while each of the other vegetables turned ripe and was picked, no one ever came to see the gourd.

One day he decided to leave the garden and look for a new home. One by one, he visited the Jewish Holy Days to see where he might be welcome.

First, he came to the festival of Hanukkah. "Wow," he thought. "What a wonderful place to be! Lots of families celebrating together. Hey, Hanukkah, do you have room for me?"

"Well you are… interesting looking," replied Hanukkah. "But we have no space for you. It's so crowded! The potatoes are here for latkes and apples for applesauce, but maybe, if you could leave your name and number we could get back to you if there is an opening."

The gourd had heard that line before. So, off he went to seek out another holy day.

The gourd came to Passover. He arrived to the big seder plate and said: "I am the lonely gourd. I have nowhere to go for the holidays. Do you have room for me?"

"We would love to give you a space," said the plate, "but look how little room we have here already! I mean, we have eggs and lamb bones and matzah and bitter herbs."

So that's where the horseradish was off to, thought the gourd.

"We don't have room for you," the plate concluded. "But listen, on your way out, could you leave the door open for Elijah?"

Sure, thought the gourd. Be nice to Elijah. After all, he doesn't eat much. But to a real living, breathing, caring gourd, just send me away.

Soon the High Holy Days rolled around. Maybe now, thought the gourd. Maybe now I will finally find a place. When he got to the Yom Kippur break-fast the guests were famished. On the table, he saw his old friends the onion and the tomato ready to be devoured by the hungry people.

"Any room up there for me?" he asked. "I am your friend, the gourd, and I have no place to go for the holy day. Can you let me stay here?"

The tomato winced. The onion grimaced. "Well, we would really like to," they stammered. "But...But..."

"But what?" said the gourd.

"But...well, after fasting all day, do you think anyone really wants to eat a gourd?"

The gourd was very hurt and very sad. Maybe he wasn't the most attractive food. After all, he had been getting bumpier and uglier as the months went by. But still...

Just then the gourd saw a whole long line of vegetables making their way down Main Street.

"Where are you going?" he asked.

"To the JCC," they replied. "We are going to decorate the Sukkah."

My big chance, thought the gourd. He took a deep breath when he arrived and asked: "Oh, sukkah, can I help decorate you too?"

"Well, of course," said the sukkah. "You're one of the most important vegetables to decorate me!"

Well, our friend the gourd was very excited and felt very proud to finally have a home here in our sukkah at the JCC on Main Street.

And with finding a home the gourd learned a very important lesson: we should welcome everyone into our sukkah and share with them, not just the beautiful and sweet smelling etrog, but also the poor, lonely, not too pretty gourd. We should open our sukkah to people who are both like the etrog and the gourd, people who are sweet smelling, beautiful, and also the people who, like the gourd, have had a hard time getting invited anywhere else.

Sukkot Crafts and Activities

Decorating the Sukkah

Rosh HaShanah Card Collage

Fruit and Vegetable Shapes

Ushpazin Life Size Paper Figure

Wind Socks

Nature Ideas

Nature Hike

Nature Bracelet

Nature Collage

Leaf Collecting

Leafed Sukkah Table

Melted Crayon Leaf Picture

Harvest Ideas

Decorating the Sukkah

ROSH HASHANAH CARD COLLAGE

MATERIALS:

Rosh HaShanah cards

Scissors

Poster board

Glue sticks

Clear contact paper

DIRECTIONS:

1 Cut words and pictures out of the cards.

2 Glue them onto the poster board to make a collage.

3 Laminate or cover with clear contact paper.

4 Hang your collage in the sukkah. Save it to hang up next year too.

5 Decorate the sukkah.

FRUIT AND VEGETABLE SHAPES

MATERIALS:

Tag board

Paper scraps

Yarn

Dried beans, corn kernels, peas, lentils CAUTION: Small objects can cause choking

White glue

Scissors

Markers or crayons

Paper punch

Yarn or string

Containers to hold materials

DIRECTIONS:

1 Using the templates on p. 274, cut the vegetable shapes out of tag board.

2 Let children glue on the dried vegetables to make a collage or glue on cut pieces of yarn to totally fill in the shapes.

Note: The yarn can either be cut into 1 inch pieces and arranged to fill in the shape or cut one long piece of yarn and looped into around itself to fill in the shape.

3 Children can also color the shapes before the gluing

4 Let the glue dry.

5 Punch a hole in the top of each shape. Thread yarn/string through and knot to make a loop. Hang the decorated fruit in the sukkah.

USHPIZIN LIFE SIZE PAPER FIGURE

A source of joy is sharing our bountiful harvest and sukkah with others. This includes sharing with those less fortunate as well as our "Ushpizin" (special Biblical guests/ancestors). According to 16th-century mystics who lived in the city of Tzfat, a different Biblical guest visited the sukkah each night. They included Abraham, Isaac, Jacob, Moses, Aaron, Joseph, and David. More recently we include Sarah, Rebecca, Rachel, Leah, Miriam, Deborah and Ruth. Can you think of any others guests you would like to invite?

MATERIALS:

Butcher block paper

Crayons and markers

Scissors

Stapler

Newspaper

DIRECTIONS:

Children should do as much as their age permits

1 Tell stories about our Jewish ancestors: Abraham being the first Jew; Jacob buying the birthright from Esau for a bowl of soup; Moses leading the Israelite people out of slavery in Egypt; Sarah having her son Isaac when she was 90 years old; Miriam dancing with the women when they crossed over the Red Sea. Books containing these stories are available through synagogue libraries, in Jewish community resource centers, in local bookstores, as well as at Jewish publishing companies.

2 Lay down 2 large sheets of butcher block paper, one on top of the other.

3 Have your child lie down on top of the papers and draw an outline around him/her.

4 Cut out the 2 sheets of paper in the shape of the child.

5 Staple the 2 shapes together, leaving enough open to allow for stuffing.

6 Color in the top shape to look like an Ushpazin of your choice.

7 Stuff the figure with crumpled newspaper.

8 Staple the body closed.

9 Put it in your sukkah - Remember to take it out if it looks like rain!

WIND SOCKS

MATERIALS:

18 x 24 inch sheet of construction paper

Markers, chalk and crayons

Scissors

Stapler and tape

Crepe paper

Three 16- to 18-inch lengths of string or yarn

DIRECTIONS:

1 Cut slits 1 inch apart and 12 inches long from one of the 18-inch sides.

Variation: Instead of cutting fringe, you could tape pieces of crepe paper to dangle from the bottom of the wind sock.

2 Turn the paper so the slits or fringe are facing you.

3 Decorate the paper with markers, chalk and crayons.

4 Staple together the 24-inch edges making a long tube with the fringe at the bottom.

5 Attach two loops of crisscrossing string to the top of the tube. Where they overlap, tie them together with one end of the third piece of string.

6 Hang it from your sukkah or near your dining room table.

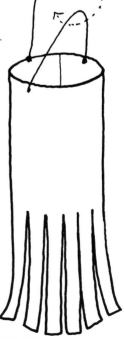

Nature Ideas

NATURE HIKE

Go "collecting" on a nature hike with your children. (Use the backpack that you made at Lag B'Omer. See p. 158 or a bag with handles.) Collect different sizes and shapes of leaves and sticks.

NATURE BRACELET

Make a nature bracelet by wrapping masking tape, sticky side out, loosely around your wrist (children and adults can do this). As you walk outside, stick things you find to your bracelet.

NATURE COLLAGES

Make a nature picture using glue and construction paper or by sticking things you find onto a sheet of clear contact paper. Use your collage as a placemat or wall hanging.

LEAF COLLECTING

Collect big and small leaves of all different shapes. You can make leaf prints with tempera paint, leaf rubbings using crayons or oil pastels, or leaf collages using clear contact paper, leaves and sequins.

LEAFED SUKKAH TABLE

MATERIALS:

Leaves

Paper tablecloth

Clear plastic tablecloth

DIRECTIONS:

1 Place the paper tablecloth over your sukkah table.

2 Scatter leaves over the cloth.

3 Cover it all with the clear plastic tablecloth.

MELTED CRAYON LEAF PICTURE

MATERIALS:

Leaves

Crayon shavings made using an old vegetable peeler

2 pieces of waxed paper, each approximately 8 x 12 inches

Iron and ironing board

Two old cloth towels

Newspapers

DIRECTIONS:

1 Cover your ironing board with two layers of newspaper. Cover paper with a cloth towel.

2 Choose some pretty leaves and arrange them on a piece of waxed paper.

3 Sprinkle the leaf arrangement with crayon shavings.

4 Lay the second piece of waxed paper on top - sandwiching the leaves and crayons.

5 Carefully move your "leaf sandwich" to the ironing board.

6 Place a towel over it.

7 An adult will turn the iron on to a low setting. **CAUTION: Adult supervision is needed. Irons are hot and can burn!**

8 Iron the towel. The crayon shavings will melt and the waxed paper will melt together.

9 Trim the edges of the finished project

10 Hang it on your kitchen windows or in the sukkah.

Harvest Ideas

Make vegetable soup

Make cut-up fruit salad

Take a trip to the pumpkin patch or apple orchard

Make caramel apples

Hanukkah

Daylight is precious now and the nights are long and cold. It is time to gather our family and friends around the menorah and celebrate Hanukkah, "The Festival of Lights." The glow of the candles is reflected in our children's faces, full of anticipation and awe. Warmth, light, miracles...this is Hanukkah.

Experiencing Hanukkah

Brightening our winters with eight days of glowing candles, Hanukkah reminds us that our God is a God of miracles. God was there when a small band of Jews defeated a mighty Greek army to reclaim Jerusalem and rededicate the Holy Temple. And God was there when these brave soldiers, exhausted and hungry, entered the Holy Temple and found only enough oil to last for one day. Imagine their faces reflected in the light of the oil, as it lasted for one, two, three, and finally, eight days. Imagine how the warmth of the flame rekindled their faith in this loving and eternal God.

Strangely enough, Hanukkah is not mentioned in the Bible. Our main sources for information on the revolt are two ancient texts called *Book of the Maccabees I* and *II*. Reading these accounts takes us back in time to Jerusalem during the Hebrew month of Kislev, in the year 165 B.C.E., over 2,100 years ago.

A man called Antiochus Epiphanies, a descendant of one of the generals of Alexander the Great, was the Syrian ruler. His goal was to impose the Greek, or "Hellenistic," culture on all the inhabitants of his empire. Practicing Judaism was strictly forbidden. The Syrians took over the Temple in Jerusalem and made sacrifices to their gods there.

A small group of freedom fighters, the Maccabees, led by Mattathias and his five brave sons, decided to take on the Syrians. Even though the Maccabees were greatly outnumbered, they were able to expel the Syrian army from Jerusalem after a terrible battle. Once this was accomplished, they worked tirelessly to clean and repair the Holy Temple in preparation for a rededication ceremony.

According to the Talmud, there was only enough holy oil to burn for one day in the menorah that was kept in the Temple. Yet, the oil lasted for eight days! In commemoration of this miracle, the holiday of Hanukkah was established as an eight-day celebration.

Traditions & Text

Our tradition offers up contradictory reasons regarding why Hanukkah is celebrated for eight days. The *Mishna* (The Oral Law—written down in the beginning of the third century C.E.) states that the holiday is celebrated because of the miracle of the oil. However, the Book of Maccabees, the account written by those who participated in the rebellion against the Greeks, doesn't mention the miracle of the oil at all. According to *Books I* and *II of the Maccabees*, the Maccabees decided to celebrate the holiday for eight days because they were unable to celebrate the holiday of Sukkot in the fall at the Temple, since, at the time, the Temple was being used for pagan Greek worship. As Sukkot is an eight-day holiday in which sacrifices are offered in the Temple, the Maccabees also celebrated their new holiday with eight days of sacrifices in the newly rededicated Temple.

The Mishna's emphasis on the miracle rather than on the creation of the holiday by the Maccabees shows that the rabbis clearly wanted to downplay the acts of human heroes in the Hanukkah story and emphasize the acts of the divine hero, the Master of the Universe. For that reason, the *Haftarah* (reading from the Prophets) for the Sabbath during Hanukkah is from the book of Zechariah (4:6) "Not by might and not by power, but by My spirit alone, saith the Lord of Hosts." Therefore, the lights of Hanukkah represent the spirit and the *spiritual* fight against oppression. The lighting of the *Hanukkiah* (Hanukkah Lamp) is a symbol of pride. In the Talmud, we are taught to light and display the Hanukkah lamp so that everyone will know of the miracle of Hanukkah. In ancient times, people hung their Hanukkah lamps on the outside of their doors as a public demonstration of pride. Today, many Jews light their lamps in their windows for all to see.

I Had A Little Dreidel

According to legend, Jewish freedom fighters holding secret meetings while plotting against the Syrians pretended they were merely gambling. Back then, people gambled with a top (called "dreidel" in Yiddish), spinning it and letting it fall to see what letter appeared on top. That is why we play dreidel games at Hanukkah and hand out *"gelt"* (coins), either real or made of chocolate.

Playing Dreidel is very simple. On each side of the dreidel is a Hebrew letter (ש,ה,ג,נ)which stands for each word of the slogan, *"Nes Gadol Hayah Sham,"* or "A Great Miracle Happened There." (In Israel the letters on the dreidel stand for, "A Great Miracle Happened Here!")

Fascinating Food Facts

Since Hanukkah is the story of "the miracle of the oil," we eat many foods that are fried in oil during this week-long holiday. The traditional favorite is latkes (potato pancakes). Some variations include sweet potato pancakes, or latkes with shredded vegetables mixed in with the potato.

In Israel it is traditional to eat sufganiyot, fried jelly doughnuts usually covered with granular or powdered sugar.

Typical Hanukkah Menu

The blessings for Hanukkah aren't as extensive as for Shabbat. Do the traditional blessings below or as many as you're comfortable with. On Shabbat, light the Hanukkah candles before the Shabbat candles. (The letter in parenthesis indicates the appropriate blessing found in "Prayers and Blessings" on p. 283.)

The following is the traditional order for the blessings.

Two blessings over the Hanukkah candles (S)
(After dark only. You might light the candles after dinner.)

The Shehecheyanu prayer (G)
(On the first night only.)

There is an additional traditional prayer "HaNerot Halalu."
(Consult traditional prayer book.)

Hanukkah songs

Before eating the following blessings are traditionally used:
Handwashing (A), Hamotzi (B)

Soup or Salad
Fruit Salad
Brisket or Fish
Latkes with applesauce (or sour cream with dairy meal)
Sufganiyot / Hanukkah cookies

Blessing after meal (*Birkat HaMazon*) (H)

GO TO RECIPE INDEX IN BACK OF BOOK FOR SUGGESTED RECIPES.

Kids in the Kitchen

Let your children enjoy the gift of giving by helping to make these delicious Hanukkah candies for family and friends.

HANUKKAH GELT

DIRECTIONS:

1 Combine all ingredients in a double boiler.

2 Place over simmering water and stir until smooth.

3 Spread quickly into a buttered or wax paper-lined cookie sheet.

4 Cool.

5 Using Hanukkah cookie cutter, a plastic lid or top of spice jar, cut circles of fudge.

6 Lift out with a metal spatula and wrap in foil to resemble coins.

7 Store in refrigerator.

COOKING EQUIPMENT NEEDED:

Double broiler

Measuring spoons

Measuring cups

Cookie sheet

Wax paper

Spatula

Cookie cutters or top of a spice jar

INGREDIENTS:

1 pound confectioners' powdered sugar

1 pound piece of chocolate

½ cup cocoa

¼ teaspoon salt

6 tablespoons butter or margarine

4 tablespoons milk

1 teaspoon vanilla extract

Read-Aloud Story

The Miracle Moon

Retold by Martin Katz
(Origin unknown)

Their bay window was no bigger than the neighbors', but it was still large enough to hold their grandmother's hanukkiah. It was the last night of Hanukkah and finally it was Sam's turn to light the menorah. Sam would light the shamash, and then help his little sister and brother light the other eight candles.

Sam knew how special this night would be since the candles would burn brighter than ever, and anyone who saw them in the window would understand the message they sent, the message of freedom.

The family gathered to recite the ancient Hanukkah prayers, and finally it was Sam's turn. One by one the candles were lit, and one by one the light from the menorah grew brighter and brighter. Sam stood back in sheer awe of its beauty.

Soon the Hanukkah songs had been sung and all the latkes had been eaten. Sam and his brother and sister liked their latkes with apple sauce, while his parents ate them with sour cream.

That night while Sam was preparing to go to sleep, his mother noticed that he seemed sad. She asked him what was wrong.

"Hanukkah is over for another whole year," he said. "How will people remember the message of our candles, the importance of freedom? Without our beautiful candles to remind them they may forget."

Sam's mother cuddled him and promised that Sam would witness a miracle the very next night, a miracle that might help others remember just how important freedom is.

Sam could hardly sleep that night. He couldn't believe that he was going to witness a miracle just like the Maccabees did hundreds of years ago. The next day seemed to drag on forever. Finally the sun set, and Sam asked his mom to show him the new miracle. They bundled up and went outside. When they came to a clear space to look up into the night sky, Sam's mom pointed towards the new moon, now four days old.

"When we began celebrating Hanukkah a week ago, the moon was getting smaller and smaller and the night grew darker and darker," she said. "Starting on the fourth day the moon began to grow again so that by today, when we have finished lighting candles, God is ready to show us his special candle, the moon."

"During the eight days of Hanukkah we need to light candles to remind the world of the miracle done in the time of the Maccabees, the miracle that led to our own freedom," she continued.

"While our work is done, God's work continues. This is the miracle I want to show you - the partnership we have with God. We share a responsibility to make our world a better place where people can live in freedom. The moon is our reminder of that responsibility."

Hanukkah Beyond Presents

When most kids think about Hanukkah, they tend to envision gifts and gelt. It's a challenge to retain the spiritual significance of the holiday that often gets lost in the abundance of gifts.

Creating an atmosphere of moderation while children are young is the key to getting back to the true meaning of Hanukkah. As a family you can start new traditions that are both fun and rejuvenating by replacing some of the material gifts with personal or spiritual gifts. Every night of Hanukkah can be devoted to a special project or activity that will initiate some thought, feelings, and conversation in your family.

Idea 1: The "Grateful" Menorah: When you light the hanukkiah, ask everyone at the table to share something they are grateful for.

Idea 2: Hanukkah *Mitzvah* Fairy: Draw names from a hat and be a secret pal for the next three days. Do a favor, leave coupons or sweet notes, complete one of their chores, or leave a small treat for the person you picked.

Idea 3: Phone a friend or a relative and as a family, sing one of your favorite Hanukkah songs over the telephone, and then wish them a Happy Hanukkah.

Idea 4: Potluck Hanukkah Brunch: Invite some friends and/or family over for a Sunday morning brunch. Assign a festive dish for everyone to bring. Have a treasure hunt for hidden gelt. Share Hanukkah songs and stories.

Idea 5: Bake and decorate Hanukkah Cookies as a family project and bring some to someone who doesn't have many family members or friends nearby.

Idea 6: Create-A-Coupon Potpourri: Use your imagination and design coupons for future services for family and friends, i.e., free back or foot massage, bake cookies, wash dishes, brush the dog.

Idea 7: Hanukkah Joke and Talent Night: Share your talents. Put together skits and make up Hanukkah jokes. For example: What has four feet and plays dreidel? (Two children.) Why are some menorahs like old cars? (They both burn oil.)

Idea 8: "*Zot* Hanukkah" (This is Hanukkah): The eighth night is called the climax of the festival. What would be a special tradition for your family to start on this night? Leave the most awesome gifts for last. How about candle-making, or a candle light dinner with all the lights turned off in the house?

Hanukkah Crafts and Activities

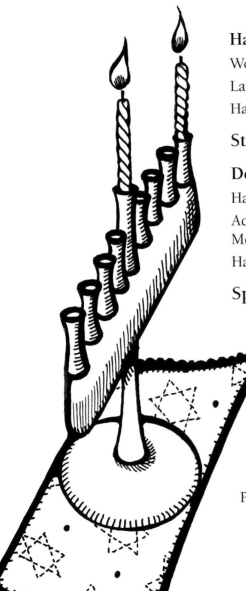

Hanukkiah/Menorah
Wooden Hanukkiah/Menorah
Layered Sand Hanukkiah/Menorah
Hanukkah Drip Tray

Striped Beeswax Candles

Decorations
Hanukkah Box
Add-a-candle-flame Refrigerator Stick Menorah
Handprint Menorah Decoration

Sponge Painted Wrapping Paper

Party Ideas
Cookie Decorating Contest
Hanukkah Gift Game
Singing

Gift Ideas
Jewelry Box
Picture Frame
Pencil Holder

Hanukkiah / Menorah

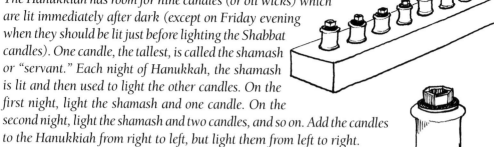

The Hanukkiah has room for nine candles (or oil wicks) which are lit immediately after dark (except on Friday evening when they should be lit just before lighting the Shabbat candles). One candle, the tallest, is called the shamash or "servant." Each night of Hanukkah, the shamash is lit and then used to light the other candles. On the first night, light the shamash and one candle. On the second night, light the shamash and two candles, and so on. Add the candles to the Hanukkiah from right to left, but light them from left to right.

WOODEN HANUKKIAH/MENORAH

Some families buy a small menorah for each child or, as they get older, allow them to make or pick one out for themselves. In this way children can really feel that they have their own part in the nightly ritual. Now lighting the menorah truly becomes a family experience, filling the home with the glow and warmth of Hanukkah.

MATERIALS:

One 11 x 2-½ x ½-inch piece of wood, with smooth sides

Tempera paint in individual containers

Paint brushes

Nine ⅜-inch hex nuts to fit your Hanukkah candles

9 pennies

10 colored wooden spools – available at craft stores

Small wooden squares or tiles – available at craft stores

Large glitter sequins and glitter

Craft glue

Spray adhesive – available at craft shops

CAUTION: Never leave a lit menorah unattended!

DIRECTIONS:

1 Paint the wood. Apply glitter now, if desired. Let the paint dry. Adults could then spray it with adhesive to help the glitter stick. Let it dry thoroughly.

2 Glue the nine wooden spools, in a row, along the top of the wood. For the shamash candle, glue a second spool on top of one other spool so that the shamash candle stands above the rest.

3 Using glue, top each spool with a penny and then a bolt.

4 Decorate the remaining painted wood as you wish with glued-on wooden squares, sequins, etc.

5 Let the menorah dry thoroughly.

LAYERED SAND HANUKKIAH/MENORAH

MATERIALS:

10 (1-ounce) crystal clear plastic shot glasses

Salt or white sand

Powdered tempera paint

Cleaned cottage cheese containers with lids to hold salt - 1 for each color planned

Plastic spoons

Toothpicks

Glue

9 metal discs (1½-inch fender washers) the size of the cup opening

Nine ⅜-inch metal nuts

Wooden base, large enough to hold nine salt/sand cups spaced 1½-inches apart

Tin foil

DIRECTIONS:

1 Divide salt/sand into containers. Put enough powdered tempera paint in each container to reach the desired shade. (Red + blue = purple; yellow + blue = green; red + yellow = orange). Mix the tempera and salt/sand.

2 Using the plastic spoons, fill the shot glasses with layers of colored sand. Make ten filled glasses. Older children and adults could make sand designs by sliding a toothpick down the inside edge of the cup as each additional layer of sand is added.

3 Cover the finished sand design with a thin layer of glue.

4 Cover the glue layer with a metal disc or when the glue is dry, turn over the cup, glue side down, and glue the metal disc on the bottom of the cup.

5 To make the shamash candle, glue one cup upside down onto the wood. Top with a second, upright, dish-covered cup.

6 Glue the metal nuts onto the discs. Allow them to dry.

7 Wrap the wooden base with tin foil. Tear a small opening to reveal the wood where each cup of sand will be placed.

8 Glue containers onto the wooden base.

HANUKKIAH DRIP TRAY

One of the best Hanukkah projects: it's fun and it saves your tablecloth from wax drippings!

MATERIALS:

Tinfoil

Pizza round or piece of card-board/ tag board cut into desired shape

Tinfoil

Colored construction paper

Stickers

Hanukkah glitter

Clear contact paper

Scissors

Glue sticks

DIRECTIONS:

1 Cover the cardboard or pizza round with tinfoil.

2 Decorate it with stickers, Hanukkah glitter, Hanukkah shapes or designs cut out of construction paper (see templates, p.275).

3 Cover the finished drip tray with clear contact paper. Make sure the contact paper covers the edges.

STRIPED BEESWAX CANDLES

MATERIALS:

Hanukkah candles

Sheets of colored beeswax, cut into 1-inch square pieces or pre-cut beeswax strips, cut into various shapes

DIRECTIONS:

1 Wrap and press pieces of wax around a candle, leaving the bottom half inch of the candle un-wrapped, so it still fits in your Hanukkiah.

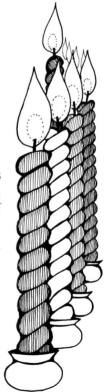

2 Decorate as many candles as you wish this way.

Decorations

HANUKKAH DECORATION BOX

Children love seeing what they made when they were younger. As one of our parents said, "These decorations become a comfortable family tradition year after year."

MATERIALS:

Empty large box with a lid

Glue

Tissue paper squares

Construction paper Hanukkah shapes - see templates on p. 275

Family photos

DIRECTIONS:

1 Decorate your box by gluing on colored tissue paper squares and construction paper Hanukkah shapes as well as family photos.

2 Store dated and signed Hanukkah decorations in box.

HANDPRINT HANUKKIAH DECORATION

MATERIALS:

12 x 4½-inch piece of tag board, white or colored

Sequins, beads, material scraps

Gold glitter

Markers

Glue

DIRECTIONS:

1 The child places his/her hands, palm side down, with thumbs touching, on the tag board.

2 Outline the hands with a colored marker.

3 Decorate the inside of the hand Hanukkiah with markers, sequins, beads, material.

4 Create flames with glue and glitter.

5 Display your Hanukkiah in the window.

ADD-A-CANDLE-FLAME
REFRIGERATOR STICK HANUKKIAH

MATERIALS:

Jumbo, 4½-inch craft sticks –
14 per picture

9 x 16-inch piece of colored tag board (Art Board)

Glue

Magic markers, crayons, glitter pens, stickers

One 9 x 16-inch piece of gold colored felt, cut into 9 x 5-inch and 9 x 7-inch pieces

Scissors

10-inch long strip of ½-inch wide magnetic tape with adhesive backing

OPTIONAL: 2 additional 8-inch strips of magnetic tape

DIRECTIONS:

1 Color the craft sticks with markers or crayons. Children can make a different design for each "candle."

Note: You could also use glitter or glitter pens. Younger children could use stickers.

2 Glue craft sticks on tag board to form a menorah. Use two craft sticks to form a horizontal base for the candles, one to make the stem, one for each of the eight nights and two to make the shamash candle.

3 Make a pocket to hold the unused "flames" by folding the 9 x 5-inch piece of felt in half to form a 4½ x 5-inch pocket. Glue the two side edges shut. Glue the pocket to the back of the tag board.

4 Cut the leftover felt into 9 flame shapes.

5 Cut 18 half-inch squares of magnetic tape.

6 Peel off the backing and attach one square of magnetic tape above each candle stick and one to the back of each flame.

7 Add a flame a night. Store flames in the back pocket when they are not being used. To use as a refrigerator magnet, place two magnetic strips on the back of the menorah.

Note: Store in Hanukkah Decoration Box.

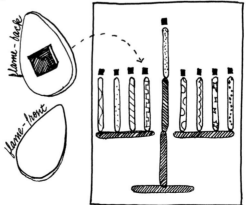

Sponge Painted Wrapping Paper

MATERIALS:

Sponges cut into Hanukkah shapes: Dreidel, Jewish star, menorah - see templates, p. 275

Variation: Many other materials, like cookie cutters dipped in paint, can be used to make prints. Be creative!!

Styrofoam meat trays

Tempera paint – one color in each Styrofoam meat tray

Large pieces of paper: white, newspaper, or colored paper

Newspaper

Glitter

DIRECTIONS:

1 Cover your table with newspaper.

2 Give each child a piece of paper.

3 Moisten sponges and squeeze out excess water.

4 Lay out the sponges, cookie cutters, etc. and the paint trays.

5 Dip the sponges into paint, scrape excess off on edge of the tray and make prints on their paper.

Hints: Cut enough sponges to have one for each color.

Try using more than one color per sponge.

Sprinkle glitter on the wet paint.

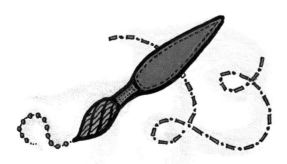

Party Ideas

Cookie Decorating Contest

MATERIALS:

Pre-made cookies (Recipe on p. 266)

Bowls filled with deeply colored frosting (Recipe on p. 266)

Cookie decorations: chocolate sprinkles, colored sugar, red cinnamon candies, silver balls, decorator gel

Paper plates

Wax paper

Plastic knives

Judges

DIRECTIONS:

1 Give each participant some cookies and a piece of wax paper on which to work.

2 Put paper plates in the center of the table.

3 Decorate cookies.

4 Put the finished cookies on large plates.

5 The judges pick the winners for:

The most beautiful

The most spiritual

The most colorful

The most international

The most funny, etc.

Everyone Should Be A Winner!

HANUKKAH GIFT GAME

DIRECTIONS:

Recommended for ages 10 and up. Younger children may have trouble understanding the rules and giving up a present they want. For younger children, adapt the rules so they can keep the present they want.

1 Each person brings a present worth $5 that is suitable for their age group.

2 Presents are put in the center of a table in the living room or family room.

3 Put a number on a slip of paper for each person attending your party.

4 Let each person pick a number.

5 Everyone gathers together in the living room or family room.

6 Person #1 chooses a gift and opens it.

7 Person #2 has a choice of taking gift #1 or choosing an unopened gift. If gift #1 is taken, that person gets to choose a new unopened gift. They cannot take back the gift they just lost, at least on this turn.

8 Person #3, and so on, has a choice of taking any opened gift or choosing one yet unopened.

9 Whoever has a gift taken from them can take an opened gift (except the one they just lost) or open a new gift.

SINGING

Following is a list of a few of the wonderful Hanukkah and Jewish holiday tapes available:

Julie Auerbach, *Seasoned with Song;* Julie Jaslow Auerbach (Shaker Heights, OH), 1989

Fran Avni, *Latkes & Hamentashen;* Lemonstone Records (Cote St Luc, Quebec), 1980

Rabbi Joe Black, *Aleph Bet Boogie;* Lanitunes Music (Minneapolis, MN), 1991

Debbie Friedman, *Miracles and Wonders;* Sounds Write Productions, Inc. (San Diego, CA), 1992

Judy Caplan Ginsburgh, *Chanuka Favorites,* Ginsburgh Enterprises; (Alexandria, LA), 1991

Doug Lipman, *One Little Candle;* Enchanters Press (Somerville, MA), 1990

Paul Zim, *Hooray for Chanukah;* Simcha, 1987

Gift Ideas

JEWELRY BOX

MATERIALS:

Cigar box for each child (Available, often free, at cigar stores)

Felt – cut to fit the inside bottom and inside lid of your box

Decorations: Choose among sea shells, different shaped noodles (plain or colored), different colored beans, feathers, sequins, faux jewels, buttons, etc.

ADULTS ONLY:

To color noodles: Soak noodles in a mixture of rubbing alcohol and food coloring. Periodically, turn the noodles, so all sides are dyed. When noodles have reached the color you desire, remove them from the liquid with a slotted spoon and lay them out on wax paper to dry overnight.
NOTE: Smelly

Scissors

Glue

DIRECTIONS:

1 Glue felt pieces to the inside bottom and inside lid of your box.

2 Cut a ¼ x 1-inch piece of felt and glue it to the inside of the front edge of the lid to form a tab that will be used as an opener. Be sure to keep the box propped open until the tab dries.

3 Glue decorations on the top of your box. Older children can make more elaborate designs.

4 Allow 24 hours to dry.

Variation: When dry, the box could be spray-painted by adults in a well-ventilated, open space. We recommend gold spray paint.

PICTURE FRAME

MATERIALS:

5 x 6-inch piece of tag board or cardboard (not needed for store-bought frame)

Materials for decorations: odd puzzle pieces, buttons, faux jewels, markers, puffy paint

Magnetic tape (available at craft and art stores)

Glue

DIRECTIONS:

1 Glue 4 tongue depressors together to form a 5 x 6-inch frame - 2 horizontal, 2 vertical, attached at the ends.

2 Let the frame dry thoroughly.

3 Decorate the picture frame as you wish with buttons, beans, etc.

4 Glue the tongue depressor frame to the 5 x 6-inch piece of tag board on 3 sides only, leaving one side open for inserting a picture.

5 When dry, attach a 2-inch piece of magnetic tape to the back top of the frame.

6 Insert a photo. Display it on your refrigerator.

Variation: Decorate a store-bought wooden frame with the same materials.

Pencil Holder

MATERIALS:

Empty, cleaned orange juice container with no sharp edges

Different colors of yarn or only blue and white

Scissors

Glue in a dish-like container

Sponge tip paintbrush

DIRECTIONS:

1 Cover the juice container with glue.

2 Coil yarn around the can, filling all the space. You can use one color, alternate colors or wrap yarn around itself, forming shapes.

3 Make yarn designs with smaller strands of yarn: squiggles, a Star of David, etc.

4 Let the pencil holder dry thoroughly.

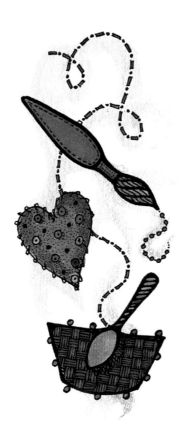

Tu Bishvat

It has been weeks since Hanukkah and snow still covers the ground. Trees lie sleeping and leafless. Yet, in the land of Israel, the rains have begun and the sap in the trees has started to rise. It is the 15th day of the Hebrew month of Shvat - the holiday of Tu Bishvat.

Experiencing Tu Bishvat

Celebrated as "The New Year of the Trees," the roots of this festival go back to ancient Israel. Mentioned in the *Mishna*, the second century book of Jewish law, as one of the four Jewish New Years, Tu Bishvat is connected to tithing (tax laws) and to calculating the age of trees. Each year, the people paid a tax on the produce of their trees. Fruits that blossomed after the fifteenth of the month of Shvat belonged to the next year's tithe; whereas fruits that blossomed before the fifteenth were counted in this year's tax. As for newly planted trees, fruit could not be eaten for the first three years after planting, the age of a tree being calculated by whether it had been planted before or after Tu Bishvat. When a young tree reached three years old, its fruit was to be dedicated to God and taken to the Temple in Jerusalem, to support the Priesthood.

In the 16th century, the great mystics of Tzfat connected Tu Bishvat with the metaphor of the Tree of Life, which symbolizes God's essence and connects the earth and heaven. The mystics created a wonderful Tu Bishvat *seder* (meal) where they ate fruit symbolizing, among other things, the various aspects of God as well as the seasons. Four cups of wine or grape juice are drunk which range from pure white (dormancy) to all red (the blooming of trees). Seven species of fruit and grain (Deuteronomy 8:8) are represented: barley, grapes, figs, olives, pomegranate, dates and wheat. Many seders present additional types of fruits representing God's concealment, God's wholeness, and the spark of God found within each of us. There are several Tu Bishvat seders available in print, and it is a fun tradition to begin with your own family.

With the rise of Zionism and the establishment of the State of Israel in 1948, the significance of Tu Bishvat has increased. It is a time when trees are planted in Israel, both by Israeli citizens and by people from all over the world who purchase tree certificates from JNF - the Jewish National Fund. Moreover, we live in a time of great ecological concern. Jewish tradition is filled with texts protecting and appreciating the bounty of God's good earth:

> *Planting is so important, that if a sapling were in your hand, and you*
> *were told that the Messiah had come, first plant the sapling, then go*
> *out to greet the Messiah. (Avot de Rabbi Natan B. Ch. 3)*

> *When you war against a city you have to besiege it a long time….*
> *you must not destroy its trees …you may eat of them, but you must*
> *not cut them down…. (Deuteronomy 20:19,20)*

Tu Bishvat is the perfect time to talk about recycling, preserving and sustaining nature. Tu Bishvat is also the perfect time to connect to the land and people of Israel and to eat together with family and friends while recalling God's goodness and the cyclical nature of the seasons.

Traditions & Text

We're used to having different New Years reckonings. We celebrate New Year on January 1st and on Rosh HaShanah. April 15th, tax day, is another sort of New Year, and so is July 1st - the beginning of the fiscal year. In ancient Israel, there were also multiple New Years. Tu Bishvat, the New Year of the Trees, is actually a kind of tax day. It was the day when the produce of trees was calculated so people would know what offerings they needed to contribute to the Temple. It was originally little more than an administrative date. It has, however, grown in importance through the generations. The mystics of 16th century Tzfat saw it as a mystical day. The Torah cryptically tells us "For a human is a tree of the field." There must be a relationship, then, between trees and people. And further, the mystics felt that they could map out God's being with a "tree of life," a configuration of God's essence.

THE TREE OF LIFE

For the 16th century mystics of Tzfat in Northern Israel, trees were a mystical symbol. Trees, after all, sink their roots in the earth and extend their branches

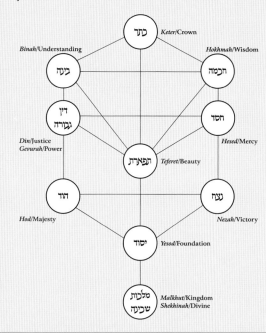

toward heaven. They felt that God's act of creating the world was done in stages—each stage corresponding to an attribute of God. They created a map of those stages or attributes (called "Sphirot") in the form of what they called the Eitz Chayim, or Tree of life. Because the tree of life represents the nature of God, and the Torah is also called the Tree of Life, the mystics related the Sphirot to Tu Bishvat. Complicated? Of course it's complicated. The mystics claimed, after all, that NO ONE should study mysticism until they were at least 40 years old!

91

Tu Bishvat

Fascinating Food Facts

After Jews were exiled from Eretz Yisrael (the land of Israel), it became the custom on Tu Bishvat to eat "fruits" that grow in Israel - particularly the seven species mentioned specifically in the Bible: "a land of wheat and barley, of vines, figs and pomegranates, a land of olive trees, dates and honey." [Deuteronomy 8:8] The Tu Bishvat seders include symbolic foods that represent different aspects of God and our relationship with the divine: fruits that can be eaten entirely (grapes, apples), those that have inedible pits, but edible outsides (dates, cherries, peaches), or those that have inedible outsides, but edible insides (walnuts, pomegranates).

Suggested Tu Bishvat Menu

One idea for a Tu Bishvat seder menu symbolizes the four mystical stages of creation as follows:

Fruits with shells - tangerine, kiwi, pomegranate, pistachio, orange, watermelon
Fruits with pits - peach, plum, date, olive, cherry
Entirely edible fruit - apple, pear, strawberry
Fruit with shell and pit - avocado

For many the edible part of the fruit represents the vulnerability of human life. There are those people who need protection from evil (the shell), and those who are spiritually strong (entirely edible fruit) and those whose sense of God comes from within (the pit). The letter in parenthesis indicates the appropriate blessing found in "Prayers and Blessings" on p. 283)

Since we eat fruit on Tu Bishvat, we should pay attention to two different b'rachot for fruit:	On Tu Bishvat we suggest using recipes that include fruits, nuts and grains:
For fruit that grows on trees (apples, pears, coconuts, avocados) *Borei Pri Ha Etz* (D)	
For fruit that grows on bushes, or vines (strawberries, bananas, watermelon) *Borei Pri HaAdamah* (E)	
The traditional blessing said at meal time. Handwashing (A) Hamotzi (B)	Mushroom barley soup Apricot chicken or honey pecan chicken Moroccan Couscous Hot fruit compote Rugalach Cookies or cakes with fruit and nuts
Blessing after meal (*Birkat HaMazon*) (H).	

GO TO RECIPE INDEX IN BACK OF BOOK FOR SUGGESTED RECIPES.

Kids in the Kitchen

On Tu Bishvat we taste many fruits that are grown in Israel. Those with seeds and those that are seedless, those we eat completely and those we shell or peel. Here is a recipe using carob, a relative to chocolate, which grows in Israel as well as other places around the world. Mix up a batch and enjoy!

EASY BAKE CAROB CRUNCH

COOKING EQUIPMENT NEEDED:

Saucepan

Measuring cups

Measuring spoons

Baking sheet

INGREDIENTS:

¾ **cup honey**

½ **cup carob* powder**

½ **cup milk (or Mocha Mix, a non-dairy creamer found in the frozen section)**

1 **teaspoon vanilla**

½ **cup margarine**

3 **cups rolled oats**

DIRECTIONS:

In a saucepan combine honey, carob, mocha mix, vanilla and margarine. Boil for 5 minutes stirring constantly. Remove from heat. Add oats and mix well. Drop by tsp. onto wax paper and let cool.

*Carob is available in health food stores.

Read-Aloud Story

Honi The Circlemaker

Babylonian Talmud Ta'anit 23a
Adapted and retold by Jody Hirsh

Honi the Circlemaker was a pretty famous man in his own time. People said that he was so close to God he was practically like family. Once when there was a terrible drought in the Land of Israel, he prayed for rain by drawing a circle on the ground and standing in the middle of the circle. "I'm not movin' out of here until it rains," he said. And you know something? IT RAINED. Oh it's true it didn't rain very much at first - just a drizzle. The people came to Honi and said, "This isn't what we need. It's not enough! Try again!" So he tried again. "This isn't what I meant," he said to God from the middle of his circle. "I meant REAL rain, not this drizzly stuff." And you know what? It rained harder. Maybe even too hard. It rained so hard that there were floods! People were taking boats to work. Everyone went up to the Temple Mount to escape the floods, and when they saw Honi, they yelled at him. "It's way too much!" they said. So Honi tried again. "We need just enough rain," he said. "Rain that will be a blessing!" And you know what? It happened. Just enough rain. Rain of blessing that was good for the flowers and especially for the trees. And mushrooms! The people immediately went out to gather mushrooms. The rain was definitely a good thing - but people just can't have too much or too little of a good thing.

Some time afterward, Honi took a walk. He was feeling proud of himself, and he liked the fact that everyone knew him. He came across a man who was planting a carob tree. "Hey there," he called out. "Hey there, Rabbi," said the man. "Tell me," said Honi. "This carob tree that you're planting . . . how long will it take until it grows carobs?" The man scratched his head and looked at Honi. "Well . . . it'll take 70 years until this tree grows fruit," he said. "What a waste of time," said Honi. "You'll never eat from this tree. Why bother planting it?" "Oh I don't know," said the tree planter. "I'm not planting this for myself. I'm planting it for my children and their children." "Life is too short," laughed Honi, and walked on his way.

Honi suddenly felt tired . . . so tired. He saw a nice shady rock, lay down behind it and fell fast asleep. He slept really soundly. In fact . . . he didn't know it, but he slept for 70 years! When he woke up, he felt so refreshed, but he didn't realize he had slept so long. He started walking home and he chanced upon the same tree. Only suddenly, the tree was a giant one. And the man was picking the carob fruit from the tree. "Hey there," called Honi. "Are you the man who planted this tree?" "Are you kidding?" said the man. "This tree was planted by my grandfather." Honi was taken aback. He realized that he must have slept 70 years! Now he understood how important it was to plant trees.

Tu Bishvat

Tu Bishvat Crafts and Activities

Tree Projects
Cardboard Tube Almond Trees
Family Tree
Tree Globes

Planters
Painted Pots
Ceramic-Tiled Pots

Decorations
Soda Bottle Windsock
Spiral Paper Plate Mobile

Tree Projects

At the Tu Bishvat Seder celebrating the New Year of the trees, the tradition is to drink four glasses of wine ranging from all white to dark red, reflecting the changing nature of the land in Israel. As Tu Bishvat nears, the barren tree branches begin to bud and by the middle of the month of Shvat, the white, full blossoms of the almond tree dot the landscape. It is Tu Bishvat.

CARDBOARD TUBE ALMOND TREES

MATERIALS:

Empty cardboard toilet paper or paper towel tubes

Brown paint

Containers to hold paint

Medium sized paintbrushes

2-inch pink and green tissue paper squares (small cotton balls colored with pink markers may be used in lieu of pink tissue squares)

Scissors

Glue sticks

DIRECTIONS:

1 Paint the cardboard tubes with brown paint. Let them dry.

2 Cut slits 3 inches down from the top of each cardboard tube, making four to six evenly spaced slits.

3 Fold the slits down to make branches.

4 Crumple pink tissue squares. Glue them onto the folded "branches" wherever you want.

5 Cut out and glue on green tissue paper leaves.

FAMILY TREE

A great project for the entire family

MATERIALS:

Photographs of the generations in your family: Grandparents, parents, sisters, brothers, (optional: aunts, uncles, and cousins)

Five pieces of 1 x 2 inch pine: 48-inch, 20-inch, 16-inch, 14-inch and 12-inch (1 x 2 inch pine boards can be purchased at a lumberyard or a home improvement center. Their personnel will cut it for you.)

Note: *The tree can be used to display pictures of your family at random or as described here, in genealogical order, in which case you may have to adjust the lengths of the wood pieces to accommodate the number and sizes of the pictures.*

Wood glue

3 feet of adhesive-backed magnetic tape

1 gallon-sized paint can – empty and cleaned

Plaster of Paris

Water

Long stirring stick or wooden spoon

Plastic bowl

Newspaper

Acrylic paint – green and brown

Paintbrushes

Hammer

½-inch nails

DIRECTIONS:

1. Cover your work area with paper.

2. When you paint the boards, paint one side and let it dry before painting the other sides.

3. Paint the 48-inch strip of wood brown.

4. Paint the 20-inch, 16-inch, 14-inch and 2-inch pieces of wood green.

5. To make the tree:

   In the following order, lay down and securely glue the 4 shorter pieces horizontally across the 48-inch length of wood. Reinforce by also hammering in a nail.

   Lay the 12-inch long piece of wood across the top for grandparent pictures.

   For parent's photos: 8 inches down, lay the 14-inch piece of wood across

   For photos of brothers and sisters: 8 inches down, lay the 16-inch piece of wood across

   For photos of aunts, uncles, cousins: 8 inches down, lay the 20-inch piece of wood across

   Let the glue dry thoroughly.

   Note: Again, picture arrangements and lengths of wood are up to you, depending on the photos you want to use and whether you chose a genealogical or random display.

6 Mix the plaster in plastic bowl, according to directions on package.

7 Fill the gallon can ¾ full with plaster.

8 When the plaster thickens, put in the 48-inch length of wood, so it touches the bottom of the can. Brace it so it remains upright until it can stand on its own. Let it set overnight. You could paint the plaster green or buy cellophane grass to lay on top of the dried plaster.

9 Cut the magnetic tape into 1-inch pieces

10 Attach magnetic pieces to the back of the photos, and corresponding pieces to the horizontal wood strips where you want the picture to be. Space your photos about 3 inches apart.

TREE GLOBES

MATERIALS:

Baby food or larger glass jar with lid

NOTE: *This is for display or decoration only. Children should not be permitted to carry the tree globe around. The glass could break.*

Tacky glue

Clay

Plastic tree(s) (available at craft supply store) or a small tree branch

Glitter

Water

Corn syrup

DIRECTIONS:

1 Remove the label and thoroughly clean and dry the jar.

2 Using the lid as a base, press a piece of clay on to its inside surface forming a small mound.

3 Arrange the "tree" in the clay.

4 Fill the jar with a mixture of 2 parts water to one part corn syrup.

5 Add 1 teaspoon of glitter.

6 Apply the glue in a circle around the inside edge of the bottle cap.

7 Carefully invert the lid and gently attach it to the jar.

8 Wipe away excess glue.

9 Let it dry thoroughly.

10 Turn your tree globe upside down and shake it gently.

Planters

PAINTED POTS

MATERIALS:

Terracotta clay pots – any size

Newspaper

Acrylic paint

Terracotta markers

Mod Podge

Paint containers: Muffin tin or individual clean plastic containers to hold paint

Paintbrushes

Large plastic or metal buttons, faux jewels, small ceramic tiles, flat marbles

Tacky Glue that holds to ceramic surfaces

DIRECTIONS:

1 Cover the workspace with layers of newspaper.

2 Ideas for painting or coloring on the clay pot:

Paint the top rim with a rainbow of vertical stripes and the rest with one solid color. When dry, paint flowers on the solid background.

Paint faces or letters

Paint dots or any other pattern overall

Use terracotta markers to enhance your designs or use them instead of paint

Paint family names

Paint handprints to look like trees

3 Let the paint dry. Cover your design with a thin coating of Mod Podge to create a protective, shiny surface. Let it dry thoroughly.

4 Glue on ceramic tiles, beads, plastic buttons, faux jewels as extra accents.

Note: Plant avocado pits, sweet potato, pineapple, carrot tops, or parsley for Passover.

Ceramic-Tiled Pots

For older children

MATERIALS:

Newspaper

Clay pots

Small ceramic tiles or broken pieces of pottery or china plates

CAUTION: *Watch for sharp edges of broken pottery.*

Plaster of Paris or grout

Ceramic glue

Measuring cup

Plastic bowl

Water

Wooden spoon

Sponge

DIRECTIONS:

1 Cover the work area with newspaper.

2 Glue mosaic tiles or broken pieces of pottery all over the outside surface of the clay pot.

3 Let the pot dry overnight.

4 Mix the Plaster of Paris according to the directions, making enough to cover your pot, or use grout.

5 Rub wet plaster or grout over your tile design, making sure to fill all the gaps between the ceramic pieces. Gently remove the excess from on top of the tiles with a damp sponge.

6 Let the plaster dry. Wipe it clean with a damp sponge and a clean cloth.

Decorations

SODA BOTTLE WIND SOCK

MATERIALS:

Top half of a 2-liter clear soda bottle, cleaned and dried

Paper puncher

Tissue paper squares, cut into smaller pieces

Paintbrush

Diluted glue or Mod Podge

Permanent markers

Different colors of shiny, curly ribbon cut into 18-inch lengths

DIRECTIONS:

1 Punch holes around the cut edge of the top half of the soda bottle.

2 Paint Mod Podge/glue onto bottle.

Apply tissue paper, covering the entire surface of the bottle.

Coat the tissue paper with another thin layer of Mod Podge or glue.

Let it dry thoroughly overnight

3 For older children or adults: Tie one piece of ribbon into each hole. Slightly curl it using the flat edge of a scissors.

4 Wrap and knot a piece of ribbon around the neck of the bottle, leaving a long end loose for hanging. Repeat with a second ribbon, leaving the loose end opposite the first.

5 Hang your windsock in a sheltered area. Keep it from getting wet.

SPIRAL PAPER PLATE MOBILE

MATERIALS:

Newspaper

Paper plate at least 9 inches in diameter

Scissors

Markers

Glitter

Sequins

18-inch length of ribbon or thick yarn

Glue or glue stick

DIRECTIONS:

1 Cover your workspace with newspaper.

2 Decorate the plate with markers, glue and glitter/sequins.

3 Let it dry thoroughly.

4 Cut the paper plate into a long spiral beginning at the outer edge of paper plate working your way into the center.

5 Leave a small circle in the middle from which to hang the mobile.

6 Poke or punch a small hole in this center circle and thread your knotted string through this hole.

7 Hang your mobile in a sheltered and breezy spot. It will twirl around and catch the glittering sunlight.

Variation: Paint Mod Podge over randomly placed colored tissue on one side of the paper plate. Sprinkle on clear "snow" glitter. Let this dry and repeat the process on other side. Cut and hang as described above.

WHEN ADAR ARRIVES משנכנס אדר

משכנס אדר

FESTIVITY THRIVES מרבין בשמחה

Cindy Benjamin

Purim

Just as winter starts to wear us down, the topsy-turvy holiday of Purim comes along. What other holiday gives you permission to make all kinds of noise in the synagogue, or includes a "Best Costume" contest? What other holiday involves carnivals, puppet shows, and parades? Purim commands us to live it up and have fun, while celebrating the rescue of the Jewish people from the evil hands of Haman.

Experiencing Purim

Our Purim celebration begins in the synagogue where the Megillah, the story of Esther, is read to young and old alike. At no other time during the Jewish year is the synagogue this lively or noisy. Wrapped up in the Scrolls of Esther, the story can also be found in the third section of the Bible called Writings. Full of melodrama and a plot that twists and turns, Purim is all about masks, hidden layers, and double meanings. On the surface the tale represents good overcoming evil. More deeply, it highlights standing up for who you are, fighting against hatred and feeling proud of being Jewish.

Purim tells the story of a beauty (Esther) and a beast (Haman), and begins with a fabulous feast in the kingdom of Persia, hosted by King Ahashverosh. The king was flaunting his riches and treasures for all to see, and decided that his beautiful wife, Queen Vashti, should also be displayed. But when the king sent for Vashti, she refused to appear before him. In anger, he threw Vashti out of the palace.

In search of a new wife, the king chose Esther, a young and very beautiful Jewish woman. Esther's uncle, Mordecai, cautioned her not to tell the king that she was a Jew.

King Ahashverosh bestowed a special honor on Haman, his power-hungry assistant, telling all the people in his kingdom to bow down to Haman. As a Jew, Mordecai refused. Haman became enraged and devised a plan to kill all the Jews. He even bribed the king into signing the declaration.

To determine the date the Jews were to be attacked, Haman drew lots ("purim" in Hebrew). Mordecai, however, discovered Haman's evil scheme and revealed it to Esther. Esther decided she must tell Ahashverosh, even if it meant her life.

King Ahashverosh was horrified to learn that his beautiful wife and her people were in danger. Haman was condemned to be hanged on the gallows and Mordecai was elevated to the position of Prime Minister. The Jews were safe once again, and Esther and Mordecai proclaimed the day to be one of feasting and merrymaking.

Today, when the Megillah is read, a great noise erupts every time Haman's name is read out loud. Young and old use groggers (noisemakers), whistles, and even bang on pot lids to make as much noise as possible.

It is a day of magic for everyone, not just a dress-up holiday for children. Adults are given permission and even commanded to drop our heavy responsibilities, lighten our load and our spirits, and resurrect the creative and imaginative parts of our being. We might put on a wig, try outrageous make-up, or wear silly clothes as we embrace the child in us to come out and play. We allow fantasy to transform reality for a day of utter enjoyment.

Traditions & Text

The central crisis of the story of Purim is the plot against the Jews. The evil Haman convinces the king that it is to his advantage to destroy the Jews and cosmically, his argument has a familiar ring:

There is a certain people, scattered and dispersed among the other peoples in all the provinces of your realm, whose laws are different from those of any other people and who do not obey the king's laws; and it is not in Your Majesty's interest to tolerate them.

(Esther 3:8)

It is the same ignorant fear that has been a source of anti-Semitism throughout the ages. Anti-Semites throughout history have claimed, "The Jews are different. They have their own laws. They don't respect your laws. They don't respect YOU."

Napoleon, before he emancipated the Jews giving them full French citizenship in the early 19th century was worried about the same thing. Consequently, he convened the "Great Sanhedrin of Paris," an assembly of 70 Jewish notables and asked them to prove to him that Jewish citizens of France would respect the laws of France. The Jews answered that, of course, they follow the laws of their country of residence, just as we do today.

In the Book of Esther, it is only when Esther reveals her background that she saves the Jewish people. Her name "Esther" means "hidden," yet it is her clever actions and her acknowledgment of her people that save the day. The message seems to be that when we are open about being Jewish, we prevent, rather than encourage, anti-Semitism.

PURIM CUSTOMS

According to the Megillah:

The same days on which the Jews enjoyed relief from their foes, and the same month which had been transformed for them from one of grief and mourning to one of festive joy, were to be celebrated every year. They were to observe them as days of feasting and merrymaking and as an occasion for sending gifts to one another and presents to the poor. (Esther 9:22)

So…the tone is set for frivolity and even a traditional time to get drunk! So drunk, in fact, that it is impossible to tell the difference between the phrase, "Cursed is Haman," and "Blessed is Mordecai!" When the Book of Esther is read publicly in the Synagogue, people use noisemakers, or "groggers" to drown out the name of Haman (which occurs 50 times in the Megillah).

Fascinating Food Facts

As on many Jewish holidays, food is a central part of the celebration. There is a traditional *se'udah* (banquet) on the afternoon of Purim with funny speeches and frivolous goings on. People give each other *mishlo'ach manot* (gifts) including at least two types of food and some money (even a couple of pennies), which the recipients can give to charity. Gift-giving was such an important Jewish tradition that the early Christian church in the Fourth Century forbid Christians from receiving Purim gifts lest they be tempted to become Jews!

The most traditional Purim food is, of course, *Hamantaschen* - triangular pastries filled with fruit or poppy seed. The word literally means "Haman's Pockets," but the tradition claims that they are shaped like either Haman's or Mordecai's three-cornered hat. In Israel the pastries are called *"Oznei Haman,"* meaning "Haman's ears."

Suggested Purim Menu

(The letter in parenthesis indicates the appropriate blessing found in "Prayers and Blessings" on p. 283)

The traditional blessings said at meal time.
Handwashing (A),
Hamotzi (B)

Soup or salad - a bean and barley soup, chicken soup with kreplach or a salad sprinkled with sunflower seeds.

Purim Challah - mix in some raisins or spread some preserves in your dough before shaping.

Fish with a sweet and sour sauce and/or roast turkey. (Because Haman was such a turkey!)

Kugel or roast potatoes.

Steamed vegetables.

Hamantashen and other sweet desserts.

Lots and lots of wine to drink and celebrate! (This is a Mitzvah after all.)

Blessing after meal (*Birkat HaMazon*) (H)

GO TO RECIPE INDEX IN BACK OF BOOK FOR SUGGESTED RECIPES.

Kids in the Kitchen

Queen Esther was a true heroine of the Purim story. We can add to the happiness of Purim by creating our own version of this heroine using canned fruit and cottage cheese. We are sure Queen Esther would have approved of this delicious dedication!

QUEEN ESTHER LOOK-ALIKE SALAD

COOKING EQUIPMENT NEEDED:

Ice cream scoop

Can opener

Plate or platter

INGREDIENTS:

Lettuce leaves

Cottage cheese

Tomato wedges

Can of pineapple

Bag of shredded carrots

Raisins

DIRECTIONS:

1 Place lettuce leaves on plate.

2 Scoop cottage cheese in center and shape into face.

3 Use raisins for her eyes and tomato wedge for her mouth.

4 Take a pineapple slice and cut it in half and create a crown on top of the cottage cheese.

5 Use carrot shavings on either side of the "face" for hair.

Read-Aloud Story

A Purim Rebus   *By Cindy Cooper*

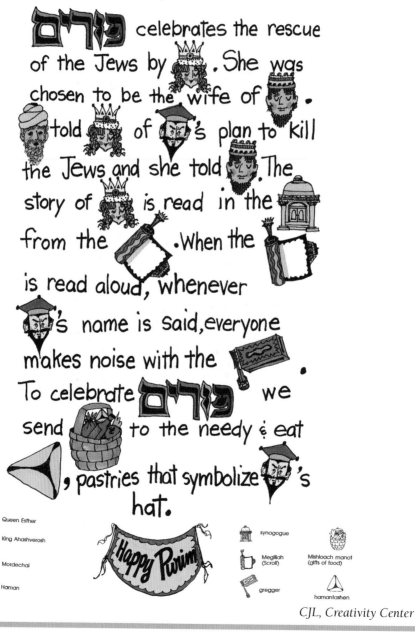

פורים celebrates the rescue of the Jews by [Queen Esther]. She was chosen to be the wife of [King Ahashverosh]. [Mordechai] told [Queen Esther] of [Haman]'s plan to kill the Jews and she told [King Ahashverosh]. The story of [Queen Esther] is read in the [synagogue] from the [Megillah]. When the [Megillah] is read aloud, whenever [Haman]'s name is said, everyone makes noise with the [gregger]. To celebrate פורים we send [Mishloach manot] to the needy & eat [hamantashen], pastries that symbolize [Haman]'s hat.

[Queen Esther] Queen Esther
[King Ahashverosh] King Ahashverosh
[Mordechai] Mordechai
[Haman] Haman

Happy Purim

[synagogue] synagogue
[Megillah] Megillah (Scroll)
[gregger] gregger
[Mishloach manot] Mishloach manot (gifts of food)
[hamantashen] hamantashen

CJL, Creativity Center

Purim Crafts and Activities

Mishlo'ach Manot Baskets
Plastic Woven Baskets
Mishlo'ach Manot Door Hanger
Woven Paper Cones

Costumes
Paper Bag Vests
Pillowcase Dress

Corrugated Crowns

Groggers
Decorated Cans
Paper Cup Shakers

Jewelry
Dough Beads
Rolled Paper Beads

Puppets
Hidden Puppets
Stick Puppets

Mishlo'ach Manot Baskets

On Purim we are obligated to send gifts of food to friends and give to the needy. This provides a great opportunity to perform a mitzvah with your children. The tradition is to make and give away at least two containers filled with hamantaschen, candy, at least two pennies and whatever else you choose. Remember to make a special card to go along with all the goodies!

PLASTIC WOVEN BASKETS

MATERIALS:

Plastic strawberry or cherry tomato baskets from the grocery store

10 or 12 colored pieces of yarn and ribbon, each cut at least 12 inches long

Multi-colored pipe cleaners

DIRECTIONS:

1 Weave ribbon, yarn, and pipe cleaners through the holes in the plastic boxes, making sure to tuck in or wrap around the loose ends of pipe cleaners. Pieces of ribbon and yarn sticking out all around add to the charm.

2 Attach two pipe cleaners twisted together to two sides of the basket to use as a handle.

3 Fill with goodies, and deliver to friends and neighbors.

MISHLO'ACH MANOT DOOR HANGER

MATERIALS:

12 x 12-inch pieces of colored construction paper

Containers (cottage cheese or yogurt) to hold paint

Tempera paint

Large paintbrushes - at least one for each color paint

Laminating machine or clear contact paper

Adhesive tape or colored masking tape

Scissors

Newspaper

DIRECTIONS:

1 Cover a large working area with newspaper and place the construction paper in the middle of it.

2 Dip your paintbrush in one color paint and then shake it all over the paper to create a splatter design. Repeat with other colors.

3 Laminate or cover both sides with clear contact paper.

4 Lay "laminated" paper in front of you in a "diamond" configuration. Face it like a kite.

5 Fold the side corners into the middle. Tape the edges together to close. Fold the bottom corner up to the middle and tape it closed.

6 Using a circular object like a glass, outline a circle in the top triangle and cut out the hole that will fit over a door handle.

7 Fill your Mishlo'ach Manot holder with goodies. When you deliver it to friends' and relatives' homes, hang it on their door handle!

Variation: Decorate an unused carry-out food container from a Chinese restaurant.

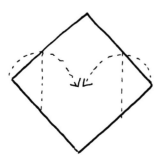 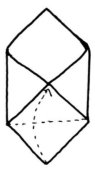 

WOVEN PAPER CONES

MATERIALS:

12 x 12-inch square piece of construction paper

12 x ¾-inch strips of different colored pieces of construction paper

Clear cellophane tape

Scissors

DIRECTIONS:

1 Fold the square of construction paper in half.

2 Beginning at the fold, cut horizontal, parallel slits stopping 1 inch from the top edge of the paper. All cuts should be 1 inch apart. Unfold the square.

3 Weave paper strips over and under the cut slits. Alternate strips first over, then under the first slit.

4 When the weaving is full, secure edges of strips by taping the ends. You could laminate the paper weaving at this point.

5 Fold the weaving into a cone shape. Close with tape. Fill it with goodies and deliver it to friends and neighbors.

Variation: For step two, you could cut zigzag or wavy parallel slits or even use fancy scissors.

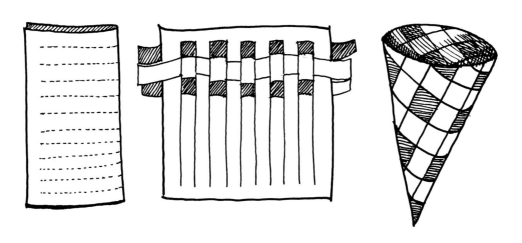

Costumes

The traditional costumes for Purim depict Queen Esther, King Ahashverosh, Mordecai, and Haman. However, anything goes at this holiday, and it is not uncommon to see children and clergy dressed in everything from cartoon characters to astronauts.

PAPER BAG VESTS

MATERIALS:

One brown paper grocery bag

Scissors

Markers or paint

Glue bottles or glue sticks

Variety of materials: Beads, yarn, sticky tape, buttons, stickers, faux jewels, colored masking tape, colored construction paper, feathers

DIRECTIONS:

1 Cut the paper bag up the middle of the front and through the bottom flap.

2 Cut a 5-inch circle out of the bottom flap, surrounding the slit you just made. This will form a head and neck hole.

3 Cut arm holes out of the two side panels.

4 If there is printing on the bag, turn the "vest" inside out at this point.

5 Older children can outline designs and fill them in. Younger children can just decorate the vest as they wish.

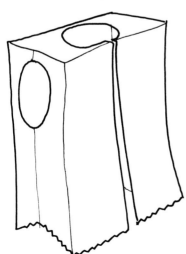

Variation: Fringe the bottom of the vest by cutting multiple slits. Use sticky tape scraps and make a pattern. String beads and attach them to the bag with tape. Make epaulets of construction paper.

Variation: Make a poncho by cutting both bag sides. Decorate as above. Punch holes along the side edges and lace it up with yarn to tie. (The front closure can also be punched and laced to close.)

Variation: Make a decorated hood using a small paper bag with a hole cut out to reveal the child's face. Decorate it with whiskers, hair, ears.

PILLOWCASE DRESS

ADULT HELP MAY BE NEEDED.

MATERIALS:

One white king-sized pillowcase

Fabric markers and puffy paints

Sticky felt

Sequins, beads

Tacky glue

Large piece of cardboard to fit inside pillowcase

Scissors

DIRECTIONS:

1 Decide who you want to dress up as.

2 Cut holes for the head and arms in the pillowcase.

3 Place the cardboard inside the pillowcase. Decorate the pillowcase with fabric markers, puffy paints, sticky felt cut to the shapes you want, sequins, and beads.

Note: The bottom edge, neck and arm holes can be fringed.

Note: Older children can sew on beads and sequins.

Corrugated Crowns

MATERIALS:

Rolls of silver and gold corrugated bulletin board borders

Scissors

Hole punch

Glitter pipe cleaners – whole and cut in half

Different size and shape beads

Stapler

DIRECTIONS:

1 Cut chosen border 1 inch longer than the circumference of the child's head. Close it by stapling.

2 Punch holes along the curving border of the crown.

3 Loop a pipe cleaner through a hole and twist to close it. Pipe cleaners can then stick straight up, be woven in and out of several holes, be looped like a coil through the holes, have beads strung on them, or connect to each other in the center to form a dome.

Note: Let the child's imagination run wild.

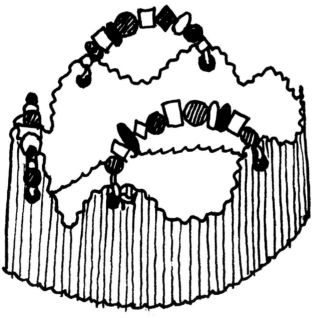

Groggers

Purim is a loud and raucous holiday. Adding to the din is the sound of "boos," "hisses," and noisemakers, called "groggers," drowning out the villainous name of Haman every time it is heard during the reading of the Purim story.

DECORATED CANS

MATERIALS:

Cleaned powdered drink or frosting cans (or any small cylindrical containers) - with lids and removed labels

Seeds or beans or stones – CAUTION: Small objects can cause choking.

Colored masking tape, stickers, sticker dots, yarn

Markers, crayons

Template designs – see. p. 276

Colored construction paper pre-cut to fit can

Glue

DIRECTIONS:

1 Decorate the construction paper with masking tape, stickers, sticker dots, markers, crayons. Use the template designs to draw hamentaschen, groggers, crowns, and megillah scrolls.

2 Once decorated, glue the decorated paper to the outside of the can. Fill the can with seeds, beans, or stones until it makes a sound the child likes. Let the child experiment with the different sounds.

3 Attach the lid by running glue along the inside edge of the lid. Let your grogger dry thoroughly.

4 Shake it when you hear Haman's name!

Variation: For older children: Cover the outside of the can with glue. Wrap layers of different colored yarns around the can.

PAPER CUP SHAKERS

MATERIALS:

Styrofoam cups

**Beans, noodles or pebbles –
CAUTION:** Small objects can
cause choking.

**Stickers and small shapes cut
out of sticky tape**

**4- to 5-inch square of colored
cellophane paper**

6-inch length of wide yarn

Plastic spoon

Strong, heavy-duty tape

DIRECTIONS:

1 Make a slit in the bottom of the cup.

2 From inside the cup, insert the plastic
spoon, handle down.

3 Inside of the cup, secure the spoon in place
with the tape.

4 Decorate the outside of the cup with stickers or sticky tape.

5 Fill the cup with beans, noodles or pebbles.

6 Cover the top of the cup with a cellophane
square and secure it with tied yarn.

7 Shake it baby, shake it!

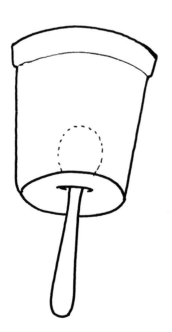

Jewelry

DOUGH BEADS

MATERIALS:

(This recipe may be doubled or tripled)

½ **cup cornstarch**

1 **cup baking powder**

5 **ounces water**

Heavy cooking pot

Long wooden spoon

Food coloring

Toothpicks

Tempera, water color, or acrylic paint

Small brushes

Mod Podge

Plastic containers for paint and Mod Podge

Waxed string (available at craft stores)

DIRECTIONS:

Note: Adult supervision is necessary.

1 Put the first 3 ingredients in a pot and mix together well.

2 Cook over a low heat, stirring constantly, until the mixture is the consistency of silly putty (about 20 minutes). Do not overcook.

3 Let the mixture cool.

4 Divide it into balls. If you wish, knead food coloring into each ball. Wrap the dough in plastic wrap or store in a covered container until ready to use. (This dough does not stay soft for long. Use it before it hardens.)

5 Shape small pieces of dough into little balls, triangles, squares.

6 Using a toothpick, make a hole, large enough for your waxed string to fit through, in the center of each bead.

7 Let the beads air dry.

8 Paint (unless you've already added color).

9 Let air dry again.

10 Cover the painted beads with Mod Podge if you wish. This helps protect the color and makes the beads shiny. Let dry.

11 String on waxed string.

Rolled Paper Beads

MATERIALS:

Triangles of paper (the base being at least 1 inch long) - cut from Sunday comics, colorful magazines, plant and flower catalogues, wrapping paper

Pencils or straws

School glue

Yarn with tightly taped end or waxed string for beading

DIRECTIONS:

1 Start at flat edge of the triangle and roll it toward the point around a pencil or straw.

2 Seal the pointed end with a dab of glue.

3 Slide the bead off the pencil or straw when it is dry.

4 String the beads onto yarn or string to make a necklace or bracelet.

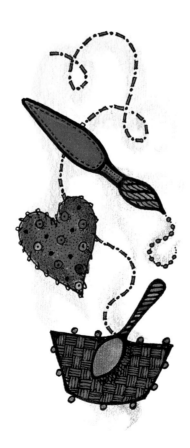

Puppets

HIDDEN PUPPETS

FOR OLDER CHILDREN

MATERIALS:

16-ounce solo cups (Poke a hole through the bottom) or a cardboard cone shape - (found in yarn factories or craft stores) or a 5-inch funnel

2½-inch Styrofoam ball

Yarn

Sticky felt – for decorations and facial features

Felt

Metallic paper

Two triangular pieces of fabric that will cover the cone for decoration (see example pattern on p. 277) and attach to the neck and cone for the costume.

Assorted trims for the costume: small buttons, lace, rickrack, felt

Tacky glue

16- to 18-inch dowel

Scissors

DIRECTIONS:

1. Decide which character they want to make. Refer to Purim story.

2. Make a hole in the Styrofoam ball with the dowel. Put glue in the hole and insert the dowel. Let it dry.

3. Make the face by decorating the Styrofoam ball:

   Glue on cut yarn for hair and beards.

   Glue on crowns or hats cut out of felt or metallic paper.

   Attach eyes, nose, and mouth cut out of sticky felt.

4. Paint glue onto your cone and cover the cone with a piece of fabric.

   Alternative: Cover the cone with wrapped-around strands of yarn.

5. Decorate the second piece of fabric to make a costume. (The narrow end is the neck.) With glue, attach small buttons, rickrack, lace, felt. Let it dry thoroughly. Do this before the fabric-covered cone is glued to the puppet.

6 Form the decorated cloth into a cone-shape. With glue, attach the pointed end tightly under the Styrofoam head. Glue the edges closed. Let it dry thoroughly.

7 Stick the dowel into the funnel through the wide end. With the puppet head and costume fully extended, the dowel will stick out the bottom of the cone shape.

8 Glue the wide, open end of the costume to the rim of the funnel/cup/cardboard cone. Let this dry thoroughly.

Note: There should be enough fabric so the puppet can stand approximately 6 inches above the rim of the cone or cup. The puppet can be raised and lowered to hide inside the cone. Make other puppets. Have a puppet show.

Purim

Stick Puppets

MATERIALS:

Purim puppet designs – page 278
(From the Coalition for Jewish
Learning's Creativity Center)

Markers and/or crayons

Masking tape

**Popsicle sticks or tongue
depressors**

Clear contact paper

Scissors

DIRECTIONS:

1 Color the puppets and cut them out.

2 Cover the puppet with clear contact paper, trimming the excess. They could be laminated instead.

3 Attach popsicle sticks or tongue depressors to the back of each puppet with clear tape.

4 Have a puppet show.

Passover

Many of us have special memories of Passover seders. The smells coming from our mother's and grandmother's kitchens, the coats piled on the bed, the noise and laughter while family members settle around the table, the taste of parsley dipped in salt water, the family member at the head of the table leading the service...What kind of memories do you want to create for your children and your children's children?

Experiencing Passover

Not long after we have put away the groggers and costumes of Purim, spring is in the air. Nature is preparing to burst into delicious smells, sounds, and colors that signal the earth emerging from the confinement of winter. In preparing for Passover, we are planning our spring festival in which the blossoming of nature symbolizes the renewal and transformation of a people from slavery to freedom.

The Pesach (Passover) experience begins with the ritual of cleaning our homes of any *hametz,* or leavened products. We look into the farthest corners of our cupboards and closets and sweep away even the tiniest crumbs. In the same way, we sweep away the cobwebs from our hearts and minds, ridding ourselves of anything that might obscure our vision of who we are and what we strive to be.

The word *seder,* the name of the special meal we have on the first and second nights of Passover, actually means "order." This is because there is a specific order to the fifteen elements of the seder which are found in a book called the *Haggadah.* There are also special songs, foods and games that make the holiday festive. There are four cups of wine, stories of the four sons, the four questions and ten plagues. Pesach is a wonderful holiday because it has so many symbols and rituals. Families can create their own memories and imagine what that first Passover was like. One of the most important lines we read from the Haggadah is "In every generation, all are obligated to see themselves as though they themselves had gone out of Egypt."

So How Did We End Up In Egypt?

The story of Passover really begins with twenty shekels of silver. That is what Joseph's brothers received for selling him to the Ishmaelites who brought him to Egypt as a slave. Because of Joseph's amazing ability to interpret Pharaoh's dreams, he quickly ascended in power. He correctly foretold of the coming of seven years of plenty followed by seven years of famine and developed a plan. Joseph oversaw the distribution of food to all who came from near and far. Because of the great drought and hunger, Jacob, Joseph's father, sent his sons to Egypt to buy grain. After an emotional reunion with his brothers, Joseph invited his father and the entire family to come and live in Egypt where there was plenty of food.

A new Pharaoh came to power who didn't know of Joseph's great deeds. The Hebrews were rapidly increasing in numbers and, out of fear and ignorance, he made them slaves. The Jews were slaves for 210 years. During that time, Pharaoh embittered their lives and gave them humiliating and difficult, back-breaking work.

God heard the Jews cry out in their misery. He called upon a man named Moses to save His people, the children of Israel. Moses went to the Pharaoh and asked him to "let my people go." One by one God sent terrible plagues to convince Pharaoh to release the Jews. But in each case, Pharaoh's heart was hardened and he refused to let the Israelite people go. Finally, God sent the tenth and most devastating plague, the death of every first-born child. The Jews marked their doors with the blood of a lamb, so that the Angel of Death would pass over them.

The smell of death and the cries of the Egyptian families filled the land. Pharaoh agreed to let the people go, but he sent his soldiers to bring them back. This time God intervened and miraculously split the Red Sea, allowing the Jews to escape into Sinai.

Traditions & Text

THE EXPERIENCE OF SLAVERY

Passover tells of the liberation of the Israelites from slavery. This experience of slavery defines and molds our entire religion. Often the Torah commands, "You shall not oppress a stranger." Why? "Because you know the feelings of the stranger. You were strangers in the land of Egypt." (Exodus: 23) Further, we are commanded to leave gleanings in the field for the poor, to support the orphan, the widow and the stranger. Why? "Because you were slaves in the land of Egypt." The fact that we were slaves in Egypt seems to be the rationale for Judaism's insistence that all people are created equal, that slavery is wrong, that all humans deserve to be treated with dignity, that we as Jews and as human beings need to fight oppression. In fact, another name for Passover is Zman Cheruteinu - "the Season of our Liberation."

DID YOU KNOW...

...there are special Passover songs in Ladino (Jewish Spanish), Arabic, Turkish, Italian, and other languages (including English, of course)?

...some families hide the afikoman, some steal it, some wear it, and some sit on it?

...Persian families hit each other with green onions during "Dayenu?"

...Yemenite Charoset is liquid and **very** spicy?

...some families eat matzah during the seder ceremony, but not during the meal?

...some Jews have never heard of matzah balls?

The Seder Plate

Made of clay, metal, glass, wood, or even plastic, the seder plate is a fixture on every Passover table. The seder plate holds five special foods. As we work our way around the seder plate, we hearken back to the story of our enslavement and journey to freedom.

Maror (bitter herb) – This can be romaine lettuce or fresh horseradish root. The sharp, bitter taste of maror is meant to remind us of the bitterness and brutality of slavery.

Roasted Shank Bone (from a chicken neck bone or, more traditionally, a real lamb shank bone) – The shank bone is not eaten, but serves to remind us of the Pascal lamb sacrifice that was eaten by our ancestors before they left Egypt. The lamb was an object of worship for the Egyptians, so this was a great and heroic act of independence on the part of each Hebrew household.

Roasted egg (boiled first) – a reminder that a special sacrifice was offered at the Holy Temple on Passover and other festivals. The egg is also a symbol of spring, fertility, rebirth and the never-ending cycle of life.

Karpas – parsley or another green vegetable symbolic of springtime. Karpas is dipped in salt water (lemon juice or vinegar), which represents the tears shed by our ancestors. While the Karpas is symbolically dipped, children should be encouraged to ask questions at the seder table so that the story of Passover can be re-told.

Charoset – a sweet dish usually made of chopped fruits and nuts. Charoset represents the mortar that the Jews used to make bricks while they were slaves under Pharaoh. The sweetness of Charoset takes the sting out of the maror, which is dipped in it as part of the seder ritual.

Fascinating Food Facts

The Jewish people have always lived in many different countries of the world and their customs and traditions can vary greatly when it comes to traditional foods.

Ashkenazic (European) Jews are forbidden to eat rice on Passover, but for Sephardic Jews (Jews of Spanish descent), rice is a traditional staple. For Ashkenazic Jews, matzah balls are a must. Arabic Jews have never heard of them!

Ashkenazic Jews use horseradish for bitter herbs, while Sephardic Jews use romaine lettuce. Ashkenazim use parsley for leafy greens, Sephardim use celery and Russian Jews use potatoes. An Ashkenazic breakfast during Passover will undoubtedly include Matzah Brei (fried matzah) while Bunuellas (a fried Passover doughnut) will grace a Sephardic table.

Of all the food, Charoset—that sweet mixture of fruits and nuts representing mortar—is the most varied. There are Italian recipes with poppy seed, Yemenite recipes with cayenne pepper, Ethiopian recipes with lemon rind and pine nuts, and Persian recipes with pomegranate seeds.

Traditional Passover Menu

The word "seder" means order. The order of the seder is laid out in your favorite Haggadah. Feel free to add your own commentaries and songs to personalize the seder.

Seder Plate (individual or a few for the table)

Charoset

Gefilte Fish - Horseradish

Chicken Soup with Matzah Balls

Lamb, Brisket, Turkey or Fish

Candied Carrots, Matzah Kugel or Sweet Potatoes

Green Vegetable

Fruit compote

Mandelbrot, Sponge Cake with Strawberries, Flourless Chocolate Cake

Kids in the Kitchen

Oh what a plague, a week without pizza! Not so. Today, we can have a new variety of pizza with a real thin crust - matzah! Make up a batch of kosher le-Pesach pizza. Hmmm…good.

MATZAH PIZZA

DIRECTIONS:

1 Preheat oven to 350 degrees.

2 Spread tomato sauce on matzah.

3 Top with sliced cheese. Sprinkle with spices. Add extra toppings.

4 Put matzah on oiled baking sheet.

5 Bake for about 5 minutes or until cheese melts.

COOKING EQUIPMENT NEEDED:

Baking sheet

Spoon and knife

Spatula

Potholder/Timer

INGREDIENTS:

1 round tea matzah (or regular matzah)

3 to 4 tablespoons tomato sauce

2 to 3 slices cheese

Oregano, garlic powder, to taste (optional)

Oil for baking sheet

Toppings if desired: olives, peppers, pineapple, etc.

Read-Aloud Story

The Passover Story   *By Cindy Cooper*

THROUGH MOSES, GOD SENT TEN PLAGUES TO EGYPT TO FINALLY CONVINCE PHARAOH TO LET THE JEWISH PEOPLE GO.

ALL RIGHT... YOU AND YOUR PEOPLE MAY GO. YOUR GOD IS TOO POWERFUL TO RESIST! GO!

...AND SO THEY PREPARED TO LEAVE EGYPT— SO QUICKLY, IN FACT, THAT THE BREAD DOUGH THEY WERE MAKING DIDN'T HAVE TIME TO RISE,

DID YOU PREPARE THE DONKEY? THIS BREAD WAS BAKED BEFORE THE DOUGH WAS READY. WE WILL EAT IT ON OUR JOURNEY.

BUT PHARAOH CHANGED HIS MIND AND SENT HIS SOLDIERS TO BRING BACK THE ISRAELITES

PRAISE GOD FOR PARTING THE WATERS OF THE RED SEA FOR US.

BUT IT'S CLOSING BEHIND US AND PHARAOH'S POOR SOLDIERS WILL BE KILLED!

THEY WERE FREE! AT PASSOVER WE CELEBRATE THAT FREEDOM BY RETELLING THE STORY, SINGING SONGS AND EATING SPECIAL FOODS.

PLEASE PASS THE MATZAH!

Passover

Some Great Ideas
For Making This Night Special

- Learn about Passover customs of Jews from all around the world.
  - Create the feeling of living in the desert by making a Bedouin tent in your living room. Drape a few large bed sheets from the ceiling. Use a fan for simulating the blowing desert winds.
  - Have your seder Sephardic-style. Place the seder plate on a low table or coffee table. Participants can then sit on the floor or lay on couches and pillows to feel like they're in the Middle East.
- Collect beautiful Haggadahs and display them for others to appreciate.
- Make homemade matzah from flour and water. Create interesting shapes.
- Because it can be hard for young children to sit through the reading of the Haggadah, place quiet toys under the table on a large tablecloth. Include snacks and figurines they can use to re-enact the story.
- Create gift bags for young children. Scratch and sniff grape stickers can be used for the wine, and apple stickers for Charoset. Include little puppets, bookmarks, and moist towelettes for spills.
- Play Passover trivia. Let each participant bring three questions. For example: What fast food is an integral part of the Seder? Who was the first Israelite to enter the Red Sea?
- Assemble "plague" bags for each participant. See Passover craft section on page 137 for more ideas.
- Play "Guess Who I Am?" Have participants pretend to be one of the characters from the Passover story (Moses, Miriam, Elijah). They can get dressed up and change their voice.
- Make up rhymes, riddles, jokes, and tongue teasers. (What did one matzah say to another? *You crack me up.* What makes the loudest noise at the Seder? *The Ma"Roar."* Who's coming to the seder? *Afi's comin.* What is the funniest thing on the Seder table? *Ha Ha Roset.*)
- Tell stories of heroic women from the Passover story, such as Miriam, Yocheved, Shifrah, Puah, and Batya.
- Name modern plagues of our society, such as AIDS, gun violence, child abuse, etc.
- Invite strangers who would otherwise not participate in a seder.
- Research the life of Elijah. Dress up like him and surprise all the guests. Answer all questions. Tell others at the table the story of your life.

Games Corner by Lenny Kass

PASSOVER CONCENTRATION

Learning Objective: Remembering Passover symbols

MATERIALS:

Create 30 or more index cards, each having a name of a Passover symbol on it. Examples are: matzah, shank bone, egg, wine cup, afikoman bag, Moses, Burning Bush, etc. (OPTION: have the children decorate the cards with appropriate pictures.)

HOW TO PLAY:

1 Turn the cards upside down and mix up.

2 Arrange the cards in 3 rows of 10 cards, all facing down.

3 Turn two cards over and try to make a match. If a match, remove from the board and set aside. If not a match, turn back upside down and next person's turn.

GO PLAGUE!

Learning Objective: Remembering the 10 plagues

MATERIALS:

Create 30 or more index cards, each having the name of one plague on it: blood, lice, hail, frogs, darkness, locusts, boils, cattle disease, flies, killing of the first born son. (OPTION: have the children decorate the cards with appropriate pictures.)

HOW TO PLAY:

1 Deal 5 or so cards to each player.

2 First player asks any player if they have a specific plague to match one of his. If they have the matching card, set aside the pair. If the player says no, pick one from the deck. First person to match all of his cards wins.

RELAY RACES

MATERIALS:

A disposable roasting pan

Large piece of cardboard or mat board

Two cones or pieces of duct tape

Small Frisbees, beanbags, or balls

Index cards with plagues written on it

HOW TO PLAY:

1 On the cardboard, draw a picture of Pharaoh's castle and tape to the back of a roasting pan so that it stands upright (serving as a backboard).

2 Have a line or cone for a start line (about 10 yards back from castle) and another line about two feet back from the castle.

3 The child stands at the start line, runs to the second line, and throws the ball, Frisbee, etc. at the castle attempting to get it into the pan.

4 If the ball lands in the pan, take out a plague card. Person who gets all 10 plague cards first wins.

Passover Crafts and Activities

Seder Plates
Homemade Seder Plate

Afikoman Bags
Zipped Plastic Afikoman Bag
Felt Afikoman bag

Elijah's/Miriam's Cup

Matzah Cover

Burning Bush Table Centerpiece

Ways to Liven Up the Seder
Plague Bags
Kefias
Parting of the Red Sea (Magic Trick)
Crossing the Red Sea
Tambourines
Frog Hats

Seder Plates

The Seder plate is found on every Seder table and holds five different foods that help the Jewish people remember what it was like to be a slave in Egypt. The Seder plate is usually near the head of the table so that whoever is leading the Seder can point to or hold up the food that is being discussed at that point in the Haggadah. There can be several Seder plates at different spots on the table. Some families even have an individual Seder plate in front of each person, with the leader's plate holding the only shank bone. The following are several ideas for making your own Seder plates.

HOMEMADE SEDER PLATE

MATERIALS:

Two 7-inch clear plastic plates

7-inch drawing of a Seder plate: a photocopy of the template found on p. 279 or design your own

Crayons and or markers

Scissors

Clear tape

Tissue paper squares, cut or torn into small pieces

Diluted glue (approx. 2 ounces glue to ½ ounce water) or non-toxic acrylic water base sealer and finish (available in craft stores) in a disposable container

Foam paintbrush

DIRECTIONS:

1 Cut out the Seder plate and color it.

2 Tape the template, face up, to the back of one plastic plate.

3 Paint the back of the template with glue and apply small pieces of colored tissue paper, collage style, to cover its entire surface. Let dry.

4 Paint glue along the outside edge of this plate and cradle the second plate to the collaged surface so that the plates will be stacked with collage-backed Seder plate in the middle. Let dry again.

Variation: Try attaching an inverted clear or tissue-covered plastic bowl to the bottom of the Seder plate, to act as a pedestal.

Afikoman Bags

At every Seder table, place three pieces of matzah on a plate covered with a special cloth, called a matzah cover. Early in the Seder, before the retelling of the Passover story, the middle piece is taken out, held up for all to see, and broken in half. The larger piece — the afikoman — is wrapped in a napkin or placed in its own special bag and hidden.

At the end of the Passover meal, all the children run to look for the afikoman. The winner gets a prize, which might be chocolate "gelt" or a silver dollar. It is a nice custom for the winner to give pieces of the afikoman to the other children so that they can "sell" back their pieces to the leader for a prize as well. The afikoman is then eaten as the last food of the Seder, the dessert.

ZIPPED PLASTIC AFIKOMAN BAG

FOR YOUNGER CHILDREN

MATERIALS:

1-quart-sized plastic bag that zips closed with no writing on it

2 x 4 inch piece of paper on which you have written the word "Afikoman"

1 roll of colored masking tape

Piece of white paper cut to the same size as the inside of the plastic bag

Various colors of sticky tape, cut into squares, rectangles, circles, triangles

Stickers – Look for Jewish stars or special Passover stickers

Markers and/or crayons

DIRECTIONS:

1 Attach the word "Afikoman" to the outside of the plastic bag by neatly framing it with colored masking tape.

2 Decorate the piece of paper cut to fit inside the bag with sticky tape, stickers, markers/crayons.

3 Place this decorated paper inside the plastic bag. Use this to hold your piece of afikoman.

Note: Start a new tradition! Give each child their own bag and their own piece of afikoman to hide, in addition to the actual afikoman. More pieces mean more fun!

Felt Afikoman Bag

For older children

MATERIALS:

Two 9 x 12 inch pieces of felt, stiffer felt may be easier to use than soft felt (available at craft and fabric stores)

Hole punch

Piece of yarn, about 45 inches long

Masking Tape

Pre-cut sticky-backed felt letters spelling A-F-I-K-O-M-A-N or cut your own out of peel and stick felt (available at craft or art supply stores)

Passover shapes and decorations cut out of sticky felt, using template shapes found on p. 280

Fabric markers and puffy paint (available at craft or art supply stores)

DIRECTIONS:

1 Put the two pieces of felt together and punch holes an inch apart along the two sides and the bottom edges. Adult assistance may be needed.

2 Wrap a small piece of masking tape around one end of the yarn, so it looks like a shoelace.

3 Starting with the top left or right hole, make a knot with the yarn and sew around the three sides of the felt pieces using a running or saddle stitch. Make another knot at the end and cut off the extra yarn.

4 Attach the sticky-backed felt letters to the front of your felt pocket to spell out A-F-I-K-O-M-A-N.

5 Decorate the front of the felt bag using fabric markers, puffy paints and sticky felt shapes. Ideas for decoration: objects and symbols from the Passover story and celebration.

6 Let dry. Use on Passover night.

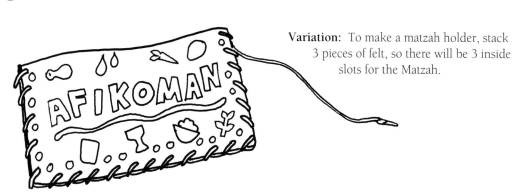

Variation: To make a matzah holder, stack 3 pieces of felt, so there will be 3 inside slots for the Matzah.

Elijah's/Miriam's Cup

Elijah was a prophet who lived a long, long time ago. Over time, many stories have been told about Elijah. It is said that he never died; instead, he was taken up to heaven in a fiery chariot. Many believe that Elijah appears as a mysterious stranger who gives help just when it's needed. Most importantly, it is thought that he will announce the coming of the Messiah or the Messianic Era. On Passover, we open our doors to welcome a visit from Elijah, who mysteriously drinks wine from the cup that is set out especially for him. In more recent times, families have also poured a cup (kos) of wine to welcome the prophetess Miriam, the sister of Moses, who led the Israelite women in dance after they crossed the Red Sea.

MATERIALS:

Masking tape

Glass or plastic stemmed cups

Glass or permanent markers

Puffy paint and/or a shiny fabric paint (found at craft or art supply stores)

Craft store jewels

Strong adhesive glue

Q-tips

Small paper cup to hold glue

DIRECTIONS:

1 Put masking tape around the top edge of the glass to mask off the lip area. This tape will be removed at the end.

2 Decorate the glass with the markers. Older children can draw a design on a sheet of paper ahead of time, and then insert the paper into the glass and trace the design.

3 Add designs with the puffy paint or the shiny fabric paint.

4 Use the Q-tip to apply a bead of glue to the cup where jewels are to be applied.

5 Carefully place jewels on these beads of glue.

6 Let dry.

7 Remove masking tape. Use your beautiful new cup on the Seder table.

8 Carefully hand wash and dry.

Matzah Cover

FOR OLDER CHILDREN

MATERIALS:

Several sheets newspaper

Plain newsprint

Man's 100% silk handkerchief or a 9 x 12-inch piece of silk fabric (available in fabric stores or art catalogues)

Silk paint (cleans with water, available in art stores). When ready to use, place each color in its own container. Dyes can be diluted with water. **CAUTION: this material stains**

Watercolor brushes

Small containers of water for rinsing brushes

Silk Wax Resist – clear, gold and/or silver - in a tipped bottle (available in art stores)

White paper (the size of the handkerchief) and a **dark marker** for creating a design, or a photocopy of a design you like

Masking tape

Note: The same silk painting technique can be used to make a challah cover.

DIRECTIONS:

1 Cover the worktable with newspaper and plain newsprint.

2 Sketch your design on the handkerchief-sized paper with a dark marker. Place face up, under the cloth handkerchief. Tape the design and material to the table.

Variation: Tape the design to the back of your fabric. Then tautly tape the fabric to an empty picture frame, to raise it off the table surface.

3 Trace over the design with Wax Resist onto the handkerchief. The gold and silver will keep its color. Let dry thoroughly.

4 Paint with the dye between the Wax Resist outlines, filling in the design. Wax Resist keeps silk colors from bleeding together. If you want colors to blend or bleed, eliminate Wax Resist outline. You could also wet the fabric before painting to encourage the bleeding.

5 Let dry.

6 Heat set by ironing between sheets of plain newsprint or put in dryer. Wax will melt away, color will remain.

Burning Bush Table Centerpiece

Though Moses grew up in the palace, he witnessed how harshly the Hebrew slaves were treated. One day, he saw an Egyptian kill one of the Hebrew slaves and, in anger, Moses killed the Egyptian. Fearing for his life, Moses ran away from Egypt and headed to the land of Midian. There he found the family of Jethro and his daughters. Moses married the eldest daughter, Zipporah, and settled into a quiet life as a sheepherder. One day while tending the sheep, Moses saw a burning bush and realized that, although there were flames all around it, the wood and leaves were not burning. Through the burning bush, God told Moses to return to Egypt and demand that Pharaoh "Let my people go."

MATERIALS:

6-inch branch from a shrub, with many side branches. It should look like a miniature bush. Spring is just starting and there may be a few budding leaves on it.

4 x 1-inch strips of red, orange, and yellow cellophane (Cellophane could be cut into flame shapes)

2-inch cube of florist's foam

Glue sticks

Container or small paper plate to hold finished burning bush

DIRECTIONS:

1 Place the tree branch in the florist's foam.

2 Attach a cellophane strip by securing one end with glue to the base of a branch and wrapping it in and around the branch, working toward the top. Glue, if necessary. Make sure the strip is securely in place. Repeat with more strips until the "bush" is covered.

3 Place the "bush" on a small plate or in a small bowl. Make several to decorate your Passover table.

Ways To Liven Up The Seder

At Passover, we are told, "In every generation, each of us should feel as though we ourselves had gone forth from Egypt…" The story of Passover takes us back to those days of slavery and deliverance. What better way to help people get into the mood than by preparing plague bags, putting on the head coverings our ancestors wore and parting the Red Sea?

PLAGUE BAGS AND A NEAT TRICK!

Giving children their own plague bag is a fantastic way to add interest to your Seder.

MATERIALS:

Plain brown lunch bags

Marker

The following items can be changed depending on what you find, either in catalogues or your favorite children's toy store, variety store, or party store:

Blood: A Neat Trick - Place red food coloring in a clear glass pitcher. Make sure no one can see it, perhaps by wrapping colored masking tape neatly around the bottom. Have water ready in a second clear glass pitcher. When naming the first plague of "blood," (Dahm) pour the clear water into the first pitcher. Very exciting!!!

Frogs: Bendable frogs, frog stickers, hopping frogs, plastic frogs

Lice: Tiny plastic bugs or paper dots made with hole punch

Wild Beasts or Insects: Rubber animal noses, plastic insects or animal/insect stickers

Cattle Plague: Cow pencils, erasers or stickers

Boils: Round band-aids or small squares of bubble wrap

Hail: Styrofoam peanuts, small Styrofoam balls, small fluorescent ball or ping pong balls

Darkness: Sunglasses or throw-away sunglasses from the eye doctor:

Death of the Firstborn: You may consider skipping this or using small plastic skeletons or black arm bands

Hint: Many of these items are available through a catalogue: Oriental Trading Co. 800/228-2269, www.oriental.com or at your local party store.

DIRECTIONS:

1 Write "Do Not Open By Order Of The Pharaoh" on the front of the lunch bags.

2 Place items in the lunch bag and tape shut.

3 Give each child his or her own plague bag before the listing of the plagues in the Seder.

4 Why not have extra items for adults to play with? This is great fun.

Kefias/Middle Eastern head coverings

MATERIALS:

Pieces of sheeting or white fabric cut into 12- to 18-inch squares

Multicolored yarn cut to at least 18-inch lengths

DIRECTIONS:

Hand each guest a piece of fabric and yarn to wrap around their head before the Seder begins.

Parting of the Red Sea (Magic Trick)

Note: Practice this trick before you perform it at your Seder. You may have to change the brand of your dishwashing liquid.

DIRECTIONS:

1 Secretly, put a drop of dishwashing liquid on the tip of your index finger.

2 Gather the children around.

3 Have a clear glass bowl of water ready that everyone can see.

4 Sprinkle red pepper or paprika in the bowl to cover the entire surface of the water.

5 When you talk about the sea parting, dip your soapy finger onto the red pepper and the pepper will separate, like the parting of the sea!!!

CROSSING THE RED SEA

A lot of Passover music about crossing the Red Sea is available:

"Dayenyu" in Fran Avni, *Mostly Matzah*; **Lemonstone Records (Côte-St.-Luc, Quebec), 1983**
"Downhome Dayenu" in Rabbi Joe Black, *Aleph Bet Boogie*; **Lanitunes Music (Minneapolis, MN), 1991**
"Miriam's Song" in Debbie Friedman, *The Journey Continues*; **Sounds Write Productions, Inc. (San Diego, CA), 1997**
"Pass Over the Water" in Debbie Friedman, *Shirim Al Galgalim*; **Sounds Write Productions, Inc. (San Diego, CA), 1992**
"Story of Nachshon" in Rabbi Joe Black, *Everybody's Got a Little Music*; **Lanitunes Music (Minneapolis, MN), 1992**

MATERIALS:

Musical tapes – see above

Tambourines (available through Oriental Trading Co. catalogue, 800/228-2269)

Tape recorder

12-foot long x 72-inch wide strip of blue polyester or satiny water-like fabric divided in half length-wise, which will result in two 12-foot x 36-inch walls of "water"

4 volunteers, 1 for each end of the 2 strips of fabric

AT YOUR SEDER:

1 Tell about Moses and the Israelites being at the edge of the Red Sea with the Egyptian soldiers racing toward them on their horses and chariots. You could play or tell Rabbi Black's story of Nachshon and say "Now, it is our time to cross the sea, just as the Israelites did so long ago."

2 Move group to an open area away from the table.

3 Have the 2 pairs of volunteers hold the fabric strips (short ends) and stand opposite each other.

4 Turn on one of the songs. When the parting of the sea is mentioned, have the 2 pairs of volunteers step sideways, away from each other, separating the 2 strips from one another so everyone can march/dance between the 2 strips of undulating sea (fabric). Sing. Dance. Play your tambourines.

Tambourines

GOOD PROJECT FOR YOUNG CHILDREN

MATERIALS:

2 paper plates

Crepe paper streamers –
Approximately 8 inches long

Curly ribbon – Approximately
12 to 18 inches long, with ends
curled

Beans

Assortment of sticky tape, cut
into various shapes and sizes

Stapler

DIRECTIONS:

1 Decorate the outside of the paper plates with sticky tape shapes.

2 Staple paper plates ¾ way around. Staple on streamers and/or ribbons as you go.

3 Pour beans into the opening.

4 Staple the plates completely shut.

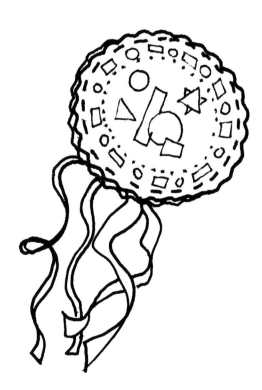

FROG HATS

MATERIALS:

Green and pink sticky tape

Scissors

8 x 12 inch construction paper:
1 sheet each of green, white and black

Glue stick

DIRECTIONS:

1 Cut a piece of green sticky tape long enough to fit around your child's head, with an extra 2 inches for overlap.

2 **Frog's head:** Cut out a large half circle from the green construction paper.

3 **Frog's eyes:** Cut out two 2- to 3-inch circles from the white construction paper. Cut out two 1- to 2-inch circles from the black construction paper.

4 **Frog's tongue:** Cut a 5-inch strip of the pink sticky tape. Trim the corners off one end to make a tongue shape.

5 Fit the green headband to your child's head.

6 Lay the strip flat on the table.

7 **Head:** Glue one green large half circle to the front center of the headband.

8 **Eyes:** Glue the white circles to the top of the green head.

9 Glue the black circles to the center of the white eyes.

10 Attach the pink tongue to the bottom of the green head.

11 Refit the green headband and lick it shut to fit the child's head.

12 Put it on and jump around like a proud frog.

Barbara Kohl Spiro

Lag B'Omer

Rabbi Akiva... "33"... Bow and Arrows... Bonfires... Picnics... Roasted Potatoes... Singing and Dancing... These are the flavors of Lag B'Omer.

Experiencing Lag B'Omer

The holiday of Lag B'Omer falls on the 33rd day between Passover and Shavuot. (Lag, spelled with the Hebrew letters "lamed" and "gimmel," means "33.") The seven weeks between the two holidays is referred to as "the counting of the Omer." (The Omer is a measure of grain. In ancient times, they counted the days from Passover to Shavuot by measuring out the Omer every day until they reached the 49th Omer.) These seven weeks are observed as a period of mourning in memory of the tragedies that befell the Jews in the second century, when observance of Jewish law and study of Torah were prohibited, and Jewish rebels died by the thousands. During this time we are to count each of the 49 days, meditate and contemplate our deeds. Marriages, haircuts, shaving and other activities are prohibited. However, on the 33rd day, called *Lag B'Omer,* we celebrate.

If you lived in Israel around the time of Lag B'Omer, you would see kids of all ages starting to collect whatever kind of wood they can find for their bonfire, or *mi'dura.* Everyone competes to see who can build the bonfire that will blaze the highest and last the longest into the night.

At home potatoes are scrubbed and wrapped in aluminum foil to throw into the fire. Families prepare platters of veggies, salads, pita breads and meat that will be grilled outdoors. Before they head out for the evening's festivities, they take in their laundry and close the windows, because soon the air will be filled with smoke!

As sundown nears, the bonfires are lit. Out comes the food, songs are sung and games are played. There are archery contests, relay races and scavenger hunts. Many marriages take place on this night, and within the Orthodox community, this is when young boys look forward to having their first haircut. Some people stay up all night, keeping the fires going, telling stories and finally straggling home at dawn under hazy skies.

Here in the United States you may want to consider beginning a Lag B'Omer tradition yourself: gather together friends and have a large bonfire where you can roast marshmallows and potatoes. Play games, run races, plan a treasure hunt or read about some of our great teachings and rabbis. Or travel to Israel for a special experience! It is said that if you fly over Israel on Lag B'Omer you can see thousands of bonfires lighting up the land.

Traditions & Text

Lag B'Omer is a holiday that is strictly a historical one: there are no commandments related to it; it is not mentioned in the Bible; and it was not celebrated before the time of Rabbi Akiva (second century C.E.). It has come to symbolize the ill-fated revolt against the Romans in the first third of the second century. The Temple had been destroyed sixty years before. Rabbi Akiva, the greatest scholar of the time (some say the greatest scholar of *all* times), believed that the rebel leader Shimon Bar Kokhba was, in fact, the Messiah. The Jews hoped to drive the Romans out of Jerusalem and rebuild the Temple, but they failed miserably. The Romans utterly destroyed the Jews and their land, causing great suffering and hardship.

The rebels succeeded, however, in keeping hope alive and sustaining the study of the Torah. Secretly, and at great risk, they studied in the forests led by Rabbi Akiva and other scholars. Ultimately, Akiva and others were captured by the Romans and tortured to death. Jewish history, however, focuses on the triumph of the spirit rather than the physical defeat. The heroic rabbis are glorified because they taught Torah at great risk. It is said in the Babylonian Talmud (Sotah 49) that: "When Rabbi Akiva died, the study of Torah was neglected, the arms of the Torah were powerless and the springs of wisdom were stopped up."

It is interesting that this obscure holiday has had powerful meaning for secular Israelis. The very fact that second-century Jews fought against all odds has persisted in the Israeli imagination. The day has been commemorated with outdoor picnics, in a sense, a secular reenactment of the secret study sessions in the forests.

THE HOLIDAY AND THE MYSTIC

In Israel, Lag B'Omer is widely celebrated with special outings. One of the most popular is the *Hillula,* or celebration of the mystical Rabbi Shimon Bar Yochai. Thousands of Jews come from all parts of Israel, walking five miles from the mystical city of Tzfat to Mt. Meron, to arrive at his grave by midnight. They light bonfires, sing and dance. It is on that day that three-year-old boys from the Orthodox community have their first haircut.

Who was Shimon Bar Yochai? A second-century student of Rabbi Akiva and a great sage, Rabbi Shimon is said to have died on the holiday of Lag B'Omer. A "great light of endless joy filled the day" because of the secret wisdom he shared with his students. Tradition tells us that these words were later transcribed as the Zohar, the "Shining Light," which reveals mystical teachings of the Torah. Because of the joy felt on that day, the modern celebration of Lag B'Omer is also a day of joy.

Fascinating Food Facts

Although roasted potatoes are the Israeli treat eaten on Lag B'Omer, any picnic items will do. If you have a bonfire, why not hot dogs and roasted marshmallows?

Suggested Lag B'Omer Menu

(The letter in parenthesis indicates the appropriate blessing found in "Prayers and Blessings" on p. 283)

The traditional blessings
said at mealtime.
Handwashing (A)
Hamotzi (B)

Cut up vegetables and dip
Sweet potato salad
Tuna or chicken salad sandwiches
cut into cookie cutter shapes
Fresh fruit salad
Homemade potato chips
Cookies and bars

Blessing after the meal
(Birkat HaMazon) (H)

GO TO RECIPE INDEX IN BACK OF BOOK FOR SUGGESTED RECIPES.

Kids in the Kitchen

Pack up your favorite picnic foods, including these wonderful homemade potato chips. Grab a blanket, Frisbee, bat and ball.

HOMEMADE POTATO CHIPS

COOKING EQUIPMENT NEEDED:

Knife

Food processor

Bowl

Cookie sheet

INGREDIENTS:

8 baking potatoes, peeled

Salt, pinch

DIRECTIONS:

1 Preheat oven to 400 degrees.

2 Slice potatoes into thin "chips" in a food processor. Keep chips in cold water to prevent browning.

3 Place chips in one layer on a well-greased cookie sheet.

4 Bake them in oven until lightly brown.

5 Sprinkle with a pinch of salt.

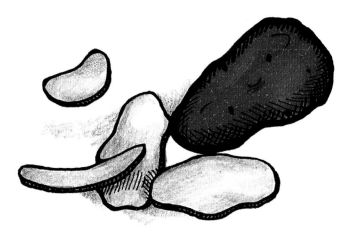

Read-Aloud Story

A Fish Out of Water

Retold by Jody Hirsh

A JEW WITHOUT TORAH IS LIKE A FISH OUT OF WATER.

Many centuries ago, the Roman Empire had conquered nearly the entire known world, including the land of Israel where many Jewish people lived. The Romans found the Jews to be rebellious and proud and made laws which forbade their study of Torah. The great Rabbi Akiva, in spite of the laws, continued to teach many groups of people in secret. One day his student, Rabbi Papos ben Yehuda, came to him.

"Rabbi," he said, "Aren't you afraid of the Romans? Why are you taking such risks?"

"I'm surprised at your question," Akiva answered. "Aren't you Rabbi Papos who people say is such a wise teacher? It seems to me that you are being foolish. Let me tell you a story."

There once was a fox that used to walk along the bank of a great river. In the river, he saw fish swimming around frantically. "What are you running away from?" he asked them. "We're running away from the nets that humans put in the river to catch us," they answered. "Why don't you come up here on the dry land?" the fox said to them. "You can live up here with me—just like our grandfathers used to live together. We'll have great fun and I'll protect you from the humans." "Are you the one that is supposed to be the cleverest of animals?" they said to him. "Why, you're being foolish! If in the river which gives us life and in which we live our lives we're in danger, then we would be in even more danger in a place where we would die without water."

"We are the same way," continued Rabbi Akiva. "It says in the Torah itself: it is our life and the length of our days. (Deuteronomy 7:5) If we're in danger when we study our Torah, think how much danger we would be in if we did not study it."

Lag B'Omer Crafts and Activities

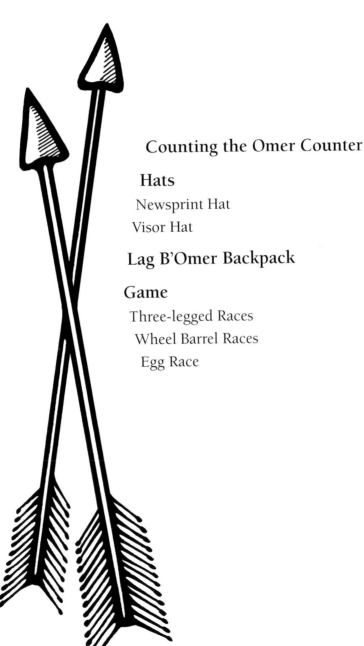

Counting the Omer Counter

Hats
Newsprint Hat
Visor Hat

Lag B'Omer Backpack

Game
Three-legged Races
Wheel Barrel Races
Egg Race

Counting the Omer

The forty-nine days, or seven weeks, between Passover (when the Israelites were freed from slavery in Egypt) and Shavuot (when the Israelite people received the Ten Commandments) is a serious time. Each day, we count the Omer and think about how to follow Torah. However, on the thirty-third day, called Lag B'Omer, we celebrate by going on picnics and playing games.

OMER COUNTER

How do we count the Omer? Say the following prayer and phrase each night (the time between sundown and sunrise) from the second night of Passover to Shavuot.

בָּרוּךְ אַתָּה יְיָ אֱלֹהֵינוּ, מֶלֶךְ הָעוֹלָם, אֲשֶׁר קִדְּשָׁנוּ בְּמִצְוֹתָיו, וְצִוָּנוּ עַל סְפִירַת הָעוֹמֶר.

Baruch atah A-do-nai Elohenu melech ha-olam
Asher kid'shanu b'mitsvotav Vetsivanu al s'firat ha-Omer

Blessed are you, O Lord our God, Ruler of the universe,
Who has made us holy with Your commandments, and has instructed us to Count the Omer

"Today is day _____ of the counting."

If the blessing is not said before dawn, you can still count the Omer, but may not say the blessing that day. If you miss counting a day altogether, you can count the Omer, but may not use the blessing for the remaining days of counting the Omer.

MATERIALS:

The "Omer" chart found on p. 281, copied and enlarged to fit on an 11 x 17-inch piece of white tag board

Glue stick

2-inch piece of magnetic tape, cut into two 1-inch pieces

¼-inch mailing dots – color of your choice...go wild!

DIRECTIONS:

1 Glue the "Omer" chart onto the tag board.

2 Attach the magnetic tape to the top two corners on the back of the chart.

3 Hang it on your refrigerator.

4 Mark off each day with a mailing dot, say the prayer and count the day.

Hats

Newsprint Hat

MATERIALS:

12 x 18 inch piece of newsprint or construction paper

Tape

Paper punch

Yarn

Glue

Feathers

Long strips of sticky tape cut into a variety of shapes

Markers

DIRECTIONS:

1 Fold the paper in half so you end up with a 9 x 12 inch piece of folded paper.

2 Turn the paper so the fold runs along the top.

3 Fold the upper left and upper right hand corners down so they meet near the center of the bottom.

4 You should now have a triangular shape with the point facing upward.

5 Fold the front bottom strip upward about 1½ inches.

6 Turn the hat over and repeat with the other side.

7 Tape wherever necessary to keep hat closed.

8 Decorate with sticky tape, markers, feathers.

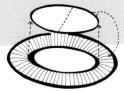

Visor Hat

MATERIALS:

Paper plate

Markers

Decorative materials: sequins, feathers, pompoms

Crayons

Glue

Scissors

DIRECTIONS:

1 Cut the embossed center circle out of the paper plate leaving just the rim.

2 Trim the hole you've cut so the rim fits easily over the child's head.

3 Take the circle you have removed and cut it in half.

4 Staple it, like a visor, to the front of the hat rim.

5 Decorate the hat as you wish.

Lag B'Omer Backpacks

It's Lag B'Omer and time for a picnic. All around are trees, acorns, interesting sticks, and bird feathers. This backpack is wonderful for storing these treasures and it can actually be worn on your front or back.

MATERIALS:

Brown grocery bag

Scissors

Backstraps: Two 18-inch pieces of thick yarn or strips of torn sheeting

Markers

Crayons

Sticky tape – cut into all different shapes

Stickers

Extra construction paper scraps for decorative shapes

Glue stick

DIRECTIONS:

1 Fold over the top edge of the paper bag three to four times to form a sturdy cuff.

2 For the backside of the backpack, cut 4 horizontal slits: two, side by side, 6 inches apart and each about 2 inches below the cuff, and two 9 inches directly below the above slits.

3 Feed the ends of the backstrap through the top and bottom slits.

4 Tie the ends into a knot, forming large loops.

5 Decorate the backpack with markers, crayons and sticky tape designs.

Games

Falling between late April and mid-May, Lag B'Omer could be the perfect opportunity for your first picnic of the year. Invite friends over for a potluck "Lag B'Omer Picnic and Games Day." Archery may be out of the question for families with young children, but there are games galore to choose from. A few ideas follow.

IDEA 1: THREE-LEGGED RACES

MATERIALS:

Old stocking legs or scarves to tie legs together

DIRECTIONS:

1 Participants choose a partner (this can be delightful fun, especially if one partner is an adult and one is a child).

2 Partners stand shoulder to shoulder. Tie their 2 inside legs together.

3 Race against other pairs to a designated spot.

IDEA 2: WHEEL BARREL RACES

1 Participants choose a partner.

2 One person kneels on the ground, with his/her hands also on the ground. The partner lifts up the kneeling person's legs, and they are ready to go.

3 Race against other pairs to a designated spot.

IDEA 3: EGG RACES

MATERIALS:

Hard-boiled eggs (For fun, you can tell the players that they're raw)

Spoons – the size depends on how difficult you want the race to be

DIRECTIONS:

1 Participants choose teams.

2 Any number of teams can play.

3 Each team divides itself in half, and each half stands facing the other from about 10 to 12 feet apart and lined up one behind the other.

4 The first person in each line walks as fast as possible across the space dividing them, holding the egg in the spoon.

5 Upon successfully reaching the first person on the other side, exchange the spoon and egg. This relay then continues until everyone on one team has completed the task.

6 If an egg is dropped, the walker has to go back to the beginning and start with a new one.

Shelly Jubelirer

Yom Ha'Atzmaut

A homeland. An inheritance from Abraham that is rich with Jewish history, culture and identity. A place that offers a sense of connection and belonging.

After 2000 years of living as exiles, the Jewish State of Israel was created on May 14, 1948. This holiday, celebrated by Jews around the world, is called Yom Ha'Atzmaut, Israeli Independence Day.

Experiencing Yom Ha'Atzmaut

Imagine it's November 29, 1947. You and Jews all over the world are listening to the live radio broadcast of the United Nations' vote on the partition of Palestine. The proposal, if passed, would grant Israel independence: it would allow the end of the British control and the State of Israel would be born.

Jews had been in exile for 2,000 years, ever since the Romans destroyed Jerusalem and decimated the Jewish population of Israel (then called Judaea). Refugees from the Nazi Holocaust illegally immigrated to Palestine. The Haganah, a Jewish defense force, had been created to protect Jewish settlements from attack by their Arab neighbors. The Jewish world was waiting for the UN's permission to create a Jewish country.

Imagine the excitement mounting as one by one the nations vote on the future of the Jewish state: Afghanistan – no; Argentina – abstain; Australia – yes . . . . At last, the final vote is tallied: 33 in favor, 13 against and 10 abstentions. The UN Partition Plan is approved! All over the world, from Tel Aviv and New York, Jews are dancing in the streets. The exile is over. Jews can begin the work of the ingathering of exiles and the building of the State of Israel.

But the real Independence Day for Israel is May 14, 1948 [5 Iyyar, 5708 on the Hebrew calendar]. The day the British departed and the armies of five Arab countries invaded the new country, Israel. Fierce battles continued for more than a year, until a final truce was signed in July 1949. Ever since, Israeli Independence Day, Yom Ha'Atzmaut, is celebrated by Jews in Israel and all over the world.

Celebration in Israel includes dancing in the streets, barbeques, entertainment and parades with the noises of great merriment. American Jewish communities celebrate with parties, parades, Israeli food, fairs and performances. Israeli entertainment brings to us the spirit of Israel, connecting the family of Jews around the world with their homeland, Israel.

The day is preceded by Yom Ha'Zikaron—Israeli Memorial Day—a day that remembers those who fell defending the Jewish State. The tone of mourning, however, changes to celebration as the events of Yom Ha'Atzmaut take over.

In the synagogue, the celebration was not without controversy. Is Yom Ha'Atzmaut a religious holiday? Although there are those who claim that it shouldn't be, the majority of the Jewish world insists that it is—the creation of the State of Israel is nothing short of a miracle! Therefore, most synagogues have special prayers on Yom Ha'Atzmaut. Some congregations even have a Torah reading on Yom Ha'Atzmaut. For those of you who remember a world with no Jewish state, and those of us for whom the existence of Israel has been a constant in our lives, Yom Ha'Atzmaut has become a significant Jewish holiday in the home, the synagogue and the community.

Traditions & Text

A JEWISH STATE

The creation of the State of Israel was fraught with controversy when Theodor Herzl first suggested a Jewish State at the First Zionist Congress in 1897 in Basel, Switzerland. Herzl predicted in 1897, that within 50 years Statehood would be a reality. Many religious Jews were horrified at the very idea of a return to the homeland and the creation of a Jewish State before the coming of the Messiah. Others insisted that the creation of Israel was a prelude to the Messiah. Still others rejected religious implications of a Jewish state and responded to the political necessities as purely secular Jews. Other secular Jews rejected Zionism as antagonistic to the Jewish identity of citizens in various countries around the world. At the Sixth Zionist Congress of 1903, Herzl himself proposed that Uganda, and not Palestine, be considered as the location of the Jewish State.

On November 29, 1947, the United Nations General Assembly passed a resolution calling for the establishment of a Jewish State in Eretz-Yisrael. The coalition of religious and secular Zionists helped make the dream a reality. The Declaration of Independence of the State of Israel makes that reality clear:

Eretz Yisrael was the birthplace of the Jewish people. Here their spiritual, religious and political identity was shaped. Here they first attained statehood, created cultural values of national and universal significance and gave to the world the eternal Book of Books.

After being forcibly exiled from their land, the people kept faith with it throughout their dispersion and never ceased to pray and hope for their return to it and for the restoration in it of their political freedom.

Impelled by this historic and traditional attachment, Jews strove in every successive generation to reestablish themselves in their ancient homeland. In recent decades they returned in masses. Pioneers, "ma'pilim" (immigrants coming to "Eretz-Yisrael" in defiance of restrictive legislation) and defenders, they made deserts bloom, revived the Hebrew language, built villages and towns, and created a thriving community, controlling its own economy and culture, loving peace but knowing how to defend itself, bringing the blessings of progress to all the country's inhabitants, and aspiring towards independent nationhood. . . .

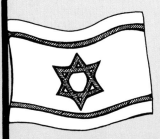

SYMBOLS OF THE STATE OF ISRAEL

By Nir Barkin, Sheliach, Milwaukee Community 2000
Sheliach is the Hebrew word for Emissary

FLAG OF ISRAEL

Unlike the flags of other countries, the flag of Israel is meant to represent Jews living throughout the world, all of whom are considered spiritual citizens of Israel.

The origins of a Jewish flag date to a red and white flag during the reign of Emperor Charles IV in 1354 Prague.

However, the modern Israeli flag found its roots in the 19th century fledgling Zionist movements in Russia. The Hibat Zion movement of the 1880s adopted a flag with a white field, two blue stripes along the sides and a blue Star of David in the center. This blue and white flag came to be used frequently with the early settlers in Palestine. The first established settlement, Rishon L'Zion, raised a blue and white flag as its official symbol in 1885. Theodor Herzl, a founding father of the State of Israel, was considering several designs for a national flag when David Wolfsohn, his personal emissary, created a design based on the tallit, or prayer shawl, which incorporated the Star of David. It is this flag, which was adopted as the official Zionist flag in 1933 at the 18th Zionist Congress, that is recognized throughout the world today as the Flag of Israel.

HATIKVAH

Originally a song of the Zionist movement, Hatikvah has become the national anthem of the State of Israel. The song was adapted from the poem "Tikvatenu" (Our Hope), which was penned by poet Naphtali Herz Imber in 1878. Shortly after the poem was completed, Samuel Cohn, who had come to Palestine from Moldavia in 1878, set the poem to a melody, which he consciously based on a Moldavian-Rumanian folk song. Soon the melancholy song became a popular folk-anthem among the early settlers in Palestine, and it was officially recognized in 1933 as the anthem of Zionism. The heartfelt words and moving melody of Hatikvah emphasize the attachment of all Jews to their homeland, Israel.

The earliest printed version of Hatikvah appeared in Breslau in 1895.

As long as deep in the heart,
The soul of a Jew yearns,
And towards the East
An eye looks to Zion,

Our hope is not yet lost,
The hope of two thousand years
To be a free people in our land,
The land of Zion and Jerusalem
To be a free people in our land,
The land of Zion and Jerusalem

Fascinating Food Facts

What is Israeli food? Some say the *felafel*—that amazing concoction of balls of ground and spiced chickpeas, deep-fried and served with salad in a pita (middle eastern pocket bread), dripping with tahini (sesame sauce). But wait - they eat felafel in Jordan, Egypt and other Arabic countries. In fact, the very word "felafel" is Arabic, and not Hebrew.

Maybe Israeli food is the salad of chopped tomatoes and cucumber served at breakfast. Or yogurt. Or perhaps fried breaded chicken breast—schnitzel. (Hmm—isn't schnitzel a German word?) What about gefilte fish (Eastern European) or stuffed zucchini (Mediterranean) or hamburgers (give me a break—what's more American than that)? The truth is that just as the goal of Zionism was "The ingathering of the exiles," Israeli food seems to be "The ingathering of the cuisines."

Israeli food is food that Jews brought with them from every corner of the globe. Restaurant critics tell us that if Israel has any distinctive type of restaurant, it is the Kosher dairy restaurants that only serve fish and vegetarian food (adhering to the Kosher principle of not mixing meat and milk). Even many Israelis who don't keep kosher feel that eating meat and milk together is somehow unnatural—hence the many gourmet dairy restaurants.

Suggested Yom Ha'Atzmaut Menu

We have yet to develop major home-based traditions on Yom Ha'Atzmaut. How about trying your hand at typical Israeli food, such as those listed below?

(The letter in parenthesis indicates the appropriate blessing found in "Prayers and Blessings" on p. 283)	
The traditional blessings said at mealtime. Handwashing (A) Hamotzi (B)	Eggplant Dip Hummus Israeli Salad Tahini sauce on felafel in pita bread Yogurts Ice Cream
Blessing after the meal *(Birkat HaMazon)* (H)	

GO TO RECIPE INDEX IN BACK OF BOOK FOR SUGGESTED RECIPES.

Kids in the Kitchen

On Independence Day (Yom Ha'Atzmaut) Israeli children enjoy a day off from school and a fireworks display which lights up the entire sky. In America, we can sample a taste of Israeli foods by making a friendly pita face.

PITA FACES

COOKING EQUIPMENT NEEDED:

Bowl

Baking tray

Knife

INGREDIENTS:

Pita

Garlic powder

Salt

Zatar

1 can hummus

1 can techina

Cooking oil spray

Olives

Carrots

Pickles

Tomatoes

Cucumbers

Red pepper

DIRECTIONS:

1 Allowing 1 pita per person. Spray with cooking spray or wipe with oil.

2 Sprinkle garlic powder, salt, Zatar (an Israeli spice).

3 Bake at 350 degrees for about 5 minutes.

4 Then, using either the hummus recipe on page 197 or using the canned hummus and techina dips imported from Israel (Mix 1 can of each to make a delicious dip), spread your pita with the hummus/techina mixture (about 3 to 4 tablespoons).

5 Decorate your "pita face" (olives for eyes, carrot for nose, pickle for mouth). Or use your imagination with tomatoes, cucumbers, red pepper, etc.

6 Finally—enjoy a fun taste of Israel for Yom Ha'Atzmaut.

Read-Aloud Story

Waking Up The Hebrew Language

by Jody Hirsh

People said that Eliezer ben Yehuda was crazy. He was born in Eastern Russia but while he was a university student in Paris, he thought long and hard about his identity as a Jew. "One thing that sets us apart," he thought, "is that we no longer have our own language. Jews have forgotten our own ancient language, Hebrew." He moved to Palestine and started speaking Hebrew even though not every Jew understood him. He published a newspaper in Hebrew and insisted on teaching math and science to Jewish high school students in Hebrew. When he brought his bride, Deborah, to Palestine, he insisted she speak Hebrew too.

Reviving a dead language wasn't easy. He had to create new words every day. How do you say "clock" in Hebrew? He looked at all the old books. Nowhere in the Bible are there any clocks—clocks weren't invented back then. So he took the ancient word, *sha'ah*–hour—and made from it a modern Hebrew word, *sha'on*–clock! He took the word lead, *oferet,* and made from it *iparon*–pencil! (Pencils had lead in them in those days.) In fact, he had to write a whole dictionary of Hebrew!

When his first child was born, he decided that he would be the first modern child in history to speak Hebrew as his mother tongue! He named him Itamar—an ancient Biblical name which means "Island of Date Palms." Ben Yehuda wouldn't let anyone in his house unless they spoke only Hebrew or agreed to be entirely silent. People said that he would damage his son— that Itamar would never learn to speak at all—that it was unnatural to speak an ancient dead language. When Itamar reached his third birthday and still wasn't speaking, everyone blamed his father. Finally Itamar did speak, and he spoke beautiful Hebrew. He later became a writer and a newspaper publisher—all in Hebrew.

★ BYTZ MSH FNL NVAYV FGTSS?

✳ WHY DON'T WE SAY IT LIKE THIS!

Yom Ha'Atzmaut

Yom Ha'Atzmaut Crafts and Activities

Israel in Art
"Jerusalem of Gold" Collage Picture
"Jerusalem of Gold" Wall Hanging
Layered Sand Jars
Clear Contact Paper Stained-Glass Windows
Fish Aquarium

Salt Dough Map of Israel

Israeli Marching Flag

Israeli Independence Day Necklace

Israel in Art

Israel is a country that boasts arid deserts, forest covered hills, sophisticated cities, agricultural wonders, a beautiful lake teeming with fish, and a history of the Jewish people that covers 4,000 years.

"JERUSALEM OF GOLD"

Over 3,000 years old, the city of Jerusalem gleams in the afternoon light. With domed roofs, peaked towers and buildings of white Jerusalem stone, its luminescence reflects the light of God's presence.

"JERUSALEM OF GOLD" COLLAGE PICTURE

MATERIALS:

9 x 12 inch piece of black construction paper

Gold wrapping or foil paper

Gold glitter

Small paper drinking cup

Scissors

Glue stick

DIRECTIONS:

1 Cut gold paper into architectural shapes: arches, squares, rectangles and half circles.

2 Glue shapes onto black paper to form the "City of Gold"—Jerusalem.

3 Pour a small amount of gold glitter into a drinking cup. Wherever you want glitter, put glue on your picture. Sprinkle on the glitter, a pinch full at a time. Pour excess glitter back into the cup. Repeat until your picture is finished.

"Jerusalem of Gold" Wall Hanging

For adults or older children

MATERIALS:

9½ x 14-inch (or you can determine desired size) piece of fabric

9½ x 14-inch (same size as your fabric) piece of white paper or newsprint

Pinking shears

Newspaper

Masking tape

Permanent black magic marker

Various colors of quality water color paint

Medium-sized paintbrushes

Container of water

11 x 16-inch tag board

Glue

DIRECTIONS:

1 Cut the edges of the material with pinking shears or hem.

2 Draw a scene of Jerusalem on the white paper using squares, rectangles, half circles, template shapes (see p. 282) to form building shapes.

3 Cover your worktable with several layers of newspaper.

4 Lay the drawn Jerusalem scene on the newsprint.

5 Tape the fabric over the drawn design, so neither will move.

6 Copy the picture onto the fabric with black magic marker.

7 Paint over the scene. It does not matter what colors are used or whether the paint follows the borders of the drawing. The paint will "bleed" into other areas.

8 Let the fabric-painted picture dry.

9 Mount it on the tag board.

Variation: This idea can be used for many themes - Israel, Hanukkah, Shabbat, Sukkot. Adapt your outlined picture to the theme.

LAYERED SAND JARS

In the south of Israel lays the Negev desert, where layers of sand and dunes cover the land. Arid and dry, the land looks uninhabitable. Yet, it is there that Israel has created fields of vegetation and growth—another miracle that is a part of the land and her people.

MATERIALS:

Clean baby food jars, with labels removed

Colored sand – available at most craft stores, or salt, colored with dry tempera paint

NOTE: *To color salt, add 1 teaspoon dry tempra paint to 1 cup salt in a large baggie. Shake until salt is colored.*

Containers

Plastic spoons

Toothpicks

Cotton balls

Glue

Gold spray paint

DIRECTIONS:

1 Spray paint baby food jar lids with gold paint and allow to dry.

2 Fill each container with a different colored sand/colored salt.

3 Spoon a layer of "sand" into a baby food jar. The thickness of the layers can vary. You may want to tilt some layers.

4 Add a second color of "sand," a third, etc.

5 After three to four layers, slide a toothpick along the inside of the baby food jar to make designs along the outside edge. Repeat as you wish with that layer and subsequent layers.

6 When the jar is full, place cotton balls on top.

7 Place a ring of glue around the inside rungs of the bottle cap.

8 Screw the cap on the jar. The sand should not be able to move.

Variation: Different-sized and shaped containers can be used.

CLEAR CONTACT PAPER STAINED-GLASS WINDOW

Marc Chagall created 12 beautiful stained-glass windows depicting the 12 tribes of Israel. Installed in Hadassah Hospital in Jerusalem, the windows glow with a beauty and intensity paralleling the light of Jerusalem itself.

MATERIALS:

9 x 12-inch piece of black construction paper

12 x 18-inch piece of clear contact paper, folded in half, making it 9 x 12-inch

Colored tissue paper cut into 1 to 1½-inch pieces

Scissors

DIRECTIONS:

1 Cut an arch shape out of the black paper, leaving a 1 to 1½ inch framed border.

2 Lift the paper backing from half of the folded piece of contact paper.

3 Carefully lay the black frame on the just exposed sticky side of contact paper.

4 Cover the sticky side of contact paper with differently colored pieces of tissue paper.

Variation: Older children could plan out a design to form with the tissue paper or they could cut the tissue paper into specific shapes: Stars of David, Menorahs, buildings. Cut-out pictures of Israel, Jewish stories, etc. could be laid, picture side down, on the contact paper before the tissue paper is applied.

5 When the arch shape is totally covered, lift the remaining backing from the contact paper and carefully press it over your "stained-glass window."

6 Hang the pictures in a window to show off the variety of colors.

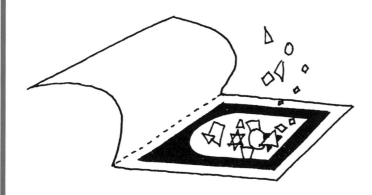

Fish Aquarium

The very southern tip of Israel meets the Red Sea (traditionally thought of as the sea Moses divided when the children of Israel fled Pharaoh and his army). At the very southern tip is the resort city of Eilat. There, travelers come to snorkel, roam the beaches, ride glass bottom boats and view the abundance of tropical fish.

MATERIALS:

Styrofoam meat tray (white or yellow) - Wash thoroughly with hot water and soap. Unused ones are available at supermarkets.

Different colors of construction paper

Blue transparent cellophane paper, cut to fit over the meat tray, with ½ inch overlapping

Blue, green, yellow, tissue paper

Large sequins (to represent bubbles)

Pipe cleaners (to represent seaweed)

Glue

Tape

Scissors

DIRECTIONS:

1 Cut fish shapes out of the construction paper.

2 Cut the tissue paper into wavy strips to represent waves and water.

3 Glue fish, waves, seaweed and bubbles onto the meat tray.

4 Cover the meat tray with blue cellophane, glued, or taped to the tray.

Salt Dough Map of Israel

MATERIALS:

12 x 18-inch mat board, masonite, plywood or heavy poster board - available at a lumber yard or hardware store (size is dependent on your needs)

Pencil

Poster paints

Dough:

1 part white flour

1 part salt

Just enough water to make it workable

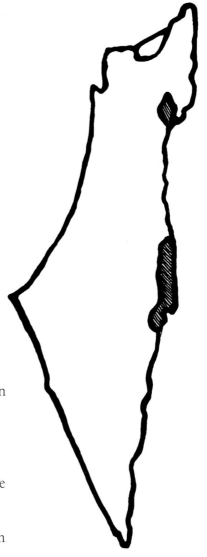

DIRECTIONS:

1 Draw an outline of the map of Israel on the board.

2 Spread dough to fill the map.

3 Add dough for mountains. Shape the dough for other geographical features.

4 Let the dough dry thoroughly. Paint it with poster paints.

Israeli Marching Flags

MATERIALS:

9 x 12-inch piece of white construction paper

Two 9 x 12-inch pieces of blue construction paper

Cut out two 1 x 9-inch stripes

Cut out 2 equilateral triangles, approximately 4 inches on each side. Refer to template on page 00

Wooden paint stirrer – available for free at most paint stores

Markers

Stapler

Glue stick

Scissors

DIRECTIONS:

1 Place the white paper with the long side on top. Glue the triangles onto the center of the white paper to make a Jewish star: Glue on one triangle. Glue the second one upside down on top of the first.

2 Glue each stripe along the long sides of the white paper, one inch from each edge of the paper.

Variation: Make an outline where the stripes should go. Cut sticky tape into smaller pieces and stick them between the outlines on the paper to make the stripes.

3 Let the star and stripes dry.

4 Color designs on the blank side of the paint stirrer.

5 Staple the flag to the top of the paint stirrer.

6 Choose some Israeli music and get ready to march.

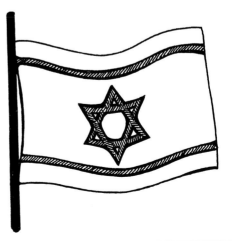

Israeli Independence Day Necklace

DIRECTIONS:

1 Punch a hole in the top or center of each star.

HINT: If you want the stars to lay flat on the necklace, punch 2 holes side by side.

2 Color the white rectangles to resemble an Israeli flag (see previous project).

3 Punch a hole in the narrow side of the flags.

HINT: If you want the flags to lay flat, punch 2 holes side by side.

4 Make your necklace by "sewing" the stars, flags, fruit loops or beads onto the yarn. When finished, cut off the masking tape, fit it around your neck and make a knot.

MATERIALS:

Drinking straws

Scissors

12- to 18-inch long piece of yarn, with a 1-inch piece of masking tape rolled tightly around one end. Tie a knot on the opposite end. (Yarn should be as long as you want your necklace.)

6-pointed 1- to 2-inch Stars of David cut out of various colors of construction paper (see template p. 282).
HINT: Cut one out of cardboard and use it as an outline for the paper stars or make an outline around a 1- to 2-inch star cookie cutter shape.

2 x 1-inch rectangles cut from white construction paper

Blue markers

Paper punch

Fruit loops or plastic beads
CAUTION: Use one or the other, so younger children don't get confused and try to eat the plastic beads.

Holly Williamson

Shavuot

Let us make our way to Jerusalem, to the house of our God, and give thanks for the fruits of the earth, which the Almighty has provided.

We shall bring with us the sweetest of our figs and grapes and offer sheaves of our finest golden wheat.

Our beasts adorned in gold shall lead the way and we shall dance together to the sound of flute and timbrel. Music and merriment will greet us and we shall rejoice with our brethren of high and low station.

For we are filled with gratitude for all that has been provided to us and humbly thank Adonai for the bounty that we have received.

Experiencing Shavuot

In ancient times we were a people who lived according to the cycle of the seasons, depending on nature's bounty to sustain us. Because of this, many of our Jewish holidays are celebrations that coincide with the harvest.

The spring, summer and fall harvests are connected to Passover, Shavuot and Sukkot. These harvests were celebrated by a pilgrimage to the Temple in Jerusalem with people coming from all over *Eretz Yisrael* as well as Babylon and Egypt to give thanks to God for the bounty they were to receive. Shavuot is known as *"Chag HaBikkurim,"* the holiday of the first fruits. When farmers would notice that the first fruits had begun to ripen, they would bundle them together, fill their baskets and join the joyous procession to the Holy Temple to give thanks to God for the bounty they were to receive.

After the Romans destroyed the Temple in the first century, it seemed as if Shavuot and much of how Judaism was practiced would cease to exist. Without the Temple, Jews no longer had a place to make sacrifices and priests lost their central role. And so, in their wisdom, the Rabbis transformed many of the rituals and holidays associated with the Temple.

The Rabbis came to emphasize the connection between this holiday of Shavuot and the giving of the Torah. Counting seven weeks from the second night of Passover, (*"Shavuot"* means weeks in Hebrew), Shavuot falls on the sixth day of Sivan. The Bible tells us that the Israelites received the Torah in the third month (the month of *"Sivan"*). Therefore, according to the Rabbis, the sixth of Sivan is the anniversary of the giving of the Torah. On Pesach, we left the slavery of Egypt. On Shavuot, we received the Torah, the gift of God's commandments.

Today, Shavuot is celebrated as the anniversary of receiving the Ten Commandments. It is also the holiday on which Reform Jews celebrate Confirmation, the ceremony in which 10th graders affirm their acceptance of Torah and a commitment to Judaism.

Introducing young children to Hebrew and Torah on Shavuot is another beautiful custom of the holiday. In some traditions, a little honey is spread over the Hebrew letters on a page. As the child licks the page, s/he begins to realize that learning is a sweet experience.

Dairy meals are often served on Shavuot, relating to the following verse from *Song of Songs:* "Honey and Milk are under your tongue." This passage refers to the sweetness of Torah. (Others suggest that once the Israelites received the Torah, they had to adopt a kosher lifestyle. Eating only dairy was an inital simple solution.)

Lastly, it is customary to decorate the synagogue and home with greens and flowers, again reminding us of Shavuot as the time of the spring harvest.

Traditions & Text

Ever since Rabbinic times 2000 years ago, Shavuot has come to commemorate the giving of the Ten Commandments on Mt. Sinai. More than anything else, our understandings of this primary event in Jewish history characterizes our various religious approaches to Judaism. Did the revelation on Mount Sinai really occur as the Torah tells us? Is the Torah the literal will and word of God? Are we bound to the commandments? The various movements within Judaism have conflicting perspectives on this event.

The different philosophies of Judaism are complex and can't really be reduced to simple statements, but a general summary might go as follows: According to a traditional view, the revelation on Sinai took place as described in the Torah. We, therefore, know that God expects us to follow the commandments in a fairly literal sense, helped by what is called the oral law, or the Talmud (also given to us by God) which interprets and illuminates the laws of the Torah. These interpretations and illuminations must be interpreted for us by rabbi/scholars in every generation, but they must be true to the wishes of God, who gave us the Torah.

The Reform movement, on the other hand, tells us that the revelation on Mount Sinai may not have happened exactly as described in Exodus. The Torah was written by humans inspired by God. In many ways the Torah reflects the realities of the age in which it was written thousands of years ago. These beliefs are not necessarily relevant nor literally binding in our own times. The "spirit" of the Torah, however, is universally true. In every generation, we are told to seek justice and to support the needy, to avoid violence and to treat our fellow human beings with kindness. All Jews can understand these basic truths and interpret the Torah on their own. In recent years, however, the Reform movement has shown an increasing reverence for Jewish law.

A Torah All-Nighter

The Midrash tells us that the Israelites overslept on the day of receiving the Torah! Therefore, the custom of staying up all night studying, reading and discussing Torah and other traditional books are to show God that we are excited to receive His words. Also, the Jewish mystics said the sky opens at midnight for just a moment to reveal Heaven on this evening. Just as all Jews—past, present and future—are said to have been present at God's giving of the Torah, Shavuot gives us each the opportunity to relive that moment of covenant.

The Conservative movement agrees with the Reform movement in a historical sense. However, in acknowledging that Jews have been committed to the Laws of the Torah for 3,000 years, it is necessary to take these laws seriously and to find relevant contemporary ways to interpret them. Only the experts, they assert, are fully capable of interpreting the laws.

Secular Jews often reject both the historical truth of events at Sinai and the relevance of the laws of the Torah. The laws, they say, are rooted in myth. Therefore, we have no obligation to follow them or even to understand them.

So what is the true way to understand the events of Shavuot? Our rabbis tell us "There are seventy faces to the Torah." That is, there are seventy different ways of understanding the Torah. Each of us must find the path which resonates with our own lives. Whether we believe that the events of Sinai are historically true or not, we must admit that the image of Sinai has affected Jewish history and our lives as Jews more powerfully than any other historical event, real or imagined.

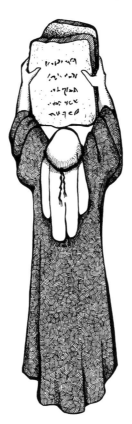

Fascinating Food Facts

BLINTZES, BLINTZES, BLINTZES!

According to legend, when the children of Israel were awaiting the revelation on Mt. Sinai, they realized that the laws they were about to be given would include dietary rules. Since they didn't know what those rules would be regarding the preparation of meat, they ate only dairy foods. Therefore, today's Shavuot feasts include dairy foods like blintzes (Jewish crepes filled with sweet cheese or fruit and served with sour cream) and cheesecake. Some traditions insist on a Shavuot dinner that includes dairy appetizers followed by a meat meal (after the required 20-minute waiting period between milk and meat). This may be an interesting concept in a Kosher home, but a pain in the neck for a homemaker who will have dirty milk and meat dishes to deal with at the same time.

Traditional Shavuot Menu

The following is a suggested order for the blessings.

(The letter in parenthesis indicates the appropriate blessing found in Prayers and Blessings on p. 283)

The following foods are traditional on most holidays, but feel free to use any of the many delicious recipes in this book.

Blessing over the candles (J)

Blessing over the wine (C)

Shehecheyanu (G)

Wine (or grape juice for children)

Blessing for hand washing (A)

Blessing over the bread (B)

Challah

Salad

Blintzes with sour cream

Fish

Ice-cream cake, Cheesecake, or Fruit Kabobs

Blessing after the meal
(Birkat HaMazon) (H)

GO TO RECIPE INDEX IN BACK OF BOOK FOR SUGGESTED RECIPES.

Kids in the Kitchen

One of the ways we celebrate Shavuot is by staying up all night and studying the Torah. Many people believe that by following the ways of the Torah you gain strength. To help promote strength, this recipe uses yogurt to help build strong bones and promote good health. These popsicles are a great treat for that late-night studying or as a dessert for your holiday meal.

YOGURT POPSICLES

Ruth Wallace

COOKING EQUIPMENT NEEDED:

Measuring cups

Knife

Bowls

Popsicle sticks

Small cups or popsicle mold

INGREDIENTS:

1 cup plain yogurt

1 banana, sliced

1 teaspoon vanilla

1 cup fruit juice or fruit chunks

Favorites: orange juice or peach

DIRECTIONS:

1 Blend ingredients together and pour into small paper cups.

2 Freeze.

3 Place a plastic spoon or popsicle stick in each cup when yogurt mixture is half frozen.

4 To serve, turn cup upside-down and run hot water over it until the popsicle slips out.

5 Let children keep the cups to use as a holder.

6 A great recipe to help teething children, as well as, a nutritious snack.

Read-Aloud Story

David's Wish

by Rabbi David Fine

Maybe this year. Maybe this year I will be able to stay up all night on Shavuot. As my father and I walked to the synagogue, I asked, "What do you think, Dad? Will I be able to stay awake this year?" My father just looked at me and smiled.

The synagogue was alive with activity. Children were weaving in and out all of the people gathering for study sessions. I quickly left my father's side and ran to the kitchen, where I knew all the special foods for Shavuot would be waiting. Cheesecakes, blintzes, and ice cream were set out for the taking.

I ate until I thought my stomach would burst. I laughed and played with all my friends. Finally I found my way to my father's side, where I settled down to listen to all the different voices studying Torah: the booming voice of the Rabbi, the rapid-fire voice of our neighbor Shmuli, the squeaky violin voice of my uncle and, of course, the gentle, warm sound of my father's voice.

My eyes became heavy and my mind was filled with pictures of the mighty Moses carrying the stone tablets down from Mt. Sinai, and of the wild waters of the Red Sea parting to let the Jewish people walk through.

The next thing I knew the bright light of morning was shining in my eyes. I smiled up at my father, and then I frowned when I realized I had fallen asleep. "Dad," I asked, "I slept through Shavuot again! Did I stay up longer than last year?"

"Yes, David," my father replied. "You made it past last year by twenty-five minutes. By that rate, you will make it all night in just a few years!"

"But Dad, why do you stay up all night, anyway?" I asked.

"Ahhh, now this is a very important question," my father answered. "Let me tell you a story."

"Once upon a time, God had a very special treasure that he wanted to give the Jewish people. The treasure was the Torah. After they had come out of Egypt and crossed the Red Sea, he told them to camp by Mount Sinai, promising them that on the third day he would give them the Torah."

All of a sudden my father stopped and asked, "Don't you think the Jewish people would have been very excited to receive such a gift like the Torah?"

I thought of how excited I got when I was waiting for special gifts and answered "Of course!"

"Well, David," my father continued, "the people were excited, but when God came the next morning to give them the Torah, they were all sleeping! God had to wake them up! So that is why we stay up all night on Shavuot, the holiday that celebrates the giving of the Torah, to make sure God never has to wake us up again to receive such a precious gift!"

As we walked home from the synagogue in the early morning warmth, I thought of the story. I looked up at my father and said, "Next year I'll do it. I know I can!"

My father looked down at me and smiled.

Shavuot

Shavuot Crafts and Activities

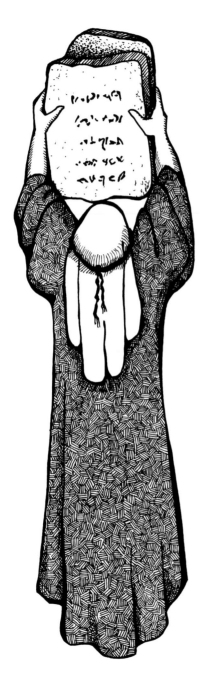

Shavuot Parade

Tissue Flowers and Garland

Foil-Tooled Mizrach

Shavuot Parade

A favorite memory of living on a kibbutz was the Shavuot parade. Tractors pulled farm wagons decorated with flower garlands and wheat sheaths and filled with the first fruits and crops of the harvest. A parade of school children, also covered in garlands of flowers, followed close behind. Everyone on the kibbutz followed out to the field where an area had been plowed flat. Soon young children appeared, dressed in simple dance costumes and performed Israeli folk dances, all relating to the harvest. Of course, we all joined in.

- Marsha Loeb

Think of Shavuot on the kibbutz in Israel and have yourself a Shavuot parade.

MATERIALS:

Wagons or bicycles

Crepe paper

Tissue paper flowers
(next project)

Kazoos and/or tambourines

DIRECTIONS:

1 Decorate bike or wagon with crepe peper and flowers.

2 March, dance and ride around neighborhood.

Note: Musical instruments can be ordered from Oriental Trading Catalogue at 800/228-2269.

Tissue Flowers and Garland

Although Mount Sinai is in the desert, Midrash tells us that the desert bloomed when the Torah and the Ten Commandments were received. Shavuot is the holiday where the first fruits were brought to the Temple and it is marked by decorating the synagogue and home with fruits, greens and flowers.

MATERIALS:

6 x 6-inch squares of tissue paper

Stapler

Pipe Cleaners

Pieces of thick green yarn or rope – Approx. 18 inches long for tissue flower garland

DIRECTIONS:

Flower:

1 Stack together three to four squares of differently colored tissue paper.

2 Accordion-style, fold them together.

3 Staple the accordion fold in the middle.

4 Crimp the middle so both ends point upward.

5 Wrap a pipe cleaner tightly around the crimped center.

6 Gently, fold back each layer of tissue paper on both sides to form the flower shape.

Flower Garland: Wrap individual flowers by their pipe cleaners around a piece of yarn or rope, leaving enough space at each end to tie it to a bike or wagon.

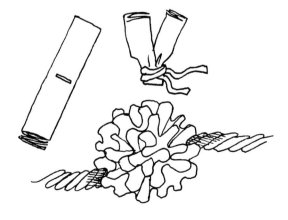

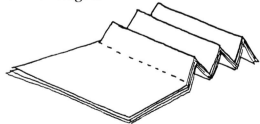

Foil-Tooled Mizrach

FOR OLDER CHILDREN

"Mizrach" means "East" and also refers to a plaque that hangs on the eastern wall of a room to indicate the direction of Jerusalem. The plaques are usually very artistic, featuring calligraphy, paper cutting, foil tooling, clay, batik, silk painting or virtually any art technique. The subject of a Mizrach can be words from any prayer or picture the artist desires. Traditional prayers used include - Psalms 16:8, "I have placed the Lord before me forever…," and Psalm 67 "God be gracious unto us, and bless us; may He cause His face to shine toward us… (often written out in micography in the shape of a menorah).

MATERIALS:

Copper tooling foil – available from a craft store or heavy-duty aluminum foil

Blunt tipped pencil or ball point pen

Magazines (for padding)

Masking Tape

White paper, the size of your desired Mizrach

DIRECTIONS:

1 On the white paper, make a sketch of a design that appeals to you. Subject ideas for Shavuot are: the Ten Commandments, the tablets of the Ten Commandments, Honoring Your Mother and Father, God giving Moses the Jewish laws, Ruth & Naomi.

Variation: Find a simple picture that you like and use that.

2 Put a small pile of magazines on the table for padding.

3 For safety, cover the sharp edges of the foil with masking tape.

4 Lay the foil over the magazine.

5 Tape your sketch to the top of the foil and the magazines to keep it from moving.

6 Go over the design with the pen/pencil. The design will be pressed into the foil. To avoid tearing, do not press too hard. You are actually stretching the foil.

7 Remove the paper design. Working on the back of the foil, rub the pen/pencil tip gently on all sections of the design you want pressed forward.

8 Turn the foil to the front. Press the opposite sections away from the viewer. You will be creating a 3-D picture in foil.

9 Frame your mizrach and hang it on an eastern wall in your home.

Recipes

In the Beginning (Appetizers, Breads, Salads & Soups)

Then There Was (Main & Side Dishes)

And in the End (Desserts)

Mock Chopped Liver

PARVE

A vegetarian version of a traditional favorite. Serve with crackers.

3	tablespoons of margarine	4-6	hard-boiled eggs
1	cup sliced mushrooms	¼	pound chopped walnuts (or other nuts)
1	cup sliced onions		Salt and pepper to taste

- Sauté mushrooms and onions in margarine until soft, but not dry. Drain well.
- In food processor, chop eggs and walnuts with metal blade. Add mushroom mixture and process until smooth. Add salt and pepper to taste. The consistency should be similar to traditional chopped liver.
- Garnish with chopped parsley or other fresh herbs.

Serves 6 to 8

Chef's tip: For a nuttier flavor, roast the walnuts for a minute in toaster oven or under broiler before adding them into recipe.

Low Fat Chopped Liver

MEAT

Nouveau Jewish!

1	pound chicken livers	1	teaspoon salt
2	medium onions, finely sliced	½	teaspoon black pepper
1	barely rounded tablespoon soft margarine		Good pinch of ground nutmeg
1	clove of garlic, crushed	3	large hard-boiled eggs, shelled and halved

- Grill the livers over medium to high heat.
- Melt the margarine in a covered frying pan, add the onions, sprinkle with the seasonings, then cover and cook over moderate heat for 10 minutes or until onions are softened and golden brown, stirring twice.
- Let mixture cool slightly. Purée until fairly smooth in processor.
- Add to the processor the grilled livers and the shelled and halved eggs and process until finely chopped and blended. Use a spatula to scrape down the sides if necessary.
- Adjust seasonings to taste. Refrigerate 6 hours or overnight.

Serves 6 to 8

Chef's tip: This is a great way to make chopped liver, only using half the normal amount of fat, binding it instead with extra onions. This will keep 5 days under refrigeration or in the freezer for 1 month.

Salmon Mousse with Cucumber Dressing

A light, sophisticated starter. The dressing is also terrific as a veggie or pita dip.

Salmon Mousse:

1	envelope unflavored gelatin	1	cup salmon (red sockeye), bones removed
2	tablespoons lemon juice	¼	teaspoon paprika
1	cup boiling water	1	teaspoon dill
1	small onion, chopped	½	cup sour cream
1	cup mayonnaise		Fresh dill for garnish

- In blender or food processor, blend onion, lemon juice, boiling water, and gelatin powder for about 1 minute. Add mayonnaise, sour cream, and seasonings and blend 30 seconds. Add salmon and blend until smooth.
- Spray a 3 to 4 cup fish mold or ring mold with cooking spray. Pour mixture into mold.
- Cover with plastic wrap and refrigerate until firm, at least 1 hour or overnight.
- To serve, unmold onto lettuce-lined plate and garnish with fresh dill sprigs. If desired, drizzle Cucumber Dressing on each slice, or in a bowl on the side. Great with party rye, pumpernickel slices, or crackers.

Cucumber Dressing:

1	cup sour cream	½	teaspoon salt
2	tablespoons lemon juice	½	teaspoon onion powder
1	teaspoon Dijon mustard	1	cup cucumber, seeded, drained and finely chopped
1	teaspoon dill		

- Blend all ingredients together in blender or processor until relatively smooth. Refrigerate 1 hour or overnight.
- Serve over slices of Salmon Mousse, or in a bowl on the side.
- Also great as a dip for pita wedges and veggies!

Serves 8

Chef's tip: If plain gelatin is not available, use lemon gelatin and eliminate 1 tablespoon lemon juice from mousse recipe.

Fresh Tomato Tart

DAIRY

Easy and tasty!

1 (10-inch) basic pastry dough pie crust (found in freezer section)	½ teaspoon salt
8 ounces mozzarella cheese, shredded	¼ teaspoon pepper
2 tablespoons fresh basil, chopped	1 tablespoon extra virgin olive oil
4-5 ripe Roma tomatoes, in ½-inch slices	Fresh basil for garnish

- Preheat oven to 400°F.
- Line 10-inch tart pan with parchment paper or foil and place pastry dough in pan. Sprinkle cheese and basil on dough. Cover with tomato slices, as evenly as possible.
- Sprinkle tomatoes with salt and pepper and drizzle with olive oil.
- Bake 30 to 40 minutes (can take twice as long depending on how juicy tomatoes are).
- Garnish with fresh chopped basil. Slice tart in wedges and serve warm or at room temperature.

Serves 6 to 8

Creamed Herring

DAIRY

Oldie, but goody!

1 (16-ounce) jar herring in wine sauce	¼ cup sugar
1 large red onion, thinly sliced	1 pint sour cream
¼ cup white vinegar	

- Drain herring fillets in colander. Lay fillets on paper toweling and pat dry. Remove and discard onions from herring.
- In a bowl, mix together vinegar, sugar and sour cream. Place a layer of herring in a glass or plastic bowl. Put a layer of sliced red onion over the herring. Put a layer of sour cream mixture over herring.
- Repeat layering of herring, onion and sour cream. Cover and marinate in refrigerator for 3 days. Stir every day.
- Serve with small pieces of rye or pumpernickel bread.

Serves 8

Passover Sweet and Sour Meatballs

MEAT

Delicious and tender, good anytime.

Meatballs:

2	pounds ground chuck	½	cup onions, minced
⅔	cup matzo meal	1	teaspoon salt
½	cup water	¼	teaspoon pepper
2	eggs, slightly beaten		

- Combine all ingredients by hand or in mixer and shape into small meatballs. Place on wax paper in fridge while preparing sauce.

Sweet and Sour Sauce:

1	large onion, diced	1	(11-ounce) can or jar tomato-mushroom sauce
½	cup fresh lemon juice		
½	cup sugar	½	cup water
½	cup brown sugar		

- Combine sauce ingredients in a pot and bring to a boil. Add meatballs, reduce heat and simmer for about 1 to 1½ hours.
- Serve with cocktail forks on skewers.

Serves 12 to 14

Baked Salami

MEAT

Never enough!

1	(2-pound) salami	2	tablespoons Dijon mustard
1	(10-ounce) jar apricot preserves		

- Preheat oven to 400°F.
- Combine the preserves with the mustard.
- Slice a 2-pound kosher salami thinly (¼-inch slices) almost to the bottom, but not all the way through. Brush apricot-mustard glaze between each slice and over the top of the salami. Place salami on a lined cookie sheet and bake uncovered at 400°F for 1½ hours.
- Serve hot with pretzel sticks and mustard sauce.

Serves 8 to 10

Gefilte Fish

PARVE

A holiday favorite.

Boil cinnamon sticks in separate pan to eliminate fish odor in your kitchen. Have the fish market trim, fillet and grind fish, but keep heads and trim for the stock. Note that the ground portion of the fish will be about ½ the weight of the untrimmed fish.

3	pounds whitefish		Top of 1 head celery, including leaves
2	pounds trout	7	teaspoons salt, divided
2	pounds walleye pike	2	teaspoons pepper, divided
3	onions, chopped in large pieces	3	tablespoons sugar, divided
2	carrots, chopped in large pieces for stock plus	2	cups matzo meal
		3	eggs
2-3	more carrots sliced in ¼-inch diagonal rounds to serve with fish	¼	cup water

Make Stock:

- Rinse trim and heads, tie in cheesecloth (or strain stock through j-cloth afterwards) and place in large pot. Add onions and 2 carrots in large pieces and top of celery head.
- Add 4 teaspoons of salt, 1½ teaspoons of pepper and 2 tablespoons of sugar.
- Cover with cold water and bring to simmer. Simmer 45 minutes.
- Remove trim, onions and carrots from stock and discard. Return stock to a slow boil to cook balls.

Make Fish Balls:

- Combine in mixer or food processor: ground fish, 3 teaspoons of salt, ½ teaspoon of pepper and 1 tablespoon of sugar, eggs, and matzo meal. Chill covered 30 minutes.
- Moisten hands with water and form 12 to 14 balls with mixture, adding more matzo meal if too soft to form. Drop balls in stock one at a time.
- Simmer balls for 3½ to 4½ hours over low heat with partial cover. Remove cover for last hour.
- Add diagonally sliced carrots (enough for 1 to 2 per person) to cook for last ½ hour.

Assembly:

- Remove fish balls from broth with slotted spoon. Top each ball with a sliced carrot or two and chill before serving.
- Serve each ball of fish on a plate with lettuce and a dollop of strong red horseradish.

Chef's tip: Save the fish stock to preserve any leftover fish in the fridge for a few days, or to make fish chowder. The stock can be frozen until needed.

Serves 12 to 14

Homemade Hummus

PARVE

A popular choice, great as a dip for pita and veggies. Try preparing this a day in advance for even better flavor.

3 tablespoons homemade tahini or 5 tablespoons store-bought	½ teaspoon salt
3 tablespoons water	1-2 large cloves garlic, minced
6 tablespoons fresh lemon juice	Parsley, olive oil and paprika for garnish
1 (16-ounce) can chick peas, drained	Bagel chips or pita bread for dipping

- Pour liquid ingredients into blender (water, lemon juice, tahini). Pulse blender while adding garlic, salt and chickpeas.
- When chickpeas are crushed, set on low speed briefly, then increase to high. Blend until smooth. Refrigerate until ready to use.
- Spoon hummus into flat dish, spread, drizzle with olive oil, sprinkle paprika and parsley.

Serves 10 to 12

Chef's tip: Thin hummus with lemon juice if it gets too thick. Serve with a few olives scattered on top.

Sticky Chicken Wings

MEAT

Great sauce! Use it on other poultry.

2-3 pounds chicken wings or drumettes	¼ cup catsup
½ cup honey	4 tablespoons brown sugar
¼ cup soy sauce	1 garlic clove, smashed

- Preheat oven to 375°F.
- Mix honey, soy sauce, catsup, brown sugar and garlic clove. Refrigerate overnight.
- Season wings with salt, pepper and garlic salt. Place on a cookie sheet with sides. Cover and bake at 375°F for 45 minutes.
- Pour off juice and pour sauce over wings. Reduce heat to 350°F, and return wings to oven, basting with sauce every 15 minutes for 45 minutes.
- Serve hot or flash freeze individually on lined cookie sheet and then keep in a baggie in freezer until needed.

Appetizers

Spinach and Mushroom Roll-Ups

DAIRY

Wonderful and beautiful - great for parties! If you don't have time to make the dough, use pre-made flour tortillas, available at your grocery store.

8	ounces cream cheese, softened	½	teaspoon salt
⅔	cup butter, softened, plus 2 tablespoons	½	teaspoon lemon juice
1	cup all-purpose flour, plus 1 tablespoon	⅛	teaspoon garlic powder
1	cup self-rising flour	¼	cup Parmesan cheese
10	ounces frozen spinach, chopped	1	egg white
2½	cups fresh mushrooms, chopped	1	tablespoon water
1	cup onion, chopped		Flour for rolling
½	teaspoon oregano, crushed		

Dough:

- Preheat oven to 400°F.
- In a large bowl, beat together cream cheese and the ⅔-cup butter. Add 1 cup of the all-purpose flour and the self-rising flour; beat until dough is smooth.
- Divide dough into two balls; wrap each in plastic wrap and chill 30 minutes.

Filling:

- Cook spinach according to package directions. Allow to cool slightly. Squeeze out excess liquid and set aside.
- In a large skillet, melt the 2 tablespoons butter. Sauté mushrooms and onion until tender. Add spinach, remaining tablespoon flour, oregano, salt, lemon juice and garlic powder. Cook and stir until mixture thickens. Stir in Parmesan cheese. Set aside to cool.

Assembly:

- On floured surface roll a pastry ball into a 12 x 7-inch rectangle. Spread half the spinach mixture on dough to within ½ inch of edges.
- Starting with a short side, roll up dough and filling, jelly roll style. Moisten edges with water and pinch to seal. Cover with plastic wrap and chill 1 hour. Repeat with remaining pastry.
- Slice logs into ½-inch thick slices. Combine egg white and water. Place on ungreased baking sheets; brush with egg mixture.
- Bake 20 minutes or until golden. Remove to wire racks; cool. Arrange on a platter and serve.

Serves 25 to 30

Easy Eggplant Dip

PARVE

A tangy treat.

3	tablespoons olive oil	1	red pepper, chopped
2	cloves garlic, minced	1	tablespoon ground cumin
1	large eggplant diced	¼	teaspoon cayenne pepper
2	(8-ounce) cans tomato sauce	2	teaspoons salt
¼	cup red wine vinegar	½	teaspoon pepper
1	green pepper, chopped		

- In large covered pan, heat oil and add all ingredients. Simmer for 20 minutes, stirring occasionally. Uncover and turn up heat to reduce liquid.
- Cool dip to room temperature, cover and refrigerate. Serve with pita chips, rye slices or crackers.

Serves 6 to 8

Chef's tip: Slice and lightly salt the eggplant for thirty minutes prior to use. Then rinse or wipe off the salt with a towel. This reduces the water content and bitterness of eggplant.

Stuffed Bleu Cheese Mushrooms

DAIRY

Wonderful as a side or appetizer.

12-14 extra large fresh mushrooms	¼	cup crumbled bleu cheese
¼ cup chopped scallions	⅓	cup fine dry Italian breadcrumbs
¼ cup butter or margarine		

- Preheat oven to 350°F.
- Remove stems from mushrooms and chop finely. Cook stems and onions in butter until tender, not brown.
- Add cheese, 2 tablespoons of breadcrumbs and salt and pepper to taste. Fill mushroom crowns with mixture and sprinkle with remaining crumbs.
- Place on baking sheet and bake at 350°F for 12 minutes, or until brown.

Serves 6 to 8

Appetizers

Banana Bread

DAIRY

Delicious and freezable!

½	cup butter	½	teaspoon cinnamon
¾	cup brown sugar	½	cup yogurt
1	egg	1-1½	cups mashed bananas (the more ripe the bananas, the more flavor)
1½	cups flour		
1	teaspoon baking soda	1	cup chocolate chips
¾	teaspoon salt	1	teaspoon vanilla

- Preheat oven to 350°F.
- In large bowl, cream butter and brown sugar until creamy. Beat in egg.
- Sift flour, baking soda, salt, cinnamon; combine and mix in small bowl. In another small bowl, combine bananas and yogurt. Add dry ingredients alternately with butter mixture and banana mixture. Add chocolate chips and vanilla.
- Pat into greased 9 x 5-inch loaf pan. Bake at 350°F for 50 to 60 minutes.

Yields 1 loaf

Chef's tip: Throw your overripe bananas in the freezer and just thaw them in the microwave when you need them. They keep for a long time frozen.

Pumpkin Bread

PARVE

This is a wonderful alternative to banana bread. Moist and sweet.

2	large eggs	¾	teaspoon ground cinnamon
½	cup vegetable oil	½	teaspoon freshly grated nutmeg or ⅛ teaspoon dry
1	cup unsweetened pumpkin purée		
2	cups all-purpose flour	½	teaspoon salt
¾	cup sugar	½	cup coarsely chopped walnuts (optional)
1	teaspoon baking soda	1	cup raisins or chopped pitted prunes

- Preheat oven to 350°F. Grease a 9 x 5 x 3½-inch loaf pan.
- Whisk together the eggs, oil and ¼ cup water. Add the pumpkin purée and stir well.
- In a large mixing bowl, combine the flour, sugar, baking soda, cinnamon, nutmeg and salt. Stir the pumpkin mixture into the dry ingredients until well blended. Add the raisins and nuts if desired.
- Transfer the batter into the prepared loaf pan. Bake until a toothpick inserted into center comes out clean, 1 to 1¼ hours. Cool on wire rack.

Yields 1 loaf

Zucchini Bread

DAIRY

Great to serve in the Sukkah!

3 cups zucchini (about 3 medium), unpeeled and shredded	1 teaspoon salt
2 cups sugar	1 teaspoon ground cinnamon
⅔ cup vegetable oil	¼ teaspoon ground cloves
2 teaspoons vanilla	½ teaspoon baking powder
4 eggs	½ cup pecans, coarsely chopped
3 cups all-purpose flour*	½ cup mini chocolate chips
2 teaspoons baking soda	½ cup raisins (if desired)

*If using self-rising flour omit baking soda, baking powder and salt.

- Preheat oven to 350°F.
- Grease bottoms of 2 loaf pans. Mix zucchini, sugar, vanilla, oil and eggs in large bowl. Stir in remaining ingredients. Pour into pans.
- Bake 50 to 60 minutes or until inserted toothpick comes out clean. Cool 10 minutes. Loosen sides, remove from pans and cool completely before slicing.
- Before eating or to store, wrap tightly and store at room temperature for 4 days or refrigerate up to 10 days.

Yields 2 loaves

Incredibly Easy Challah

PARVE

This is a Camp Interlaken favorite!

2 packages dry active yeast	3 eggs plus 1 yolk
7½ cups all-purpose flour	½ teaspoon salt
1½ sticks margarine	1¼ cups sugar
1 cup hot (not boiling) water	1 egg to coat Challah

- Sift yeast and flour. In a large bowl, mix margarine and water until margarine is melted. Add eggs, yolk, salt and sugar. Keep mixing. Gradually add flour mixing well (a wooden spoon works great). Cover bowl with warm damp towel and leave covered for 3 hours, more is better.
- Smash down, divide into 12 balls. Roll into snakes. Braid snakes into 4 loaves. Put on cookie sheet. Cover with damp towel for 1 hour.
- Brush loaves with beaten egg. Bake at 350°F for 30 minutes.

Yields 4 loaves

Breads

Challah with a Twist

PARVE

2	packages quick rise dry yeast	1	tablespoon salt
1	teaspoon sugar	2	large eggs
½	cup warm water	2	tablespoons margarine
9	cups unbleached flour	3	cups warm water
4	tablespoons sugar		Non-stick cooking spray (optional)

Topping:

1	egg	1	teaspoon sugar

- Dissolve yeast and 1 teaspoon sugar in warm water. Let stand until mixture bubbles.
- Pour 5 cups of flour and all of the other dry ingredients into a large bowl. Make a well in the center. Add warm water, eggs, margarine and yeast mixture. Mix and gradually add rest of flour as needed.
- Knead well until smooth and dough separates from the bowl. Cover and let rise in warm place until double in bulk. Punch down and reform into a ball. Let rise another 20 minutes.
- Preheat oven to 350°F.
- Divide the dough into 2 to 3 parts and braid. Place on greased baking sheets. Let rise in warm place for another 20 minutes. Brush with egg mixture (1 egg and 1 teaspoon of sugar mixed well). Bake at 350°F for 20 to 30 minutes, until golden brown.

Fun Challah Options:

Rainbow Challah:
Divide the dough into 3 or 4 sections, depending on how many strands you will need for braiding. Add 6 to 8 drops of food color to each section of dough and knead in. Braid the different colors into one another.

Honey of a Challah:
Dip strands into honey then braid, or paint each strand with honey, using a pastry brush. Cover challah with foil if it gets too dark

Raisin or Nut Challah:
Add a cup of raisins or nuts (or both!) at end of kneading to create a sweet loaf.

Onion Challah:
Chop onions and sauté in olive/garlic oil. Flatten 3 balls of dough one at a time, into rectangles. Fill with onion and roll up. Seal each end. Lastly, braid and bake.

Traditional Sprinkling:
After brushing dough with egg, sprinkle with sesame or poppy seeds. For the kids, it might be more fun to use colored sugar sprinklings. Then bake.

Challah with a Twist continued

Monkey Bread Challah:
Roll dough into lots of little balls. Prepare a dish of melted butter, a dish of cinnamon, sugar, and a dish of finely chopped walnuts. Grease a deep round pan or an angel food cake pan. Dip each ball into butter, then into cinnamon mixture. Place balls on top of each other until pan is filled. No need to brush with egg before baking.

Freezing Challah:
Make the challah ahead of time and freeze it. To defrost, simply sprinkle water on challah and place in 325°F oven. It is also a good idea to have a pan of hot water in the oven to keep the challah moist.

Yields 2 large challahs

Onion Bread

PARVE

Simple yet satisfying.

1	package yeast	3	cups flour
1	cup warm water	2	tablespoons margarine, melted
1	teaspoon salt	½	medium onion, chopped
1	teaspoon sugar		

- Dissolve yeast and sugar in water and set aside until bubbling. Add 1 cup flour and mix well. Then add the other 2 cups of flour and salt. Knead until smooth and shape into a ball. Cover with a damp kitchen towel, set in a warm place and let rise 1 hour.
- Place dough in a greased 9 x 13-inch pan. Spread with melted margarine, then press in onions on top. Let rise again for 1 hour, covered.
- Preheat oven to 450°F. Sprinkle with salt. Bake at 450°F for 20 minutes.

Pizza Dough Option:
- Let rise for 1 hour for thicker crust or not at all for thinner crust. Roll out and top with pizza sauce, mozzarella cheese, and desired toppings.
- Bake at 400°F until cheese is bubbly.

Yields 1 pan

Chef's tip: Try adding some fresh chopped herbs such as rosemary, as well as, or instead of the onions.

Passover Cherry Muffins

PARVE

Good for breakfast or a snack.

⅓	cup margarine	½	cup matzo cake flour
1	cup sugar	¼	cup potato starch
1	teaspoon vanilla	½	teaspoon salt
	Add 3 eggs and beat	1	can pitted cherries, drained

- Preheat oven to 350°F.
- Combine wet ingredients and dry ingredients separately. Add the wet ingredients to the dry, and combine thoroughly. Add cherries.
- Pour batter into lined muffin tins. Bake 350°F for 45 minutes.

Yields 6 muffins

Chef's tip: Try this recipe with sun-dried cherries or cranberries.

Italian Pizza Bread

DAIRY

Serve as an appetizer or light entrée.

1	small onion, diced	½	teaspoon Italian seasoning
1	clove garlic, minced	¼	teaspoon salt
1	tablespoon olive oil	1	loaf Italian bread, cut horizontally
1	(10-ounce) package frozen chopped spinach, thawed and drained	2-3	tomatoes, sliced very thin
1	tablespoon Parmesan cheese, grated		Mozzarella cheese, shredded
			Parmesan cheese

- Preheat oven to 400°F.
- In a large skillet, sauté onion and garlic in oil. Add spinach, cheese and seasonings.
- Slice bread in half lengthwise and top each half with the cooked mixture. Top with tomato slices, mozzarella and Parmesan cheeses.
- Bake at 400°F for 10 minutes. Cut each half in 4 to 6 pieces.

Yields 1 loaf

Easy Passover Popovers

PARVE

So easy...and tasty, too!

2	cups water	1	teaspoon salt
1	cup vegetable shortening (Crisco)	4	tablespoons sugar
1	cup potato starch	12	eggs
1	cup cake meal		

- Preheat oven to 425°F.
- Bring the water and the vegetable shortening to a boil until shortening dissolves. Stir in (or use mixer) potato starch, cake meal, salt and sugar. Add 12 eggs, one at a time, beating constantly in mixer.
- Grease muffin tins. Fill each ½ to ¾ full. Bake at 425°F for 35 to 40 minutes.

Yields 2 dozen muffins

Chef's tip: For larger popovers, place in greased oven-proof ramekins and bake.

Rosemary and Coarse Salt Focaccia

PARVE

Making focaccia is a very easy way to begin making bread if you have never tried it before. Serve this bread as an appetizer with some balsamic vinegar and olive oil in a bowl. It's amazing!

1	package active dry yeast	6	tablespoons olive oil
¾	cup warm water	2	tablespoons fresh chopped rosemary
3	cups all-purpose or bread flour		Coarse salt to sprinkle on top
1	teaspoon salt		

- Dissolve the yeast in ½ cup of the warm water, and let sit 10 minutes until bubbly.
- In a large bowl, combine the flour, the teaspoon of salt, the yeast mixture and the remaining water. Knead by hand or machine until smooth, about 5 minutes by machine. Place in a well-oiled bowl, cover with plastic wrap, and let rise until doubled, about 1½ hours.
- Punch down and place on an oiled cookie sheet with sides, or a lasagna pan, forming into a rectangle to fill pan. The dough should be about 1-inch thick at this point. Cover loosely with plastic and let rise another 20 to 30 minutes.
- Preheat the oven to 425°F.
- Dimple the top surface all over with your finger tips, and then drizzle with the oil and sprinkle with rosemary and coarse salt. Bake about 20 to 25 minutes or until golden. Serve warm or at room temperature.

Yields 1 large pan

Chef's tip: Instead of the rosemary, you might add 2 to 3 tablespoons of fresh chopped sage to the dough with some Fresh Parmesan on top. Other alternatives are sliced olives, thinly sliced zucchini or thinly sliced onions. Grated Parmesan, mozzarella, or Fontina are also good.

Festive Chicken Salad

MEAT

Colorful and delicious!

1	cup celery, diced	1½	tablespoons French dressing
¾	cup toasted salted almonds	4	hard-boiled eggs, halved or chopped (optional)
1	teaspoon capers		Salt and pepper to taste
2	cups cooked and boned chicken pieces		Water chestnuts (optional)
⅔	cup mayonnaise or salad dressing		

- Cut chicken into generous size pieces. Marinate chicken in 1½ tablespoons French dressing. Allow to stand at least 1 hour.
- Mix chicken, ½ cup of the almonds, and the rest of the ingredients together, lightly. Add the hard-boiled eggs if desired. Pile lightly on crisp lettuce.
- Garnish with remaining almonds.

Serves 6

Tuna Salad with a Twist

DAIRY

Not your average tuna dish and very easy to make!

2	(7-ounce) cans white solid pack tuna, drained	1	cup water-packed quartered artichokes, drained
1	(11-ounce) can Mandarin oranges, drained	1	cup sliced water chestnuts, drained
¼	pound fresh mushrooms, sliced	½	cup canned fried onion rings
4	ounces slivered almonds, toasted		

Dressing:

¼	cup mayonnaise	2	teaspoons sugar
¼	cup sour cream	1	bunch green onions, sliced
1	tablespoon lemon juice		

- Mix salad ingredients together in large bowl. Combine dressing ingredients and toss with salad.
- Serve immediately.

Serves 3 to 4

Chef's tip: Go gourmet! Try this recipe using fresh broiled or grilled tuna steaks!

Israeli Salad

Great pita stuffer!

4	tomatoes	4	green onions or 1 large red onion finely chopped
2	large cucumbers	½	head lettuce
1	large green pepper	½	cup chopped calamata olives
6	radishes		

Dressing:

3	tablespoons olive oil	½	cup feta cheese, crumbled
	Juice of 1 lemon		Salt to taste

- Chop all vegetables into very small cubes.
- Drizzle on oil, lemon juice and salt. Sprinkle with feta cheese, toss and serve.

Serves 8

Chef's tip: Garnish with chopped parsley or cilantro for added color and flavor.

Oriental Cole Slaw

PARVE

Crunchy and tasty.

1	pound bag prepared coleslaw or 1 pound shredded cabbage	¼	pound pea pods, halved
1	bunch green onion, chopped	3	packages chicken-flavored kosher ramen noodles, broken up
1	green or red pepper, chopped		Sunflower seeds
1	can sliced water chestnuts		

Dressing:

5	tablespoons white or red wine vinegar	¼	teaspoon pepper
⅔	cup salad oil		Chicken broth packets from ramen noodles
4	tablespoons sugar		

- In bowl, mix cabbage, onions, peppers, water chestnuts and pea pods.
- Combine dressing ingredients and shake vigorously. Dress salad and top with broken ramen noodles and sunflower seeds.
- Refrigerate 1 to 2 hours before serving.

Serves 4

Chef's tip: Add a chicken breast for an entrée salad.

Shabbat Salad

PARVE

Add color to your Shabbat table with this salad!

1	red pepper, diced	1	can artichoke hearts, drained, rinsed, and quartered
1	green pepper, diced		
1	orange pepper, diced	3	scallions, chopped
8	ounces fresh mushrooms, sliced		

Dressing:

¼	cup vinegar	2	teaspoons dill weed
½	cup olive oil		Salt and pepper to taste
1	tablespoon sugar		Hot pepper sauce, to taste

- Place all chopped vegetables in a medium salad bowl.
- Mix dressing ingredients together and pour over vegetables. Stir well. Let marinate for 4 hours or overnight before serving.

Serves 4

Cornucopia Salad with Lime Vinaigrette

DAIRY

A delightful salad that everyone will enjoy.

1	small head leaf lettuce	1	avocado
1	small head romaine	½	cup of crumbled blue cheese (for a meat meal, omit cheese)
1	cup of chopped celery		
4	green onions, chopped	½	cup candied almonds*
¼	cup of currants	1	(11-ounce) can Mandarin oranges
1	red apple		

Dressing:

4	teaspoons lime juice	⅛	teaspoon grated lime rind
3	tablespoons olive oil		Salt and pepper to taste
1	teaspoon honey		

To candy nuts, caramelize 3 tablespoons of sugar in a fry pan and sauté almonds until golden brown.

- Add all salad ingredients to a bowl. Mix dressing ingredients together and toss with salad. Sprinkle candied nuts on top.

Serves 4 to 6

Chef's tip: For an entrée salad, add 3 grilled chicken breasts chopped.

Ramen Noodle Salad

PARVE

Fast and delicious.

1	head green leaf lettuce	½	pound sautéed sliced mushrooms
1	head red leaf lettuce		Ramen noodles, broken up
½	red pepper		

Dressing:

4	teaspoons white vinegar	1	veggie kosher ramen noodle seasoning package
½	cup olive oil		
4	teaspoons sugar		

- Toss all ingredients in a garbage bag or bowl.
- Combine dressing ingredients separately. Dress just before serving, or the salad will get soggy.
- Pound ramen noodles in package to break them up; sprinkle over salad.

Serves 6

The Best Strawberry Salad

PARVE

Delicious!

2-3	heads assorted leafy greens (red or green leaf lettuce, romaine, Boston, or spinach)	1-2	cups pecan halves browned at 350°F for 5 minutes in toaster oven
1	pint to 1 quart fresh strawberries		

Dressing:

⅓	cup raspberry vinegar (option: white vinegar)	1	teaspoon dry mustard
1	cup oil (preferably canola)	1	teaspoon salt
½	cup sugar (or artificial sweetener equal to ½ cup of sugar)	1½	tablespoons onion, minced
		1	tablespoon poppy seeds, added right before serving

- Mix dressing ingredients together. Combine greens, pecans, strawberries (sliced in half) and toss with homemade dressing.

Serves 6 to 8

Chef's tip: If you don't want to make your own dressing, use Walden Farms Raspberry dressing.

Sweet Potato Salad

Refreshing and colorful!

2½ pounds sweet potato (5 cups diced)	¾ cup green onions, thinly sliced
1¼ cups celery, diced	1 cup daikon radish, peeled and diced
¾ cup parsley, minced	½ cup sweet red pepper, minced
¾ cup cilantro, minced	

Dressing:

⅓ cup low fat sour cream	2 tablespoons Dijon mustard
⅔ cup low fat mayonnaise	1 teaspoon garlic, finely minced, about 2 cloves
½ teaspoon hot pepper toasted sesame oil (Eden)	1 tablespoon grated fresh ginger or more to taste
½ cup fresh lemon juice	¾ teaspoon salt
1 tablespoon light honey (clover)	

- Peel and dice sweet potato into ½-inch pieces. Makes about 5 cups. Steam potatoes until just tender, check at 7 to 10 minutes. Do not overcook. Assemble dressing while potatoes are cooking.
- While potatoes are still warm, toss them gently in one half of the dressing and chill. Add remaining salad ingredients and dressing and gently mix before serving.

Serves 8

Pasta Salad

Eye pleasing!

16 ounces uncooked tri-color spiral noodles	1 cup broccoli pieces, blanched
½ cup green or yellow peppers, diced	8 ounces mozzarella cheese, cut in ½-inch cubes
½ cup red peppers, diced	8-10 ounces Italian dressing
1 cup cauliflower pieces, blanched	Grated Parmesan (optional)
½ cup olives, halved or quartered	

- Boil noodles and drain. Add vegetables, cheese and dressing to noodles. Toss in large bowl.

Serves 6

Mediterranean Bean Salad

PARVE

Yummy! Salad for four or more!

1	can garbanzo beans (chick peas), rinsed and drained	2	tomatoes, finely chopped
1	small red onion, finely chopped	2	pickling cucumbers, finely chopped
		1	small green pepper, finely chopped

Dressing:

2	tablespoons balsamic vinegar	¼	teaspoon kosher salt
3	tablespoons olive oil	¼	teaspoon pepper
1	clove garlic, minced		

- Combine garbanzo beans, red onion, tomatoes, cucumbers and green pepper.
- Prepare vinaigrette with the remaining ingredients and adjust seasonings to taste. Pour vinaigrette over vegetables, mix and refrigerate for 1 hour or more.

Serves 4

Green Bean, Avocado & Tomato Salad

PARVE

1-2	pounds green beans	1	tablespoon sugar
1	avocado	¼	cup olive oil
1	pint grape tomatoes		Salt and pepper
4	limes		

- Steam green beans. Combine green beans, avocado and tomatoes.
- Squeeze juice of limes. Combine lime juice with sugar. Slowly whisk olive oil into mixure. Add salt and pepper to taste. Dress vegetables.

Serves 6

Salads

Farmers Chop Suey

DAIRY

Serve as a side-dish or as a main course.

4	cups chopped romaine or iceberg lettuce	1	can artichoke hearts, drained and chopped
3	cups assorted chopped vegetables (carrots, onions, peppers, cucumbers, etc)		

Dressing:

1	cup sour cream	1	small envelope Italian salad dressing mix

- Mix sour cream and salad dressing. Chill for 30 minutes.
- Toss lettuce, vegetables and artichokes in large bowl. Toss with desired amount of sour cream mixture just before serving.

Serves 6

Potato Salad

DAIRY

A classic recipe.

6	cups potatoes, peeled, sliced, or diced	1	cup celery, cut fine
2	tablespoons onion greens, cut fine	6	hard-boiled eggs, sliced or diced

Dressing:

2	cups mayonnaise		Garlic powder to taste
½	cup heaping sour cream (or more, to taste)		Seasoned salt
1	tablespoon lemon juice	1	small pimento (optional)
1	teaspoon dry mustard		

- Boil potatoes until tender and let cool.
- Cover eggs with cold water, bring to a boil, and reduce to a simmer for 12 minutes. Run eggs under cold water to remove shells.
- Mix dressing ingredients thoroughly, pour over salad and toss thoroughly.
- Garnish with fluted cucumbers, fringed celery, radish accordions and carrot curls.

Serves 8

Chicken Soup

MEAT

This is from Monya Tolkan as passed on to her niece June Wallace of Milwaukee, WI. It can be served for any holiday or on Shabbat.

1	whole chicken, cut up (4 pounds)	1	clove garlic, sliced
4	quarts water	2	stalks celery, sliced
2	onions, diced	5	carrots, sliced
¼	cup parsley	1	tablespoon sugar (optional)
1	parsnip, sliced	2	teaspoons salt
½	green pepper, diced	4	teaspoons chicken bouillon powder

- Bring chicken and water to boil. Skim. Add vegetables, sugar, salt, and bouillon. Return to a boil. Reduce to simmer. Cook 2½ hours.
- Strain soup and return pieces of chicken and vegetables into soup as desired. Discard chicken bones and skin. Refrigerate or freeze.
- Remove fat before reheating.

Serves 6 to 8

World's Lightest, Fluffiest Matzah Balls

PARVE

A must have for Passover.

2	large eggs	½	teaspoon salt
2	tablespoons margarine	½	teaspoon pepper
½	cup matzah meal	⅛	cup chopped parsley (fresh is better)
2	tablespoons cold water		

- Mix all ingredients together. Refrigerate at least 30 minutes.
- Form into balls. Drop into boiling water.
- Put the lid on the pot and do not, I mean do not, open for 30 minutes! Take them out with a slotted spoon.

Yields 12 matzah balls

Chef's tip: You can make these and freeze them ahead of time in soup, bouillon, or Carmel soup mix. When you thaw them out, throw away that soup and put them into your delicious home made soup.

Vegetarian Southwestern Soup

PARVE

An original recipe you won't find anywhere else.

1	onion, chopped	1	can parve chicken broth or vegetable broth
2	tablespoons margarine	1	can hominy (undrained - the liquid has a nice flavor)
1	can kidney beans, drained		
1	can pinto beans drained (or substitute black beans or both)	1	small jar green chilies, optional (If you don't rinse them, the soup will be good and hot. If you prefer milder, then rinse first.)
1	can corn, drained		
1	can tomatoes, broken up (do not drain)	1	envelope taco seasoning
		1	envelope ranch dressing mix

- Sauté onions in margarine until soft. Add other ingredients and simmer for at least ½ hour.

Serves 8

Chef's tip: Before serving, crumble in ½ box (or more if you prefer) baked vegetarian patties.

This makes a very thick hearty soup. Add more broth if you like it thinner.

Gazpacho

PARVE

Perfect for a hot summer day.

1	large can tomato juice (about 5-cups)	1	tablespoon lemon juice, and the juice of a fresh lime
1	small bunch scallions, chopped finely		
2	large tomatoes, diced	2	tablespoons wine vinegar
1	large green pepper, minced	1	tablespoon olive oil
1	diced cucumber		Tabasco to taste
2	tablespoons honey		

- Combine all ingredients. Add a few drops of Tabasco to get the hot taste of your choice, but be careful, as the soup will get hotter as it stands. Add salt and pepper to taste.
- Chill for several hours or overnight before serving.

Serves 6 to 8

Chef's tip: Garnish this great soup with fragrant summer herbs such as basil, parsley, cilantro or mint. If you want a smoother soup, pulse it in a processor until desired consistency is reached.

Mushroom Barley Soup

PARVE

Great on a cold day.

1	medium onion, peeled and quartered	¼	teaspoon thyme
1	pound mushrooms, rinsed and dried	1	bay leaf
1½	tablespoons margarine	3	tablespoons wine
6	cups vegetable soup stock, (fresh or canned)	2	cloves garlic, minced
⅓	cup pearl barley	1	tablespoon soy sauce
¼	teaspoon black pepper	⅛	cup parsley

- In a food processor, slice onion. Set aside. Slice mushrooms and set aside.
- Melt margarine in 3-quart pot and sauté onion over medium heat until onion absorbs margarine. Add mushrooms and cook over high heat, stirring constantly for 5 minutes. Add stock, barley, pepper, thyme, bay leaf, wine, garlic; bring to a boil; simmer covered until barley is tender, about 45 minutes. Stir in soy sauce and simmer 5 minutes more.
- Remove bay leaf. Add parsley.

Serves 6 to 8

Vegetable Soup

DAIRY

A healthy vegetarian soup.

2	tablespoons oil	1	small can tomato paste
2	tablespoons butter	2	quarts boiling water
1	cup onions, chopped		Salt and pepper to taste
1	cup carrots, chopped	½	cup macaroni
½	cup celery, chopped	2	ounces shredded spinach
2	cloves garlic, chopped	1	tablespoon chopped parsley
1	cup shelled peas or green beans		Freshly grated Parmesan cheese to taste
¼	small cabbage, shredded		

- Heat oil and butter in pot. Add onions, carrots, celery and garlic and cook slowly 10 minutes, covered. Add peas or beans, cabbage, tomato paste, water, salt and pepper. Bring to boil. Add macaroni. Simmer slowly until all ingredients are tender.
- A few minutes before serving, add spinach and parsley. Sprinkle cheese on top if desired.

Serves 6

Cabbage Soup

MEAT

Simple and wholesome.

1	(1 to 1½-pound) soup bone (ask butcher or select beef shanks)	1	onion, sliced
1	cabbage, sliced	1	large tomato juice
12	ounces apple cider concentrate (frozen)	1	tablespoon honey (optional)

- Combine all ingredients in large pot. Simmer covered for 3 hours.
- Add salt and pepper to taste. Add 1 tablespoon honey or more to taste, if you like it sweet.

Serves 4

Curried Vegetable Stew

PARVE

Hearty and flavorful.

3	cloves garlic, cut up	¼	teaspoon pepper
1	inch cube ginger, peeled and cut up fine or grated	¼	teaspoon ground cinnamon
3	tablespoons water	1	small acorn squash, peeled, cut into 2-inch pieces
1	tablespoon vegetable oil	2	cups cauliflower, cut in 2- to 3-inch florets
1½-2	cups onions, in chunks	2	cups zucchini, cut in 1- to 2-inch pieces
1	tablespoon curry powder	1	cup cooked or canned chickpeas
½	teaspoon ground cumin	¼	cup currants or raisins
1	cup broth or water	2	tablespoons fresh lemon juice (optional)
1	cup canned crushed tomatoes	2	tablespoons chopped fresh cilantro (optional)
½	teaspoon salt		

- In a food processor or blender, combine garlic, ginger and water. Purée until smooth and set aside.
- In large (4-quart) Dutch oven or heavy saucepan, heat oil over medium heat. Add onion. Cook, stirring until tender, about 10 minutes. Add curry powder and cumin and cook 1 minute, stirring. Add garlic and ginger purée; cook 1 minute. Add broth, tomatoes, salt, pepper and cinnamon. Stir well.
- Bring mixture to a boil, reduce heat and simmer 10 minutes. Add squash, cauliflower, zucchini, chickpeas and currants. Simmer covered 40 to 50 minutes or until vegetables are tender, stirring occasionally.
- Sprinkle with fresh lemon juice and chopped cilantro. Serve over rice if desired.

Serves 6

Fannie's Fabulous Beet Borscht

DAIRY

Borscht is my favorite dish. My mother made it for me as a special treat when I was a child and I can remember visiting with her over a cup of cold borscht during my summers home from college. After I married, my mother would schlep many a mason jar full of this magenta liquid to our house. It's a terrific dish and I hope you enjoy it as much as I have. - Stuart Brafman

2	bunches fresh beets	½	cup lemon juice
8	cups water	½	cup sugar
1	large onion, chopped	4	eggs
2	tablespoons salt (or more to taste)	½	pint sour cream

- Trim off beet stems and leaves and set aside. Peel beets and slice very thin. Chop up about 4 or 5 stems and leaves and add with beets to pot. Cover with water, onion and salt.
- Bring to boil and reduce to a simmer for about 30 minutes. Add sugar and lemon juice and simmer another 10 minutes. Remove soup from heat. Add more salt if desired.
- Beat eggs until foamy and fold them into the sour cream. Whisk the sour cream mixture into 1 cup of hot soup to temper the soup, then add this all back into the remaining soup. Stir soup until blended, cool and chill in refrigerator 2 hours or overnight.

Serves 8

Chef's tip: Garnish this fabulous soup with fresh chopped dill and finely chopped scallions. Use low-fat sour cream to cut calories if desired.

Cream of Springtime Soup

PARVE

The taste of a creamy soup without the extra calories and cholesterol!

3	yellow Finnish potatoes the size of a small fist, quartered with skins	1	large bunch of asparagus, cleaned and broken at the base, break off and save tips
3-5	cloves of garlic, peeled	2	tablespoons fresh basil
1	stalk of celery, halved	2	tablespoons fresh parsley
1	medium onion or 3 green onions, quartered	½	teaspoon salt or to taste
			Lemon wedges

- Place asparagus tips in small pot of salted water and cook to al dente - set aside. Place potatoes, onions, celery and garlic in a 4-quart pot, with 1 quart of water. Boil gently for 20 minutes. Add remaining asparagus and simmer 10 minutes more, or until tender. Let cool slightly.
- Purée soup to smoothness in two batches in a blender. When the second batch is done, add salt and herbs, pulse several times to be assured the herbs have been blended, but are still in pieces.
- Combine both batches in a pot or serving container. Stir in the asparagus tips. Adjust seasonings. Serve with lemon wedges.

Serves 4 to 6

Tomato and Artichoke Pasta

DAIRY

Quick to make and easy to double for company!

2 tablespoons olive oil	2 teaspoons oregano
1 medium onion, chopped	1 (6½-ounce) jar marinated artichoke hearts, quartered, marinade reserved
3 large garlic cloves, sliced thin	
1 (28-ounce) can Italian plum tomatoes crushed with puree, or fresh diced tomatoes	12 ounces bowtie pasta
	1½ cups grated Parmesan cheese
2 teaspoons basil	3 tablespoons roasted pine nuts

- Add onions and garlic to oil and sauté 5 minutes. Add tomatoes and seasoning. Simmer for 8 minutes. Add artichokes and their marinade. Cook slowly for 5 to 10 minutes. Add ½ cup Parmesan cheese and pine nuts. Season with salt and pepper.
- Let sit 6 hours or overnight for best flavor.
- Cook pasta following directions on package and add to sauce.
- Serve with additional Parmesan cheese and freshly chopped herbs.

Serves 6 to 8

Matzo Brie Recipe

PARVE

Breakfast, lunch…anytime!

1 egg for every 2 matzos	Salt and pepper to taste

Matzo Brie:
- Soak matzos in boiling water for 5 or 6 minutes to cover matzos (this allows matzos to hold its shape and makes it fluffy) Squeeze out excess water.
- Beat eggs until frothy. Pour eggs over matzos. Season with salt and pepper.
- Heat oil or margarine in fry pan. Pour in matzos mixture. Stir while cooking until brown.

Chef's Tip: Serve with sugar, cinnamon, apples, jelly, syrup or honey for a sweet treat.

Matzo Brie with Salami:

MEAT
- Preheat oven to 350°F.
- Cut salami into chunks. Put on cookie sheet. Bake for 10 minutes at 350°F (get rid of some fat).
- Add to matzo brie towards end of cooking and mix thoroughly.

Serves 1 to 2

Chef's tip: Serve with scallions or fried onions sprinkled on top.

Passover Lasagna

DAIRY

A taste of Italy for Pesach.

4	eggs		Milk as needed
1½	pounds cottage cheese	½-1	pound mozzarella cheese, shredded
	Clove garlic minced or ⅛-teaspoon garlic powder	1	jar tomato sauce
9	whole matzos		Salt and pepper to taste
			Oregano to taste

- Preheat oven to 350°F.
- In a bowl, combine the eggs, cottage cheese, salt, pepper, garlic and oregano. Wet matzos in the milk.
- Pour a little tomato sauce into the bottom of a casserole or lasagna pan. Layer ingredients as follows: matzos, cheese mixture, tomato sauce, mozzarella cheese. Continue layering until you have finished all the ingredients. End with a layer of mozzarella cheese. Sprinkle the top with Parmesan cheese.
- Bake at 350°F for 45 to 50 minutes.
- Let the lasagna rest for 5 to 10 minutes before cutting.

Serves 6

Passover Macaroni and Cheese

DAIRY

Kids and adults love this!

3½	cups matzo farfel	1	cup milk
3	large eggs	1	pint sour cream
½-1	pound Cheddar or American cheese		Salt and pepper to taste
1	pound cottage cheese	1	stick butter or margarine

- Preheat oven to 350°F. Grease a 9 x 13-inch casserole.
- Beat the eggs well with a wire whisk and pour over the farfel. Add the cottage cheese and milk. Stir with a wooden spoon until moistened. Add salt and pepper.
- Grate the cheese into another bowl. Layer the mixture in the casserole, as follows: farfel, cheese, sour cream (spread the sour cream over the entire layer), butter, repeat. Top your casserole with an extra layer of cheese.
- Bake for 30 minutes covered, and then uncovered for 10 more minutes.

Serves 4

Artichoke Pizza

DAIRY

Not your ordinary pizza!

1	(6½-ounce) jar marinated artichokes, chopped and drained, marinade reserved	½	red onion, thinly sliced
2	tomatoes, thinly sliced	½	cup Greek olives, pre-pitted
4	ounce package or jar Mediterranean seasoned feta cheese	2	tablespoons capers

- Preheat oven to 425°F.
- Buy or prepare pizza crust. Brush dough with 1 tablespoon marinade from artichokes.
- Top dough with artichokes, tomatoes, cheese, onion, olives and capers. Drizzle 1 tablespoon marinade over top.
5 Bake at 425°F for 15 to 18 minutes.

Serves 2

Unbelievable Blintzes

DAIRY

Traditional Shavuot dish.

Batter:

4	eggs, well-beaten	1	teaspoon salt
1	cup flour	1½	cups water

- Beat eggs, then add salt and water. Gradually sift in flour. Chill, covered for 30 minutes.
- Pour on to a hot buttered skillet, adding just enough batter to cover the bottom.
- When lightly brown on bottom, turn out onto waxed paper.

Filling:

1	pound dry cottage cheese (or ricotta)	3	tablespoons sugar
4	ounces cream cheese	¼	teaspoon salt
1	egg		Optional: grated lemon rind, blueberries or strawberries
2	tablespoons butter		

Assembly:

- Combine ingredients and place 1 to 2 tablespoons of the filling at the bottom of crêpe on the browned side.
- Fold like an envelope.

Serves 4

Steak Diane

Great, try this on the grill!

4	New York strip steaks	1	tablespoon Dijon mustard
	Garlic to taste	3	tablespoons lemon juice
	Crushed black pepper to taste		Dash Worcestershire sauce to taste
8-10	sliced mushrooms (or a 13-ounce can)	¼	cup red wine
4	tablespoons margarine	½	teaspoon cornstarch
3	green onions, chopped		

- Preheat broiler or grill. Season steaks and broil to desired doneness.
- Sauté onions in margarine, add mushrooms and sauté 7 to 9 minutes.
- In bowl, add mustard, lemon juice, Worcestershire, wine and cornstarch - mix until smooth. Add mixture to onions and mushrooms; cook until smooth. Pour over hot steaks.

Serves 4

Beef Tenderloin

MEAT

Company will love this!

1	(5-pound) beef tenderloin or 2 (2½-pound) roasts	1	teaspoon paprika
5	tablespoons cracked black pepper (to taste)	½	teaspoon garlic powder
		1	cup soy sauce (option: low sodium soy sauce)
½	teaspoon ground cardamom	¾	cup red wine vinegar
1	tablespoon tomato paste		

- Preheat oven to 425°F.
- Coat tenderloin with tomato paste, then coat with pepper and cardamom. Place in meat sized pan. Mix together remaining ingredients and pour over meat.
- Roast at 425°F, basting every 5 minutes, for 35 to 40 minutes or until desired degree of doneness is reached on meat thermometer.

Serves 8

Sweet and Sour Brisket

This recipe should be prepared at least one day in advance or can be frozen. Remember, brisket shrinks, so make lots!

3½-5	pounds beef brisket	4	tablespoons lemon juice
½	cup celery, chopped	½	cup brown sugar
1	large onion, sliced fine	½-1	cup water
½	cup green pepper, seeded and sliced fine	1	cup catsup
2	tablespoons oil	3	tablespoons Worcestershire sauce
2	tablespoons vinegar	1	teaspoon yellow mustard

Brisket:

- Preheat oven to 300°F.
- Trim excess fat from brisket. Place brisket in a large covered roaster. Add no water or seasonings. Roast at 300°F for 3½ to 4 hours.
- While brisket is in oven, prepare sauce.

Sauce:

- In a large skillet or electric fry pan, heat oil. Brown celery, onion, and green pepper. Add remaining ingredients; bring to boil. Reduce heat, cover and simmer for 1 hour.

Brisket Assembly:

- Cool and slice roasted brisket across the grain. Place slices into 9 x 13-inch pan. Add drippings to sauce. Pour sauce over brisket.
- Cover with foil; refrigerate or freeze. When fat has congealed (there will be a lot) remove hard layer from top.
- Reheat and serve - from frozen, covered at 300°F for 3 to 4 hours.

Serves 8

Brisket

A traditional holiday choice.

2½	pounds beef brisket	2	tablespoons onion flakes
	Meat tenderizer	1	can mushroom gravy
½	cup catsup	½	cup brown sugar
¾	cup water		Seasoned salt
3	carrots		Pinch of sugar
2	stalks celery	1	teaspoon of Kitchen Bouquet
1	whole head of garlic, peeled		Additional catsup (if necessary to increase gravy)
1	package onion soup mix		

- Preheat oven to 325°F.
- Sprinkle tenderizer on meat and pierce with a fork all over. Place in roaster with catsup and water. Cut celery and carrots and place around meat and sprinkle with onion soup mix.
- Option: Add peeled white potatoes, halved or quartered, and onion wedges. Cover and bake in 325°F oven for 2 hours.
- When done, place meat on a platter and gravy in a bowl. Cool and refrigerate overnight.
- The next day, skim fat off gravy.
- Preheat oven to 325°F.
- Add onion flakes, mushroom gravy, season salt, sugar, Kitchen Bouquet and brown sugar to gravy. Add additional catsup to increase gravy. Slice meat, place in roaster and pour gravy mixture over this.
- Cover and heat at 325°F for 1 hour.

Serves 6

Chef's tip: Check the tenderness of your meat throughout cooking. The longer a brisket cooks, the more tender it becomes.

Cholent: Beef or Kishka
with Shabbat Eggs

MEAT OR PARVE

Traditional Jews do not cook on Shabbat. However, dishes prepared in advance can be kept hot in a previously lit oven or crock pot. This easy crock pot recipe is a main course, traditionally served on Saturday for lunch with salad and Shabbat Eggs.

Beef Cholent:

1	cup dried lima or mixed beans (soaked in water overnight)	2	teaspoons salt (to taste)
1	medium large onion, diced	¼-½	teaspoon pepper
8	cloves garlic, peeled and diced	½	teaspoon ginger
½	cup medium pearl barley	1	teaspoon paprika
½	cup bulgar wheat	1-2	bouillon cubes
4	medium potatoes, peeled and quartered		Water to cover
3	tablespoons olive oil	2	pounds meat, beef soup bones, stewing meat, etc.

- Place all ingredients in crock pot with beef on top. Cover and cook on low temperature for 12 to 24 hours. The longer, the better. If in a hurry, bake in oven at 350°F for 4 to 5 hours.

Cholent with Kishka:

2	cups flour	¼	teaspoon black pepper
⅔	cup water	¼	teaspoon chile powder
⅓	cup olive oil	½	teaspoon paprika
1	teaspoon salt	1	teaspoon or 1 cube beef bouillon

- Mix cholent ingredients without beef and put in crock pot. Place flour in a deep bowl. Make a well in the center. Fill well with the water and the olive oil. Add salt, pepper, chile powder, paprika and beef-flavored bouillon.
- Mix with hands or wooden spoon and form into a ball or long, thick tube and place on top of the cholent. Cook as previously explained.

Cholent with Kishka and Shabbat Eggs continued

Shabbat Eggs:

- Take 4 fresh, jumbo, uncooked eggs in shells and place on top of your ingredients in the crock pot. Allow to cook with Cholent.
- Before serving remove eggs and run cold water over them. Crack and peel.
- Chop some fine Vidalia onions or fresh scallions. Chop up the eggs (make sure you have some chunks unmashed). Add onions and 1 tablespoon (more or less) mayonnaise. Salt to taste. Mix well.
- Spread on shallow plate, garnish with garlic chives and paprika and green and black olives with slivers of red peppers on the edge.
- Serve the eggs before the cholent with salad or warm challah. But don't eat too much - remember that the cholent is the real filler.

Teriyaki London Broil

MEAT

An impressive dish.

½	cup soy sauce	2	tablespoons vegetable oil
1	clove garlic, crushed	1	tablespoon honey or brown sugar
1	London Broil steak, 2-inch thick (round or flank steak)		

- Use meat tenderizer on steak, then marinate in sauce made by combining remaining ingredients. Marinate for 2 hours, turning once.
- Preheat broiler and broil steak 5-inches from broiler in leftover marinade, 8 to 10 minutes per side (longer if desired). Cut slit in center of steak to test for tenderness. Best at medium-rare (pink inside).

Serves 2 to 4

Chef's tip: To test a steak for doneness, just poke it with your finger instead of cutting it. For a medium rare steak, the steak will offer some resistance, but not too much.

Stuffed Cabbage

MEAT

Traditional and delicious. A wonderful Sukkah dish.

1½	pounds ground beef (or ground turkey)	¼	cup lemon juice (depending on how sour you like it)
¼	cup uncooked rice		
1	egg	½	cup brown sugar (depending on how sweet you like it)
½	teaspoon salt		
10-12	cabbage leaves (2 small cabbages)	2	large (28-ounce) cans tomatoes, crushed
2	onions	6	gingersnaps

- Preheat oven to 325°F.
- Combine beef, rice and egg. Add salt. Form balls of meat with the mixture and set on a sheet pan in the fridge while preparing cabbage leaves.
- Core the cabbages and place in boiling water for 3 to 5 minutes. Take the leaves off one at a time. Cut the remaining core away and place it in a deep roaster with the sliced onions. Place onions, extra cores and extra cabbage in the roaster to make a bed for the balls.
- To assemble rolls: take a cabbage leaf and place a ball of meat on the side where the core was cut, fold it over and "diaper" it. Combine the tomatoes, lemon juice and sugar to taste and pour over the balls.
- Cover and cook for 2 hours at 325°F.
- Crunch up the gingersnaps and add some gravy from the roaster to soften cookies and pour this over the bed of balls.
- Cook for another 1½ hours.

Serves 4

Chef's tip: Instead of boiling the cabbage leaves, simply core the head of cabbage and place it in freezer overnight. As it thaws (takes about 8 hours), the leaves will be soft and will peel right off, ready to be used! To thaw quickly, place the frozen cabbage in the microwave for a few minutes.

Terrific Chili

Sweeter than regular chili and kids love it!

2	pounds ground sirloin	1	teaspoon cinnamon
1¼	cups sweet onion, chopped	1	teaspoon ground cumin
¾	cup red pepper, chopped	1	teaspoon pepper
1	large garlic clove, minced	½	teaspoon ground coriander
2	(14½-ounce) cans chili tomatoes	1	(15-ounce) can light red kidney beans, drained
2	(14½-ounce) cans chili tomato sauce (or regular tomato sauce)	1	(15-ounce) can chili beans, undrained
1	tablespoon chili powder		

- Brown ground sirloin for about 5 minutes. Break up meat during browning. Drain fat from meat.
- Add onion, red pepper, and garlic; continue cooking until the meat is well browned. Add tomatoes, tomato sauce, chili powder, cumin, pepper, cinnamon and coriander. Stir to combine. Cover and simmer for 1 hour.
- Add the beans and simmer uncovered for an additional 30 minutes.

Serves 6

Apricot Chicken with Cranberry Option

MEAT

Surprisingly easy and impressive. Can be made for Passover also. Serve apricot chicken over noodles or rice.

2	pounds chicken pieces - with or without bones and skin	1	package dry onion soup mix
1	(12-ounce) jar apricot jelly	½	cup white wine
1	small bottle of western-style French dressing	1	cup dried apricots (or more)

- Mix all ingredients, except chicken. Pour over chicken and allow it to marinate in fridge for at least an hour or overnight.
- Preheat oven to 350°F.
- Bake for 1 hour at 350°F for boneless breasts, 1½ hours for bone in breasts.

Cranberry Option:
- This is stickier, but with a wonderful flavor.
- Omit apricot jelly, wine, and dried apricots. Add instead 1 (16-ounce) can whole cranberries, one cup dark French or Russian dressing, and ½ package onion soup mix.

Serves 6

Honey Pecan Crusted Chicken

MEAT

Crunchy and sweet!

8	pieces skinless chicken breast halves	¼	teaspoon paprika or seasoned salt
¼	cup honey	⅛	teaspoon garlic powder
	Salt and pepper to taste	1½	cups corn flakes, crushed or Matzah Meal
2	tablespoons Dijon mustard	¾	cup chopped pecans

- Preheat oven to 400°F.
- Combine honey, dash of salt, pepper, mustard, paprika and garlic powder in a bowl. Combine corn flakes and pecans in a shallow dish.
- Brush chicken pieces with honey mustard and then dredge in the cornflake mixture. Lightly spray chicken with vegetable spray and place in a baking pan.
- Bake at 400°F for about 40 minutes or until done.

Serves 8

Chicken Marsala

MEAT

Great over rice.

2	boneless chicken breast halves, skinned	¼	cup flour
½	cup white or marsala cooking wine	¼	teaspoon black pepper
4	tablespoons parve margarine	1	cup sliced mushrooms
¼	teaspoon paprika	2	tablespoons minced parsley

- Preheat oven to 200°F.
- Mix flour with peppered paprika and lightly dust the chicken breasts.
- Melt margarine in hot skillet. Sauté chicken gently over low heat, until golden on both sides and juices run clear. Remove to a platter and keep warm in 200°F oven.
- Pour cooking wine into skillet. Scrape skillet to incorporate brown bits. Add mushrooms and continue to cook until wine is reduced by one half. Add any juices that might have accumulated around the chicken pieces.
- Pour sauce over chicken breasts and sprinkle with parsley.

Serves 2

Chicken Fricassée
with Meatballs and Knaidlach

MEAT

Warms the heart, and reminds you of grandma's cooking. Serve chicken fricassee with knaidlach or plain white rice or, as my father does, with mashed potatoes that have been mixed with fried onions.

1	whole chicken, cut up	2	carrots, cut up
2	onions, cut up	¼	cup white wine (or more to taste)
2	cloves garlic, minced oil	1	bay leaf
1	(28-ounce) can tomatoes of choice	1	teaspoon thyme
1	(8-ounce) can tomato sauce		

- Sauté onion, garlic and chicken in a little oil until chicken begins to brown.
- Add all other ingredients. Simmer gently until done, adding water if necessary.

Meatballs for Chicken Fricassée:

1	pound ground beef	Garlic powder to taste
1	egg	Onion powder or minced onions to taste
	Matzos meal as needed	Water as needed

- Mix all ingredients. Form into balls and add to the chicken fricassée about ½ hour before done.

Knaidlach:

- Follow any knaidlach recipe and add uncooked knaidlach to the chicken fricassée about ½ hour before done.

Serves 4

Potato Chip Chicken Strips

MEAT

Great finger food.

4	chicken breast halves (boneless and skinless)	1	cup Italian dressing
2	ounces potato chips, crushed really fine		Seasoning to taste: pepper, garlic, onion powder

Honey Mustard Sauce:

1	tablespoon margarine	2	tablespoons Dijon mustard, to taste
1	tablespoon honey		

- Cut chicken breasts into strips. Marinate in Italian dressing 1 hour.
- Preheat oven to 400°F.
- Remove chicken from marinade.
- In a plastic bag, crush potato chips with back of a spoon. Season chips to taste. Add chicken strips to bag and shake. Sprinkle remainder of chips on top.
- Bake for 20 minutes at 400°F, turning chicken once after 10 minutes.
- Mix ingredients for Honey Mustard Sauce; use for dipping or for drizzling over chicken.

Serves 4

Smoked Turkey Breast

MEAT

Wonderful!

1	(5 to 6-pound) turkey breast	1	apple, cored and sliced
1	carrot, sliced	1	orange with rind, chopped
1	rib of celery, chopped		Seasoned salt
1	onion, chopped		Few drops liquid smoke flavoring
2	cloves garlic, minced	¾	cup teriyaki sauce

- Put all ingredients in plastic zip lock bag overnight.
- Preheat oven to 350°F.
- Make mound of veggies and place turkey breast on top. Roast uncovered at 350°F until internal temp is 170°F, or when pierced with fork juice runs clear and skin is brown.

Serves 6

Veal Daube

Warms you on a cold day.

1	(4 to 5-pound) veal shoulder roast	½	teaspoon sage
1	clove garlic	2	bay leaves, crushed
¼	cup flour	2	tablespoons oil
1	teaspoon salt	4	carrots, sliced
⅛	teaspoon pepper	1	medium onion, chopped
¼	teaspoon allspice	2	ribs celery, chopped
½	teaspoon thyme	1	cup boiling water

- Cut garlic in half and rub it all over the roast.
- Combine the flour and the spices in a shallow pan. Dredge the roast with the flour mix, shaking off excess flour. In a heavy pan, brown the roast in hot oil until it is crusty on all sides. Remove meat.
- Brown veggies and replace meat in pan. Add water. Cover and cook slowly 2½ hours at low heat or until tender.

Serves 8

Stuffed Veal Breast

An unusual version of a traditional dish.

1	(4-pound) veal breast with pocket		Garlic
	Salt	2	slices of onion
	Pepper	1	bay leaf
	Paprika	½	cup warm water

Stuffing:

½	cup vegetable shortening	1	small onion, grated
1	tablespoon seasoned salt	1	teaspoon salt
2	cups breadcrumbs	¼	teaspoon pepper
½	cup flour		

- Preheat oven to 350°F.
- Rub salt, pepper, paprika and dash of garlic powder over meat and inside of pocket.
- Mix all ingredients for stuffing together, crumble as for pie crust. Fill cavity.
- Use skewers and lace together open end of veal breast (or tie roast with string). Place in roasting pan and add 2 sliced onions, one bay leaf, ½ cup warm water. Cover and bake at 350°F for 3 hours.
- Remove cover and continue to bake for 30 minutes or until brown and tender.

Serves 8

Chef Jeffrey Nathan's
Famous Nori Wrapped Salmon with Salad

DAIRY

1	pound salmon fillet, skinless, pin bones removed	½	cup julienned carrots
2	tablespoons soy oil	½	cup julienned snow peas
1	tablespoon minced fresh ginger	1	teaspoon sesame oil, toasted
½	cup julienned shiitake mushrooms	6	sheets nori
			Soy sauce, as needed

Salmon:

- Divide the salmon fillet lengthwise into six pieces, approximately 5 inch x 1 inch. With a paring knife, make a pocket slit lengthwise down each piece of salmon, leaving ½ inch remaining uncut on each end. Do not cut through the salmon.

- In a medium sauté pan, add soy oil, ginger and vegetables. Quickly sauté until just wilted. Add sesame oil and gently toss to combine. Remove from fire and allow to cool. Evenly divide the vegetables into the pockets of each salmon portion.

- Place the nori sheets on a flat surface, shiny side down. With a brush, moisten with soy sauce. Place a filled portion of salmon on the bottom third of the nori wrapper. Roll into a cylinder shape, leaving the seam side down. Repeat with all nori wrappers and salmon.

- In a large sauté pan, place in soy oil, add salmon rolls and cook on all sides. Remove from pan. Finish cooking in a 350°F oven until desired doneness is achieved, or serve rare, direct from the sauté pan.

Yield 6 rolls

Wasabi Rémoulade:

1	tablespoon wasabi powder	½	teaspoon sesame oil, toasted
	Rice wine vinegar, as needed to moisten	1	tablespoon soy sauce
¼	cup mayonnaise		

- In a small bowl, combine wasabi powder with the rice wine vinegar until a paste is formed. Add in the mayonnaise and mix well. Season with the sesame oil and soy sauce. Set aside.

Abigael's Ponzu Sauce:

⅓	cup soy sauce		Juice of ½ orange
⅓	cup water	1	teaspoon minced ginger
⅓	cup lemon juice	1	tablespoon honey

- In a small bowl, combine all ingredients and mix well. Set aside.

Asian Salad:

½	pound pea shoots	1	tablespoon toasted sesame seeds
1	red bell pepper, julienned		Sesame oil, to taste
4	shiitake mushrooms, julienned		

- In a medium bowl, combine all salad ingredients and toss to evenly combine. Drizzle with Abigael's Ponzu Sauce until evenly dressed. Add a hint of sesame oil, as desired.

Assembly:

- Arrange salad in the center of a large plate. Cut Salmon Rolls into 1-inch pieces and arrange around the salad. Drizzle entire plate with Wasabi Rémoulade and Abigael's Ponzu Sauce.

Salmon with Brown Sugar and Mustard Glaze

DAIRY OR PARVE

Wonderful!

1	tablespoon brown sugar	1	tablespoon soy sauce
1	teaspoon honey	1	tablespoon olive oil
2	teaspoons unsalted butter or margarine	2	teaspoons fresh ginger
2	tablespoons Dijon mustard	1	whole salmon fillet, skin on (2½ pounds, ¾ to 1 inch thick)

- Preheat grill to medium heat.
- Melt brown sugar, honey, and butter in saucepan. Whisk in mustard, soy sauce, olive oil and ginger. Allow to cool.
- Place salmon skin side down on aluminum foil. Leave a foil border of ¼ to ½ inch. Coat salmon with mixture.
- Grill salmon indirectly over medium heat until edges begin to brown and inside is opaque, 15 to 25 minutes - depending on thickness of fish and desired degree of doneness. Cut salmon crosswise into 6 to 8 pieces. Do not cut through skin.
- Slide a spatula between skin and flesh to remove pieces to serve.

Serves 6

Sea Bass

Fish lovers' favorite.

1½	pounds sea bass fillets	1	tablespoon minced garlic
½	cup spicy breadcrumbs	⅛	cup Italian dressing
½	teaspoon seasoned salt	⅛	teaspoon pepper
4	tablespoons frozen orange juice concentrate	¼	teaspoon onion powder
½	cup water	¼	teaspoon fresh cilantro
¼	cup teriyaki sauce	1	tablespoon lemon juice

- Preheat oven to 350°F.
- Mix above ingredients except for breadcrumbs and seasoned salt. Place fish in glass Pyrex pan. Combine liquid ingredients and pour over fish. Cover with all-purpose seasoning. Bake at 350°F for 20 minutes.
- Cover with breadcrumbs. Bake another 10 minutes or until fish flakes with a fork.

Serves 4

Really Simple Fish

Use this recipe to prepare your favorite fish.

8	fillets of your favorite fish	1	slice of onion
	Salt and pepper to taste	1	slice of tomato
	Fresh chives, chopped	2	cups frozen or canned corn
	Minced garlic	2	sliced oranges to garnish
2-3	stalks asparagus		

- Preheat oven to 400°F.
- Season fillets with salt, pepper, chopped fresh chives and a touch of minced garlic. Place atop of fish 2 or 3 stalks of thin or blanched asparagus, 1 thin slice of onion, 1 thin slice of tomato and a small handful of frozen or canned corn. Wrap the fish loosely in parchment paper or foil - like a present, with the tomato slice placed on the top.
- Bake on baking sheets at 400°F for 10 to 20 minutes, depending on thickness of fish. Snip open parchment or foil and serve right out of the paper on a plate.
- Serve with sliced oranges or favorite mixed fruits as garnish.

Serves 6 to 8

Matzo Meal Stuffing

PARVE

Great with poultry or veal.

3	tablespoons margarine, plus 4 teaspoons	1	potato
¼	cup celery	3	eggs
¼	cup onion	1	cup Matzo meal
2	carrots	½	cup water

- Preheat oven to 350°F.
- Grate carrots and potato into a large bowl and set aside.
- Sauté celery and onion in 3 tablespoons of the margarine.
- Mix all ingredients together, except the 4 teaspoons margarine, and spoon into greased round 3-quart casserole dish. Distribute the 4 teaspoons margarine evenly over top.
- Bake at 350°F for 1 hour, covered for first 50 minutes and uncovered for last 10 minutes to brown.

Serves 8 to 10

Chef's tip: If you wish to make this a one dish meal, use uncooked stuffing on bottom of a 9 x 13-inch pan and place 10 to 12 pieces of chicken on top. Season with salt, pepper and garlic powder. Add a little chicken soup just for moisture. Cover and bake for 1 to 1½ hours.

Parve Mushroom Kugel

PARVE

1	pound egg noodles	1	(10-ounce) frozen package chopped spinach, thawed and drained well
2	envelopes (1 box) onion soup mix	1	small non dairy liquid coffee creamer, thawed
½	stick margarine, melted		
6	eggs		
2	cans mushrooms stems and pieces		

- Preheat oven to 350°F.
- Boil the noodles less than al dente. Drain well. Mix in remaining ingredients, except coffee creamer.
- Pour into greased 9 x 13-inch pan. Pour coffee creamer over the top.
- Bake at 350°F for 45 minutes to an hour.

Serves 8

Apricot Kugel

DAIRY

Easy to make. A favorite of Fannie Brafman Bloom's!

1	pound medium egg noodles	½	cup apricot preserves
4	eggs	½	cup apricot filling
8	ounces cream cheese	¼	cup applesauce
16	ounces baker's cheese (ricotta)	1	stick butter or margarine
16	ounces sour cream		

- Preheat oven to 350°F.
- Cook noodles according to package directions. Drain well and add 1 stick of melted butter or margarine.
- In mixer, beat the eggs, cream cheese, bakers' cheese and sour cream until well blended. Add this to the buttered noodles and mix well.
- To the Solo apricot filling, add ¼ cup of applesauce and the apricot preserves.
- Grease a 9 x 13-inch pan and fill with half of the noodle mixture. Spread the apricot mixture over the noodle mixture already in pan, and top with the rest of the noodles.
- Bake at 350°F for 1 hour.

Chef's tip: Top with Crumb Topping after 1 hour of baking if desired.

Crumb Topping:

1	cup crushed corn flakes	1	teaspoon brown sugar
½	stick butter or margarine	½	teaspoon white sugar
1	teaspoon cinnamon		

- Melt butter or margarine and toss with remaining crumb mixture ingredients.
- After baking for 1 hour, remove kugel from oven and sprinkle with the crumb mixture. Return to oven to bake another 15 minutes at 325°F.

Serves 8

Puffy Noodle Kugel

DAIRY

A not-too-sweet kugel that can be enjoyed by company and kids! Egg Beaters, "no yolks" noodles and low fat cottage cheese can be substituted for a low-fat version of this recipe.

8	ounces wide egg noodles	¾	cup cottage cheese
2-3	tablespoons butter, in small pieces	½	teaspoon cinnamon
6	ounces light cream cheese	4	eggs
⅓	cup sugar	½	cup milk

Topping:

1	tablespoon sugar	¼	teaspoon cinnamon

- Preheat oven to 375°F.
- Boil noodles in a pot of rapidly boiling, salted water until tender, about 10 minutes. Place butter in shallow 1½ to 2-quart baking dish. Drain noodles and toss with butter until butter is melted. Set aside.
- Beat cream cheese and sugar with electric mixer. Beat in cottage cheese, cinnamon, eggs and then milk (mixture will be lumpy). Pour over noodles. Top with cinnamon and sugar.
- Bake in preheated 375° oven 30 to 45 minutes, until "puffed."
- Serve hot, warm or cold.

Serves 6

Crustless Spinach Quiche

DAIRY

Easy to make!

1	(10-ounce) package frozen chopped spinach, thawed and drained well	3	eggs
4	ounces canned sliced mushrooms, or fresh sautéed and drained	8	ounces grated Cheddar cheese
1	cup sour cream	1	large can French-fried onions, or fresh sautéed onions

- Preheat oven to 350°F.
- Mix all ingredients, with ½ of the onions. Pour into a 9-inch pie plate. Sprinkle remaining onions on top.
- Bake at 350°F for 1 hour.
- To reheat: 350°F for 15 minutes, sprinkle with onions last 5 minutes.

Serves 4 to 6

Side Dishes

Squash Soufflé

PARVE

This has converted many squash haters to squash lovers! A good friend gave this recipe to my mother. We have been making it at holiday get-togethers for years.

1	package frozen yellow squash, defrosted	3	eggs
½	stick melted margarine	2	cups coffee creamer
½	cup sugar		Pinch salt
½	cup flour		Cinnamon to taste

- Preheat oven to 350°F.
- Mix squash with margarine. Mix all dry ingredients together in a separate bowl then add to squash.
- Beat eggs in coffee creamer until blended and add to other mixture. Pour into greased casserole dish.
- Bake at 350°F for 1 hour or until firm.

Serves 4 to 6

Matzos Apple Kugel

PARVE

A sweet kugel.

4	boards matzos	2	teaspoons cinnamon
3	large eggs	½	cup golden raisins (or more to taste)
	Pinch of salt	3	apples (I like to use Cortland, Empire or Ida Reds)
½	cup sugar		
1	teaspoon cinnamon	½	cup chopped almonds or grated rind of 1 orange (optional)
½	stick butter or margarine melted		

- Preheat oven to 350°F.
- Peel, slice, and chop apples (leave some bigger slices). Break matzos into pieces (break in half 2 to 3 times). Soak matzos in water until soft (about 5 to 10 minutes). Drain excess water from matzos so they remain soggy.
- Beat eggs lightly with a fork. Add salt, sugar, margarine and cinnamon to eggs. Add sugar, margarine, and cinnamon to eggs. Add the egg mixture to the softened matzos. Stir in raisins and apples. Stir in ½ cup chopped almonds or grated rind of 1 orange.
- Bake in square baking dish in a 350°F oven for 45 minutes, until lightly brown. Add extra apples and raisins on top to taste.

Serves 6

Carrot Kugel

PARVE

Great way to feed vegetables to kids. Can be easily adapted for Passover.

3	pounds carrots, cooked in chunks	3	teaspoons vanilla (omit for Passover)
6	eggs	¼	teaspoon cinnamon
1½	cups sugar	2	teaspoons salt
9	tablespoons flour (for Passover, use cake meal)	1	teaspoon lemon juice (or a little more)
3	teaspoons baking powder (omit for Passover)	2	sticks margarine, softened
			Cornflake crumbs, nuts or cinnamon, (optional)

- Preheat oven to 350°F.
- Blend carrots in a food processor. Mix in all other ingredients. Sprinkle with corn flake crumbs, nuts or cinnamon, if desired.
- Bake at 350°F in 9 x 13-inch pan, 1 hour 10 minutes to 1 hour 20 minutes.
- Freezes beautifully.

Serves 8 to 10

Noodle Rice Casserole

MEAT

Your kids will love this!

2	sticks margarine	1	(8-ounce) can sliced water chestnuts, drained
½	package very fine egg noodles	1	teaspoon soy sauce
2	cups instant rice		

Either:

4	cups boiling water,
3	teaspoons onion bouillon and
3	teaspoons chicken bouillon

Or:

2	cans chicken soup and
2	cans onion soup

- Preheat oven to 350°F.
- Melt margarine in skillet. Add noodles and cook until brown. If using bouillon, heat water until it boils, and then dissolve the bouillon in boiling water.
- Stir well so bouillon is not stuck to bottom. Add the soy sauce to this soup mixture. Add remaining ingredients to the browned noodles. Mix well. Pour into a 3-quart casserole baking dish.
- Bake in 350°F oven for 30 minutes.
- Tastes best if top of casserole is lightly browned and forms a crust.

Serves 6

Side Dishes

Sweet Tsimmes

You must try this creative version of tsimmes.

6	canned sweet potatoes, halved	1	(6-ounce) can frozen orange juice
12	dried prunes, soaked in water 30 minutes, drained	¼	cup butter or margarine
12	dried apricots, soaked in water 30 minutes, drained		Brown sugar to taste
1	(20-ounce) can pineapple chunks		Maraschino cherries and chopped pecans to garnish

- Preheat oven to 350°F.
- Arrange sweet potatoes in a shallow baking dish. Arrange prunes and apricots in open spaces. Drain and reserve pineapple juice. Arrange chunks in casserole.
- Blend pineapple syrup and orange juice concentrate. Heat with the butter until butter is melted. Pour over fruit. Sprinkle with brown sugar.
- Bake at 350°F for 1 hour, basting occasionally.
- Before serving, garnish with cherries and pecans if desired.

Serves 6

Sweet Potato Latkes

PARVE

A new twist to an old favorite. Great with applesauce and sour cream. Enjoy!

4	sweet potatoes	1	tablespoon sugar
2	large eggs		Raisins (optional)
2	tablespoons flour	½	cup vegetable oil

- Line a cookie sheet with paper towels. Grate sweet potatoes finely and lay on paper towels to drain liquid.
- Beat eggs with sugar in small bowl and add the potato mixture. Add flour and mix thoroughly. Add some raisins if desired.
- Heat oil over medium-high heat in non-stick frying pan until drop of water sizzles. Add spoonfuls of mixture; flatten with spoon and fry until golden brown and crisp. Let latkes rest on paper towel to drain grease.
- Serve immediately or reheat to serve.

Serves 4 to 6

Great Vegetable Side Sauces

DAIRY OR PARVE

Three great sauces to top your favorite cooked vegetables!

Sauce 1: Sesame Lemon Sauce

2	teaspoons sesame seeds	½	teaspoon salt
3	tablespoons butter or margarine	¼	teaspoon hot pepper sauce
2	tablespoons lemon juice		

- Brown sesame seeds in butter in skillet; add lemon juice, salt, and hot sauce.
- Pour over cooked vegetables and serve.

Sauce 2: Herbed Butter with Parmesan Cheese Sauce

4	tablespoons unsalted butter or margarine at room temperature	1	tablespoon fresh dill
1	tablespoon chopped Italian parsley (fresh)	1	tablespoon chopped fresh rosemary or 1 teaspoon dried rosemary
1	tablespoon chopped fresh or freeze dried chives	1	teaspoon black pepper
		½	cup shredded Parmesan cheese

- In a small bowl combine butter or margarine with chopped herbs and pepper.
- Melt butter in skillet and toss with vegetables. Remove from skillet to platter and sprinkle with Parmesan cheese.
- Serve immediately.

Sauce 3: Tangy Dijon Sauce

½	cup butter or margarine	1½	teaspoons Worcestershire sauce
3	tablespoons honey Dijon mustard		

- Melt butter in saucepan (or microwave) and whisk in mustard and Worcestershire. Pour over vegetables and serve.

Serves 4 to 6

Apple Pudding

PARVE

A sweet family favorite.

¾	cup flour	⅛	cup water
1	cup sugar	3	apples peeled and thinly sliced
2	beaten eggs	1	tablespoon lemon juice
¼	pound butter or margarine, melted	⅓	cup cornflake crumbs

- Combine flour, sugar, eggs, butter and water together in large bowl. Add apples and mix lightly. Pour into greased 2-quart baking dish. Sprinkle lemon juice over apple mixture. Sprinkle with cornflake crumbs so top is covered.
- Bake uncovered at 350°F for 60 to 75 minutes or until no liquid remains. Or microwave on high for 20 to 25 minutes.

Serves 6

Rum Glazed Tsimmes

DAIRY OR PARVE

A great side dish for company.

3	pounds sweet potato, pierced 3 to 4 times with a fork	1	cup pecan halves or vacuum-packed roasted chestnuts
3	Golden Delicious apples, peeled and cut into eighths	½	cup honey
¼	cup fresh lemon juice	2	tablespoons dark rum
6	tablespoons unsalted butter or parve margarine	½	teaspoon cinnamon
		½	teaspoon ground ginger

- Preheat oven to 400°F.
- Bake sweet potatoes for 45 minutes to 1 hour until tender. Let them cool then peel and cut diagonally into ¼-inch slices.
- Peel apples and cut them lengthwise into eighths. Toss apples with the lemon juice.
- Layer the apples with the sweet potato slices in buttered 14-inch gratin dish. Sprinkle nuts over top.
- In stainless steel or enamel saucepan, cook the remaining ingredients over medium heat, stirring often until sugar is dissolved. Spoon mixture over the potatoes and apples and bake covered in middle of oven, basting occasionally - about 30 minutes.
- Bake uncovered for 40 additional minutes, basting occasionally.
- Optional: After baking, broil tsimmes until edges brown.

Serves 8

Chef's tip: The uncooked gratin can be assembled a day ahead and kept in fridge - covered.

Mock Kishka

PARVE

Great with brisket and gravy!

1	box of tam tams (use the "everything" kind)	3	stalks of celery
1	large onion	2	tablespoons oil or soft margarine
2	large carrots	½	teaspoon salt
		½	teaspoon pepper

- Preheat oven to 425°F.
- In food processor, turn tam tam crackers into very course crumbs. Grind the onion, carrots and celery and combine with tam tam crumbs.
- Divide mixture in half and mold each half into a long roll about 10 to 12 inches long on a very well oiled strip of foil. It should look like either a very fat hot dog or thin salami.
- Bake in a 425°F oven for 30 to 40 minutes.
- Remove from oven and slice into 1 to 2-inch rounds.

Serves 6

Sour Cream Potatoes

DAIRY

Easy to prepare ahead of time, then bake later.

8	large red potatoes	Salt and pepper to taste
1	cup butter or margarine	Chopped parsley or dill
1	pint sour cream	

- Preheat oven to 350°F.
- Bake potatoes at 350°F for 1 hour and allow to cool slightly. Peel and dice the potatoes.
- Increase oven temperature to 475°F. Place half the potatoes in a greased 4-quart casserole. Dot with half the butter or margarine. Sprinkle with salt and pepper. Cover with remaining potatoes and butter or margarine. Sprinkle with salt and pepper.
- Bake at 475°F for 15 to 20 minutes until browned.
- Stir in sour cream. Reduce temperature to 350°F and bake for an additional 20 minutes or until hot. Garnish with parsley or fresh dill.

Serves 8

Passover Matzos Farfel and Spinach Kugel ◆p◆

MEAT

2	cups chicken broth (fresh or canned), boiling	2	stalks celery, chopped fine
16	ounces matzo farfel	3	tablespoons margarine
4	large eggs, beaten	1	large carrot, chopped fine
1	large onion, chopped	2	(10-ounce) packages frozen chopped spinach, well drained
1½	pounds mushrooms, chilled		Salt and pepper to taste

- Preheat oven to 350°F.
- In a large bowl, stir together matzo farfel and broth. Mix well. Let the mixture stand for about 5 minutes and gently stir in the eggs.
- In a skillet cook the onion in the margarine over moderately low heat, stirring until it is softened, add the celery, mushrooms and carrot; cook the mixture for 5 minutes or until the veggies are tender and slightly brown. Stir in the chopped spinach; continue to cook over moderate heat until the liquid is absorbed. Stir the veggie mixture into the matzo farfel and add lots of salt and pepper. It needs a lot of seasoning to give it flavor.
- Bake at 350°F in a greased 9 x 13-inch pan, covered for 30 to 40 minutes and then uncover to let it brown.
- Add turkey or brisket drippings while it's cooking.

Serves 8 to 10

Chef's tip: Can be prepared two days ahead, cover and chill. Half of recipe can be made in an 8-inch square pan (9 pieces).

Simple Crunchy, Crispy, Passover Potato Kugel

PARVE

Fabulous! Sure to become a family favorite.

1	box Manischewitz Stuff-It Mix		Vegetable oil for frying
2	large packages frozen hash brown potatoes	1	pound fresh mushrooms sliced (optional)
1	large package frozen chopped onions (or 4 large fresh onions)	1	red peppers, green peppers, or both, sliced (optional)

- Preheat oven to 375°F.
- Sauté potatoes, onions, mushrooms and peppers until golden brown.
- Prepare Stuff-It mix as directed on package. Place potatoes on the bottom of shallow roasting pan with mix on top. Sprinkle salt and pepper to taste.
- Bake for 1 hour at 375°F.
- May be baked in 2 (3-quart) round casserole dishes. Use same time and temperature as above.

Serves 10

Broccoli Cheese Soufflé

DAIRY

An easy soufflé!

3	eggs	2	(10-ounce) packages of chopped frozen broccoli (substitute spinach or eggplant)
1	cup cottage cheese		
4-6	ounces Cheddar cheese (½ to ¾ cup)	1	cup seasoned breadcrumbs
3	tablespoons flour	½	cup Parmesan cheese
	Dash of salt, pepper, garlic, and oregano to taste	4	tablespoons butter

- Preheat oven to 350°F.
- Cook broccoli in water in microwave until boiling. Drain really well. Mix all ingredients well.
- Butter a 9 x 9-inch glass pan. Pour mixture into the pan and sprinkle with seasoned breadcrumbs and Parmesan cheese. Dot the top with butter.
- Bake at 350°F for 30 to 35 minutes.

Serves 8

Potato Latkes

PARVE

A traditional Hanukkah favorite. Great adapted for Passover too!

4	large potatoes	1	tablespoon grated onion (or more, if you like onions)
2	eggs		
1	teaspoon salt	½	teaspoon baking powder (eliminate on Passover)
1	teaspoon pepper		
3	tablespoons flour (on Passover, substitute matzo meal)	1	teaspoon chopped parsley (fresh is great if you have it)
			Oil for frying

- Peel and grate potatoes. Rinse in water and drain most of the liquid.
- Beat eggs and add to potatoes. Add all the other ingredients (except oil).
- Drop spoonfuls of the mixture into a hot well-greased frying pan with the oil.
- Turn with a spatula to lightly brown on both sides.

Serves 4 to 6

Serve hot with sour cream for a dairy topping and/or applesauce.

Chef's tip: Potatoes may be grated ahead of time and stored in fridge in cold water. Just strain them and squeeze out excess liquid before using them. This will make a crispier latke, too!

Applesauce

PARVE

Great with latkes.

3	pounds Jonathan or Royal Gala apples, washed, peeled, and cored	½	cup sugar (or less, to taste)
		½	teaspoon cinnamon
1	cup water		

- Chop apples into small pieces.
- Combine water, sugar, cinnamon and apples in a pot. Cover and cook on medium heat for 30 minutes or until soft. Sir occasionally.
- Cool and refrigerate.

Chef's tip: The apples can be chopped the day ahead and kept in water in fridge, with a few drops of lemon juice to prevent discoloration.

Spaghetti Squash Primavera

DAIRY

Delicious as a main course too!

1	(3-pound) spaghetti squash	3	tablespoons olive oil (divided use)
2	garlic cloves, minced	½	sliced mushrooms
2	large tomatoes, coarsely chopped	2	teaspoons dried oregano
2	tablespoons chopped olives (black)	2	tablespoons pine nuts
1	teaspoon salt	½	teaspoon pepper
1	cup shredded Romano cheese		

- Preheat oven to 375°F.
- Place spaghetti squash on baking sheet. Pierce squash in several places. Bake until tender to center when pierced with knife, 55 to 60 minutes. Cut squash open and let stand until cool enough to handle.
- Meanwhile, in large frying pan, heat 2 tablespoons olive oil over medium heat. Add garlic and mushrooms and cook until mushrooms turn limp, 2 to 3 minutes. Add tomatoes, oregano, olives, pine nuts, salt and pepper. Cook, stirring occasionally, until most of the liquid evaporates, 3 to 4 minutes. Set aside.
- When squash is cool, discard seeds. With fork, scoop out squash strands onto serving platter.
- Toss with remaining tablespoon of olive oil. Reheat sauce, if necessary, and pour over squash. Sprinkle cheese on top.
- Serve hot.

Serves 4

Chef's tip: Bake the squash whole in the microwave to save time. Just pierce and bake for 10 to 15 minutes, or until tender.

Marinated Asparagus

PARVE

A new way to serve asparagus.

1	pound asparagus	½ bottle balsamic vinegar and oil dressing

- Break asparagus off at bottom. Peel the stalk with carrot peeler. Steam in salted shallow water until tender, but not limp. Place in shallow pan.
- Pour dressing over. Let stand for 1 to 2 hours.
- Serve at room temperature.

Serves 4 to 6

Chef's tip: To reduce fat: pour oil off the top of dressing.

Couscous

DAIRY

Mediterranean style cuisine!

1	teaspoon olive oil	1	(16-ounce) can rinsed and drained garbanzo beans
1	cup shredded carrots	¼	cup Italian salad dressing
1	cup each yellow and green zucchini, julienned	1	package couscous
1	medium red onion, cut into wedges	3	tablespoons sliced kalamata olives
1	medium red pepper, sliced and roasted	4	ounces feta cheese
		¼	cup artichokes, chopped

- In large skillet, heat oil. Sauté carrots, zucchini, and onions until soft. Add peppers, beans, and dressing. Cook 5 minutes.
- Prepare couscous according to directions, without oil. Add olives, feta, and artichokes to couscous and veggies and serve.

Serves 4 to 6

Israeli Charoset

PARVE

Delicious on Passover, or as a nosh.

2	cups pitted dates	1	banana
1	cup roasted almonds	2	tablespoons red wine

- Process all ingredients in a food processor with a steel blade. The charoset should form a thick paste.

Yields 3 cups

Dried Fruit Charoset

PARVE

Wonderful!

8	ounces dried or fresh diced apples	1	cup coconut
8	ounces chopped dates	½	cup chopped nuts (pecans or walnuts)
8	ounces craisins or dried cherries	1	cup sweet wine
8	ounces chopped prunes	3	tablespoons cinnamon

- Combine all ingredients and serve.

Yields 6 cups

Moroccan Couscous

PARVE

Colorful variation of an old favorite. Great as a meal with Baba Ganoush.

1½ cups dry organic whole-wheat couscous	1 cup cut green beans, cook until become dark green
½ teaspoon salt	
½ teaspoon turmeric	⅓ cup currants
1¼ cups boiling water	½ cup almonds, toasted whole at 200°F for 10 to 15 minutes, then chopped
1 cup penny-sliced carrots, steam-cooked 3 minutes	⅓ cup red onions, finely sliced and diced
1 large green and 1 large red pepper cut into thin strips, then crosswise again	

Marinade:

¼ cup olive oil	6 tablespoons orange concentrate
¼ cup vegetable oil	4 tablespoons chopped fresh parsley
4 tablespoons fresh lemon juice	1 tablespoon fresh spearmint (or 1-teaspoon dried)
½ teaspoon salt or more to taste	Pinch of cayenne pepper
¼ teaspoon cinnamon	

- Place the couscous, salt and turmeric in a large bowl and stir in the boiling water. Cover; let set 10 to 15 minutes then fluff with a fork.
- Meanwhile, steam the carrots and beans separately. As soon as each vegetable is barely tender, add to couscous. Stir in the red onions, currants and almonds.
- Whisk together the marinade ingredients. Toss the couscous and vegetable mixture with the marinade. Chill at least 1 hour before serving.

Serves 4

Hot Fruit Compote

PARVE

Use whatever fruits you want to.

3 small jars applesauce	2 cans Mandarin oranges
1 can sliced peaches	1 tablespoon sugar
1 can black cherries	1 tablespoon grenadine or fruit liqueur or orange juice
1 can purple plums	Cinnamon to taste
1 can sliced pears	

- Preheat oven to 350°F.
- Drain and pit all fruit. Place applesauce and drained/pitted fruit in the casserole that you want to serve it in. Add sugar, grenadine and cinnamon. Adjust to taste.
- Bake at 350°F for 1 hour.

Yields lots

Oreo Cheese Cake
with Sour Cream Topping

DAIRY

Decorate this with chocolate shavings and strawberries. It's gorgeous!

Graham Cracker Crust:

2	cups graham cracker crumbs	½	cup melted butter
½	cup sugar		

- Preheat oven to 350°F.
- Mix crust ingredients together and pat into a 10-inch springform pan. Bake at 350°F for 8 to 10 minutes and let cool.

Filling:

4	(8-ounce) packages cream cheese	4	whole eggs plus 1 extra yolk
1⅓	cups sugar	2	teaspoons vanilla

- Cream together the cream cheese and the sugar. Add the eggs and the vanilla and beat well. Pour half of the batter into pan.
- Layer with 1⅓ cups broken-up Oreo cookies (small pieces). Gently pour in other half of the batter.
- Bake at 350°F for 50 to 60 minutes. Add topping.

Topping:

1	large container sour cream	1	teaspoon vanilla
½	cup sugar		

- Combine all ingredients and spread on top of cheesecake. Bake 5 minutes more at 425°F.

Serves 12

Jewish Apple Cake

PARVE

Make the cake in the morning and cut in the evening. Chop the apples after the batter is mixed. After the cake is done, turn the tube upside down on an empty soda bottle until the cake is cool.

5	cooking apples (Rome or Jonathan)	3	teaspoons baking powder
2	teaspoons cinnamon	½	teaspoon salt
2⅓	cups sugar, divided	⅓	cup orange juice
1	cup margarine	1½	teaspoons vanilla extract
4	eggs	1	teaspoon almond extract
3	cups sifted flour		

- Preheat oven to 350°F.
- In mixer, combine margarine and 1⅔ cups of sugar. Cream at medium speed until fluffy. Add eggs, one at a time, mixing well after each addition.
- In a separate bowl, stir together flour, baking powder, and salt. Add to batter. Add juice and extracts. Combine until batter is smooth.
- In another bowl peel and quarter apples, core and slice. Combine apples, cinnamon, and ⅓ cup of sugar. Mix well.
- Place a small amount of batter in bottom of greased and floured 10-inch tube pan. Arrange a layer of apple slices over batter. Continue layering, ending with batter.
- Bake in a 350°F oven 1½ hours or until cake tests done. Cool on wire rack.

Serves 8

Chef's tip: If you want to peel and quarter apples in advance, then pour a little lemon or orange juice over apples. This prevents apples from turning brown.

Quick and Easy Flourless Chocolate Cake DAIRY

Chocoholics dream!

1 package (12-ounces) semisweet or bittersweet chocolate chips	¼ cup strong freshly brewed coffee
1 stick butter (4-ounces)	2 tablespoons of your favorite liqueur (Chambourd, Amaretto, Kahlúa)
¼ cup sugar	3 eggs

- Preheat oven to 425°F.
- Butter an 8-inch springform pan. Sprinkle additional sugar to coat sides and bottom of pan.
- In a medium glass bowl, combine the chocolate, butter, sugar, coffee and liqueur. Microwave on high for 1 to 2 minutes or until the chocolate and butter are melted and smooth when stirred. Whisk in the eggs until smooth and well blended. Turn the mixture into the prepared pan.
- Bake for 10 to 15 minutes. The cake will not completely set in the middle. The sides should pull away slightly from the pan.
- Cool to room temperature, then refrigerate until cold.

Serves 10 to 12

"I Scream" Cake
DAIRY

Impress your guests with this decadent dessert!

Crust:

1 box chocolate wafers, crushed finely	½ cup butter or margarine, melted
½ cup sugar	

Filling:

12 Heath bars, crushed	1 quart chocolate ice cream (slightly softened)
1 quart coffee ice cream (slightly softened)	1 jar Hershey's fudge topping

- Preheat oven to 375°F.
- Make crust, adding sugar and melted butter to crushed chocolate wafers. Line the bottom and sides of an 8-inch springform pan with wafer mixture.
- Bake in preheated 375°F oven for 8 minutes and remove to cool. When cool, sprinkle ⅓ of crushed candy bars on bottom of crust. Then spread coffee ice cream, ⅓ of crushed candy bars, chocolate ice cream, and then the last ⅓ of crushed candy bars. Cover with chocolate fudge topping.
- Cover with double thickness of foil and freeze until ready to use.

Serves 8 to 10

Chef's tip: Slice with a sharp knife dipped in hot water.

Perfect Parve Chocolate Cake
with Bittersweet Icing

PARVE

This is not a Pesach recipe, but a great Shabbat dessert!

1 cup cocoa	1 teaspoon vanilla
2 cups water	2¾ cups flour
1 cup margarine, melted and cooled (or butter, for a milchig recipe)	2 teaspoons baking soda
2½ cups sugar	½ teaspoon salt
4 eggs	½ teaspoon baking powder

- Preheat oven to 350°F.
- In a medium pitcher, whisk together cocoa and boiling water until smooth. Set aside to cool.
- In a large mixing bowl, beat margarine, sugar, eggs and vanilla for 5 minutes. Alternate the sifted dry ingredients and the cocoa mixture. Beat only until combined. Pour the batter into three greased and floured cake pans.
- Bake at 350°F for 30 to 40 minutes until the centers of the cakes spring back when lightly touched.

Bittersweet Icing:

6 ounces bittersweet chocolate	4 tablespoons strong coffee
2½ ounces margarine	1 teaspoon vegetable oil

1. Microwave chocolate, margarine and coffee on medium until melted. Careful not to burn.
2. Add oil and beat well.
3. Frost cakes immediately and allow to cool before slicing.

Serves 16 to 20

Holiday Chocolate Roll

DAIRY

Tastes as good as it looks! Garnish with fresh berries.

Dough:
6	egg whites (at room temperature)	1½	teaspoons vanilla
¾	cup sugar		Confectioners' sugar
⅓	cup unsweetened cocoa		Dash salt
6	yolks		

- Preheat oven to 375°F.
- Grease bottom of a 15½ x 10½ x 1-inch jelly-roll pan and line with lightly greased wax paper.
- In a large electric mixer bowl, at high speed, beat egg whites just until soft peaks form. Add ¼ cup sugar, 2 tablespoons at a time, beating until stiff peaks form when beater is slowly raised. With same beaters in a separate bowl, beat yolks at high speed, adding remaining ½ cup sugar, 2 tablespoons at a time. Beat until mixture is very thick - about 4 minutes. At low speed, beat in cocoa, vanilla and salt, just until smooth.
- With wire whisk or rubber scraper, gently fold the cocoa mixture into the beaten egg whites, just until they are blended (no egg white should show). Spread evenly in pan. Bake 15 minutes, just until surface springs back when gently pressed with fingertip.
- Sift confectioners' sugar, in a 15 x 10-inch rectangle, on clean linen towel. Turn cake out on sugar; lift off pan; peel paper off cake. Roll up, jelly roll fashion, starting with the short end, towel and all. Cool completely on rack, seam side down - at least ½ hour.

Filling:
1½	cups heavy cream, chilled	2	teaspoons instant coffee
½	cup confectioners' sugar	1	teaspoon vanilla
¼	cup unsweetened cocoa		

- Combine ingredients in medium bowl. Beat with electric mixer until thick, and then refrigerate.
- Unroll cake, spread with filling to 1 inch from edge; re-roll. Place seam side down, on plate; cover loosely with foil. Refrigerate 1 hour before serving.

To serve:
- Sprinkle with confectioners' sugar; decorate with angelica and cherries. Or, you can freeze this in foil. Let stand for 1 hour before serving.
- Garnish with strawberries or raspberries.

Serves 10

Anise Honey Cake

PARVE

My parents were both profoundly deaf and even though they were unable to hear the Rabbi's voice at their Jewish wedding speaking the traditional blessings, they knew that a Jewish way of life was what they wanted.

During their school years my father attended a residential school and lived away from home, thus losing contact with Jewish celebrations. My mother, however, lived at home and helped her mother prepare weekly for Shabbat. She learned to make all of the traditional foods and to participate in the rituals associated with the major holidays just by watching her mother, Tillie Nathenson. When she married my father, she continued the rituals and holiday food preparation that she had learned at home.

Although neither of my parents had any kind of formal Jewish education my mother was able to perpetuate a strong Jewish feeling in our home through the foods she prepared. Shavuos became "cheese holiday" to us as we ate cheese pie and made blintzes by the hundreds. Rosh Hashanah was the time to eat honeyed taiglach and honey cake and Passover became the time for poppy seed cake.

Had it not been for my mother's persistence and her knowledge of Jewish cooking and traditions, my brother and I may not have grown up with the strong sense of Judaism we have today. We definitely developed our love for Judaism through our senses, which eventually led to an emotional bonding with our traditions. My mother did not always intellectually understand why she was doing something connected with a tradition. She just knew it was what her mother had done and that it was the right thing to do. With a strong feeling of pride, I share my great grandmother's recipe for Honey Cake passed on to me by my mother, Hilda Nathenson Barash.

- Eva B. Dicker Eiseman

6	eggs, beaten	4	cups flour
1	pound honey	1	teaspoon cinnamon
2	scant cups of sugar	1	teaspoon nutmeg
1	cup cooking oil	2	tablespoons anise seed
½	cup sweet wine (i.e., Manischewitz or Mogen David)	1⅓	cups white soda (i.e., Sprite)
		1	teaspoon baking soda
1	cup raisins, optional	2	teaspoons allspice
1	cup chopped nuts, optional	1	teaspoon baking powder

- Preheat oven to 350°F.
- Mix and sift dry ingredients. Add beaten eggs, honey, oil, wine, white soda, and mix together. Add nuts and raisins, although these are optional.
- Line 3 loaf pans with wax paper, which should be sprayed with non-fat oil.
- Bake at 350°F for 1 hour until brown and shiny.

Yields 3 loaves

Passover Sponge Cake Madness

While living in San Francisco, I decided to add shaved chocolate to my usual sponge cake recipe. After whipping up the beautiful mixture, I was feeling very good as I placed it in the oven.

When my timer went off, I checked to see if the cake was done and was very proud of myself when I realized that the cake not only smelled good, but had risen high above the top of the cake pan.

I turned my cake pan over on a bottle on the counter and went out of the kitchen feeling very excited that my new concoction had turned out so wonderfully.

When I returned to the kitchen a short time later, I thought I saw something on the floor by the counter, there the cake was resting. As I bent down, I felt something hot hit my back, and before I knew it, my three children had jumped on top of me screaming excitedly, "this is delicious!" I then realized that the hot thing on my back was my cake, which had obviously fallen out of the pan onto my back.

When the kids finally got off my back and I was able to straighten up, they begged me to make another one just like it, as it was so yummy! I couldn't believe it. When I turned the pan over to see what was left (so I could figure out what I had done wrong), I realized that I had put too much shaved chocolate in the cake and, obviously, didn't fold it in correctly; so when it baked, all of the chocolate went to the bottom of the pan.

Even though I had one less cake for Passover, my kids had had a great time, and enjoyed every bite of my mistake. To this day, I smile and have a good chuckle whenever I think of my San Francisco Sponge Cake fiasco as I make my first Passover sponge cake for the holiday. Oh, yes, I still make them with or without chocolate, and, so far, the rest of the cakes have stayed in the pan after baking!

- Elaine Callif

9	eggs	¾	cup potato starch
1½	cups sugar	¼	cup cake meal
1	lemon (juice and rind of whole) or 3 tablespoons fresh	3	tablespoons water (hot) into yolks
½	orange (juice and rind of ½) or 3 tablespoons fresh	1-2	unsweetened grated chocolate bars (optional)

- Preheat oven to 350°F.
- Separate whites from yolks. Put in separate bowls. Beat yolks with ½ of sugar (¾ cup). Add all the juice, water and flour in the yolks. Beat egg whites into peaks. Add the remaining ¾ cup sugar into the beaten egg whites slowly, with a pinch of salt. Fold the yolk mixture slowly into the whites until thoroughly mixed. Optional: if using chocolate bars, slowly fold into entire mixture until mixed entirely. Slowly pour entire mixture into ungreased sponge cake tin.
- Bake at 350°F on second rack of oven for 45 minutes to 1 hour, depending on your oven. Remove when lightly brown on top, and there is no residue on toothpick after testing for doneness.
- Invert cake over a large bottle to cool. Don't remove from bottle until entirely cooled off. Then take off bottle, remove the outer part of tin, run a knife under the entire cake, and around inner cake, and gently remove to a platter.
- ENJOY!! It should be a very moist and delicious cake!

Yields 1 cake

Carrot Cake with Cream Cheese Frosting

DAIRY

Use to celebrate any occasion!

2	cups flour	1½	cups oil
2	teaspoons baking powder	4	eggs
1½	teaspoons baking soda	1	cup carrots, grated
1	teaspoon salt	1	(8½-ounce) can crushed pineapple, drained
2	teaspoons cinnamon	½	cup chopped nuts
2	cups sugar		

- Preheat oven to 350°F.
- Sift together flour, baking powder, baking soda, salt and cinnamon. Add sugar, oil and eggs and mix well. Stir in carrots, drained pineapple and nuts.
- Grease and flour a 9 x 13-inch pan or 3 (9-inch) round pans
- Bake at 350°F for 35 to 40 minutes.

Cream Cheese Frosting:

1	pound icing sugar	1	teaspoon vanilla
1	package cream cheese	½	cup butter or margarine

- Let cream cheese and butter come to room temperature. Cream them together. Add vanilla. Add powdered sugar, slowly. Whip until fluffy and frost.

Serves 16 to 20

Chef's tip: If you don't have time to bring the cream cheese and butter to room temperature, whip them up in a food processor for a couple of minutes before using them in recipe.

Banana Coffee Cake

DAIRY

Sweet tooth delight.

8 ounces cream cheese at room temperature	2¼ cups flour
1 stick butter, softened	1½ teaspoons baking soda
1¼ cups sugar	1½ teaspoons baking powder
2 eggs	1 teaspoon vanilla
1 cup mashed ripe banana	

- Mix topping ingredients and set aside.
- Preheat oven to 350°F.
- Cream together cream cheese and butter. Add sugar, eggs, banana, and vanilla. Add dry ingredients. Pour ½ batter into 9 x 9-inch greased baking pan; sprinkle ½ topping over batter; repeat.

Topping:

½ cup chopped nuts	½ cup brown sugar
1 teaspoon cinnamon	2 teaspoons cocoa - optional

- Bake at 350°F for 1 hour or more.
- Test center of cake with toothpick. When it comes out clean, it's done.

Serves 8

Chef's tip: If you don't have time to bring the cream cheese and butter to room temperature, whip them up in a food processor for a couple of minutes before using them in recipe.

Key Lime Pie

DAIRY

Easy to make! Great to make ahead of time and serve right out of the freezer. Garnish with chocolate shavings or candied lime slices.

Crust:

1½ cups crumbs, either graham cracker or vanilla wafer
¼ cup sugar
⅓ cup melted butter

½ cup coconut flakes
⅓ cup nuts, finely grated or chopped (pecan dust)

1 Preheat oven to 350°F.
2 Mix all crust ingredients together and pat into 9-inch freezer-safe pie plate.
3 Bake at 350°F for 8 to 10 minutes.

Filling:

¾ cup key lime juice (found in specialty stores) or can use fresh limes
1 (12-ounce) can Eagle brand milk

12 ounces Cool Whip
1-2 dots green food coloring (optional)

• Whip all filling ingredients together. Spoon into cooled pie crust. Freeze and serve frozen or cold.

Serves 6 to 8

Chef's tip: Slice with a sharp knife dipped in hot water.

Apple Crisp

Crunchy and sweet, what a treat! Serve warm with ice cream.

1 cup flour	½ cup margarine
1½ cups brown sugar	½ cup oatmeal
½-1 cup of chopped pecans (optional)	8-10 apples

- Preheat oven to 375°F.
- Grease 9 x 9-inch baking dish. Mix above ingredients except for apples and margarine. Crumble in the margarine to form a chunky mixture.
- Peel apples and slice into small pieces.
- Beginning with the sugar/flour mixture, layer this with the apples in pan. Finish with a layer of the sugar/flour mixture, being sure to pack the baking dish full, because it shrinks when you bake it.
- Bake at 375°F for 1 hour or until the apples are soft.

Serves 6 to 8

Chef's tip: If you want to peel and quarter apples in advance, then pour a little lemon or orange juice over apples. This prevents apples from turning brown.

Rugelach

DAIRY

Serve for special family gatherings. Use this dough with other fillings.

Dough:

1 cup butter	2 cups flour
6 ounces cream cheese	¾ cup powdered sugar

Filling:

1 cup raisins	¾ cup nuts
¾ cup sugar	2 teaspoons cinnamon

- Mix dough ingredients together and chill for 1 to 2 hours.
- Preheat oven to 350°F.
- Combine all filling ingredients in a bowl. Beat 1 egg yolk with 1 tablespoon water. Divide dough into 8 parts. Roll into circles and cut into 8 wedges. Put in filling and roll up. Place point down on greased cookie sheet. Brush with yolk and sprinkle with sugar.
- Bake at 350°F for 10 to 12 minutes.

Yields 64 cookies

Buttermilk Cinnamon Bars

DAIRY

When our grandchildren were very young we would visit them frequently in Boston, Cincinnati and Deerfield, Illinois. I would always carry my special, light blue suitcase filled only with cookies and such for them. Each time they greeted us at the airport, they only wanted to carry the special "blue suitcase!" To this day our grandchildren, now in their 20's, ask for Grandma's cookies…and here is a taste!

- Ethel N. Gill

1¼	cups white sugar	½	cup butter, softened
¾	cup brown sugar	½	cup coconut
2	cups flour	½	cup chopped nuts

- Preheat oven to 350°F.
- Cream butter, slowly add the sugars, then the flour. Mix as you would for pastry. Combine 2 cups of this mixture with coconut and nuts.
- Press the coconut mixture lightly in bottom of a greased 9 x 13-inch pan. Set aside.

Combine the following ingredients in separate bowl:

1	egg, well beaten	1	teaspoon baking powder
½	teaspoon salt	1	cup buttermilk
1	teaspoon cinnamon	1	teaspoon vanilla

- Stir in remaining butter mixture and spread over first layer in pan. Bake at 350°F for 45 minutes.
- Frost while warm with confectioners' sugar. Cut into bars.

Serves 10 to 12

Chocolate Farfel Nut Clusters

DAIRY

So easy, your kids can help. These are addictive!

16	ounces semi-sweet chocolate	1	cup toasted chopped pecans
½	cup toasted matzo farfel		Handful of raisins (optional)

- Melt chocolate in a double boiler. Combine in bowl with farfel and nuts.
- Spoon into paper cups or onto waxed paper-covered cookie sheet. Refrigerate to set.

Yields 12 to 16 clusters

Scrumptious Strudel

Amazing! Mouth Watering!

2	cups flour	½	pound butter
1	small carton sour cream	2	tablespoons sugar

- Mix all ingredients together by kneading with your hands until dough is smooth.
- Form into four balls. Wrap each in plastic wrap and refrigerate overnight.

Filling Options:

1	jar apricot all fruit		Cut up maraschino cherries
½	cup white raisins and ½ cup dark raisins	1	cup chopped pecans
1	cup coconut		

- Preheat oven to 350°F.
- Roll out each ball and cut into 12 to 14 inch squares on floured surface. Spread each square with ¼ of the filling or more. Roll up tightly into long strips and place on greased cookie sheet.
- Score each roll with 15 cuts through top crust with pointed end of knife. Sprinkle with cinnamon and sugar mix if desired.
- Bake at 350°F for 25 minutes until brown.

Yields 60 slices

Sari Balls

Child-friendly recipe and they will love to help!

1	cup butter	1	cup almonds or pecans, ground
½	cup powdered sugar	1	cup chocolate chips - can use milk
1	teaspoon vanilla		chocolate or small chips
2	cups flour		

- Preheat oven to 375°F.
- Mix all ingredients together. Roll into balls.
- Bake at 375°F for 12 minutes, until lightly brown. Let cool. Roll the balls in confectioners' sugar.

Yields 2 to 3 dozen

Mandel Brot

PARVE OR DAIRY

Mandel bread lovers will ask for more of these.

6	eggs	¾	cup potato starch
½	pound butter or margarine	1	tablespoon orange juice
1¼	cups sugar	1	cup parve chocolate chips
2	cups cake meal		

Topping:

½	cup sugar	½	teaspoon nutmeg
2	teaspoons cinnamon		

- In a large bowl, cream butter and sugar together. Add eggs one at a time. Mix cake meal and starch together. Add other ingredients. Freeze for 20 minutes.
- Preheat oven to 375°F.
- Divide dough into 4 portions. Roll into loaves. Bake for approximately 40 minutes at 375°F. Remove from oven and slice into ½-inch slices.
- Sprinkle with cinnamon, sugar and nutmeg mixture. Return to cookie sheet and return to oven to brown for approximate 10 to 12 minutes.

Yields 2 dozen

Raspberry Meringue Kisses

DAIRY

Try this with yellow lemon gelatin for a Sukkoh flair.

3	eggs whites	3½	tablespoons raspberry gelatin crystals (or lemon)
⅛	teaspoon salt	1	teaspoon vinegar
¾	cup sugar	1	cup mini chocolate chips

- Preheat oven to 250°F.
- Beat egg whites with salt until foamy. Add sugar then gelatin. Slowly beat until dissolved. Add vinegar. Fold in chocolate chips.
- Spoon tablespoon-sized cookies onto parchment paper-lined cookie sheets. Bake at 250°F for 25 minutes.
- Turn oven off and leave cookies in for 20 minutes, until dry. Remove carefully.

Yields 2 dozen

Desserts

Filled Cream Cheese Cookies

DAIRY

Rolls out really well! Create your own with different fillings.

Dough:

2	(3-ounce) packages cream cheese	2	cups cake flour
2	sticks butter or margarine		

- Mix cream cheese and butter. Add flour 1 cup at a time. Combine ingredients for dough. Chill 1 hour or overnight.

Filling:

1	cup strawberry jam	2	tablespoons graham cracker crumbs
¼	cup grated walnuts (pulse in food processor)		

- Preheat oven to 375°F.
- Roll out ¼-inch thick on floured board. Cut with 2-inch round cutter that has been dipped in flour. Fill each with filling mixture. Pinch edges together.
- Bake at 375°F for 12 to 15 minutes. Cool and sprinkle with confectioners' sugar.

Yields 3 dozen

Caramel Brownies

DAIRY

For caramel lovers.

1	German chocolate cake mix (not moist)	50	caramels
1	(12-ounce) package chocolate chips	1	cup chopped nuts
⅔	cup evaporated milk	¾	cup melted butter

- Preheat oven to 350°F.
- Butter and flour 9 x 13-inch pan. Mix ⅓ cup evaporated milk and caramels in a pan, melt over low heat, stirring so it does not burn.
- Combine cake mix, butter, chocolate chips, nuts and ⅓ cup evaporated milk. Press ½ cake mixture into 9 x 13-inch pan. Bake 6 minutes. Remove from oven.
- Spread caramel mixture over brownies. Spread the rest of brownie mixture over caramel. Drop some caramels every couple inches. It will be hard to spread.
- Bake 16 to 18 minutes more. Let set for up to 12 hours.

Serves 10 to 12

Passover Caramel Pecan Squares

PARVE

Can't stop eating these on Passover!

4 plain matzos	1 cup chopped nuts, pecans, or walnuts (optional)
1 cup margarine	1 cup parve chocolate chips
1 cup brown sugar (packed)	½ cup sliced almonds (optional)

- Preheat oven to 350°F.
- Line a 10 x 15-inch pan with tin foil. Grease it really well. Fit the plain matzos in the pan, breaking them up if necessary to fit.
- Cook the margarine and brown sugar in a medium size pot to about 234°F on a candy thermometer, stirring constantly. If you are using nuts, when sugar mixture reaches 234°F, add them in, off of the heating element. Pour over matzos.
- Bake at 350°F for 15 to 20 minutes. Remove from oven and sprinkle with chocolate chips.
- Turn oven OFF and place back in oven for 2 minutes to melt the chips. Take out and spread the chocolate chips to make a smooth top. Sprinkle with sliced almonds, if desired.
- Immediately cut into triangles and serve.

Serves 10

Passover Brownies

DAIRY

Chocoholics delight!

4 ounces baking chocolate	1 cup butter
4 eggs	2 cups sugar
½ teaspoon salt	2 teaspoons vanilla
1 cup matzo cake meal	

- Preheat oven to 325°F.
- Melt chocolate and butter in double boiler (or microwave). Beat eggs and gradually add sugar. Beat until frothy. Blend in salt, chocolate mixture, cake meal and vanilla.
- Pour into greased 9 x 13-inch pan. Bake at 325°F for 25 to 30 minutes.

Serves 10 to 12

Hanukkah Cookies

DAIRY

Great fun! Decorate these with your children.

1½ cups sifted confectioners' sugar	½ teaspoon almond flavoring
1 cup butter or margarine	2¼ cups flour
1 egg	1 teaspoon baking soda
1 teaspoon vanilla	1 teaspoon cream of tarter

- Mix confectioners' sugar, butter and egg. Mix in vanilla and almond flavorings. Mix in flour, baking soda and cream of tarter. Wrap in plastic wrap. Refrigerate 2 to 3 hours or overnight. Dough will be hard.
- Preheat oven to 375°F.
- In small amounts, roll out on floured cutting board. Cut into fun shapes. Sprinkle with sugar. Place on greased cookie sheets.
- Bake at 375°F for 7 to 8 minutes. Cool and frost.

Frosting:

1 cup confectioners' sugar	½ teaspoon vanilla
¼ teaspoon salt	1½ tablespoons cream or milk or 1 tablespoon water

- Combine all ingredients then add food coloring. Decorate cookies as desired.

Yields 4 dozen

Israeli Doughnuts (Sufganiyot)

DAIRY

Fried in enough oil to last the eight days of Hanukkah.

Frozen sweet dough, defrosted	Oil, for frying

- Buy frozen sweet dough and defrost.
- Preheat oil for deep-frying.
- Lightly coat a large tray with flour. Roll out half the dough on a floured surface until it is ½ inch thick. Cut dough into rounds. Transfer rounds to tray, placing them ½ inch apart. Continue with remaining dough.
- Cover rounds with a damp cloth and let rise in a warm place about 30 minutes. Line a tray with paper towels.
- Pour oil into a deep fryer or deep, heavy saucepan. Fry doughnuts about 3 minutes on each side or until golden brown. Drain on paper towels. Pat the tops gently with paper towels to absorb excess oil.
- To insert jam, make a small hole in the side with a skewer and stuff with jam, using a small piping bag. Sift powdered sugar over them.

Yields 1 to 2 dozen

Chef Jeffrey Nathan's Fabulous Apple Cobbler

DAIRY

8	ounces almond paste	10	ounces parve margarine
1	pound sugar	1	teaspoon almond extract
8	ounces shortening	1	pound flour

- In a mixer with paddle, combine the almond paste, sugar, shortening, and margarine. Blend until smooth. Add almond extract and flour until just combined. Cover with plastic wrap and refrigerate overnight until well chilled.

Filling:

5	pounds apples, sliced	1	teaspoon cinnamon
2½	ounces sugar	½	ounce brandy
1	ounce fresh lemon juice	1	teaspoon vanilla extract
4	ounces light brown sugar	8	ounces golden raisins
3	tablespoons cornstarch		Nutmeg

- In a large bowl, combine all ingredients. Pour into a well greased casserole, or individual ovenproof serving bowls. Lightly grate topping over the filling. Bake at 350°F until golden brown.

Desserts

Hamantaschen

DAIRY

A traditional Purim favorite!

2	cups flour	¼	pound soft butter or margarine
2	teaspoons baking powder	1	teaspoon vanilla
½	cup sugar		Solo brand filling or make your own
2	eggs slightly beaten		

- Mix all ingredients as you would pie dough (use a pastry blender and knead). Refrigerate for one to two days before using.
- For filling, use a can of cherry pie filling mixed with enough tapioca to thicken it (1 to 2 teaspoons). Or use your own favorite filling.
- Preheat oven to 350°F.
- Take a small ball of dough and place on floured wax paper. Roll out with a lightly rolling pin. Cut out a 2-inch circle. Use a glass or mug to get a circle shape if need be. Fill with 1 to 2 teaspoons of filling. Fold into triangle shape and pinch well.
- Bake at 350°F for 30 to 35 minutes.

Yields 3 dozen

Hamentaschen

DAIRY/PARVE

A sweet Purim treat.

1½	cups sugar	1	cup butter or parve margarine
4	cups flour	2	beaten eggs
4	teaspoons baking powder	4	tablespoons orange juice
½	teaspoon salt		Solo filling or make your own

- Mix dry ingredients either by hand or with a mixer. Add butter, then eggs and juice. Refrigerate dough 1 hour. Dough should be fairly hard.
- Preheat oven to 350°F.
- Roll out on floured or powdered sugar surface. Cut circles. Fill with 1 tablespoon filling. Form triangles.
- Bake at 350°F for 20 to 30 minutes until lightly brown.

Yields 3 to 4 dozen

Hamentaschen Fillings

An updated favorite!

Prune Raspberry and Marmalade Filling:

2	(10-ounce) boxes pitted prunes	1	(9-ounce) jar marmalade
1	(15-ounce) box seedless raisins	1	(8-ounce) jar raspberry jam
1	lemon cut into small pieces	1	cup walnuts, chopped

- Grind prunes, raisins, and lemon in grinder or food processor. Add the jam, walnuts and marmalade. Spread on dough.

Apricot Pineapple Filling:

1	(12-ounce) package dried apricots		12-16 ounces of pineapple preserves
½	box of white raisins	½	small jar of apricot preserves
	Juice from small orange		

- Pour hot water over dried fruits and let stand for a few minutes; drain; then put through food grinder and add remaining ingredients.

Poppy Seed Filling:

1	cup of Solo poppy seed filling	½	cup chopped walnuts
½	cup of dark raisins		Juice of ½ an orange and ½ lemon

- Put all ingredients in food processor for a minute.

Quick and Easy Filling:

- For a quick and easy filling, use a can of cherry pie filling mixed with enough tapioca to thicken it (1 to 2 teaspoons).

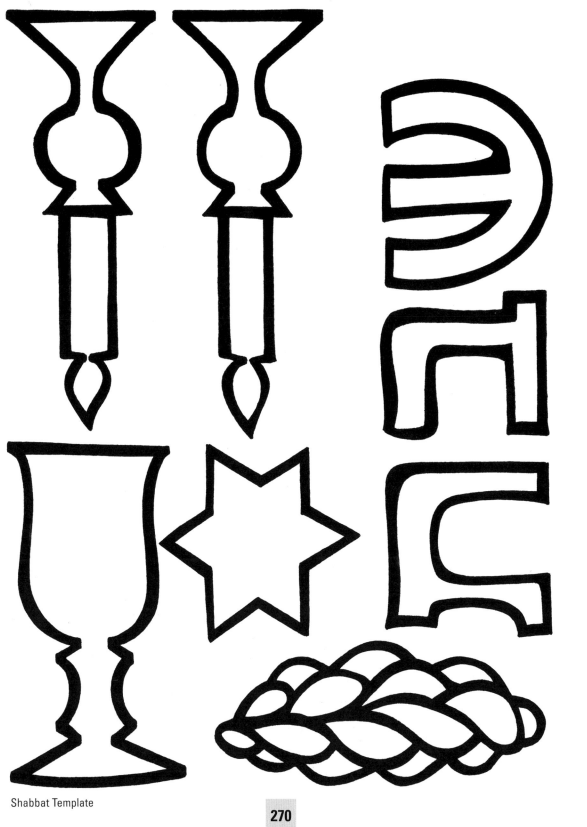

Shabbat Template

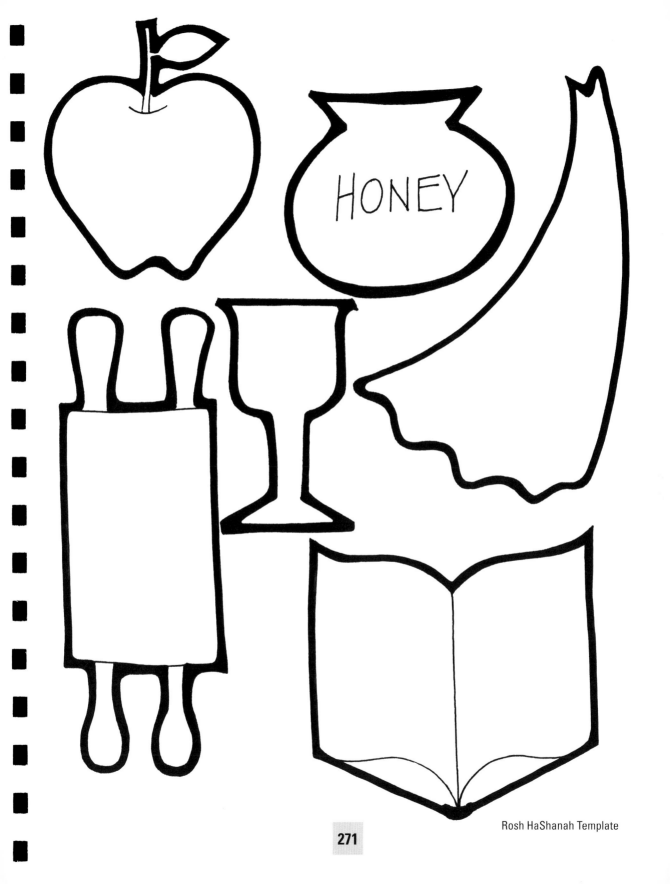

HONEY

Rosh HaShanah Template

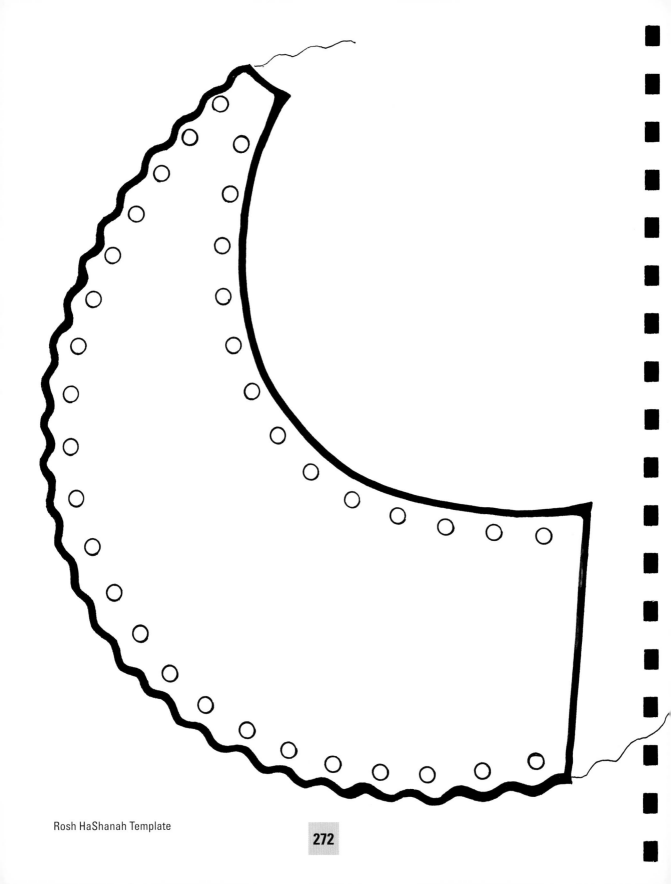

Rosh HaShanah Template

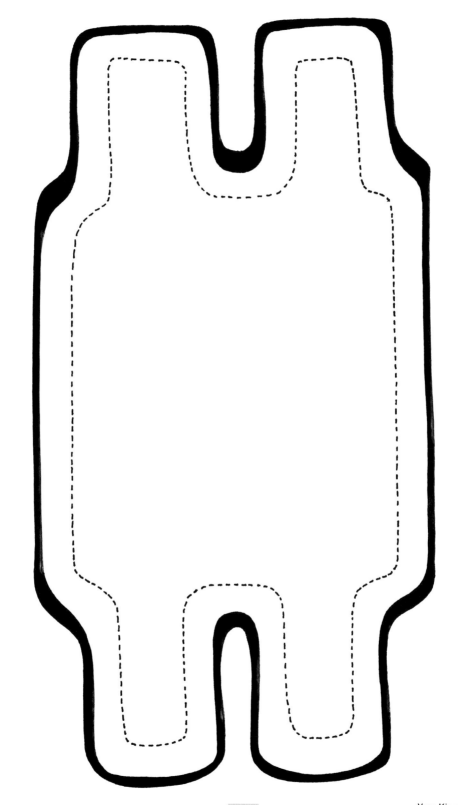

Yom Kippur Template

Sukkot Template

Hanukkah Template

Purim Template

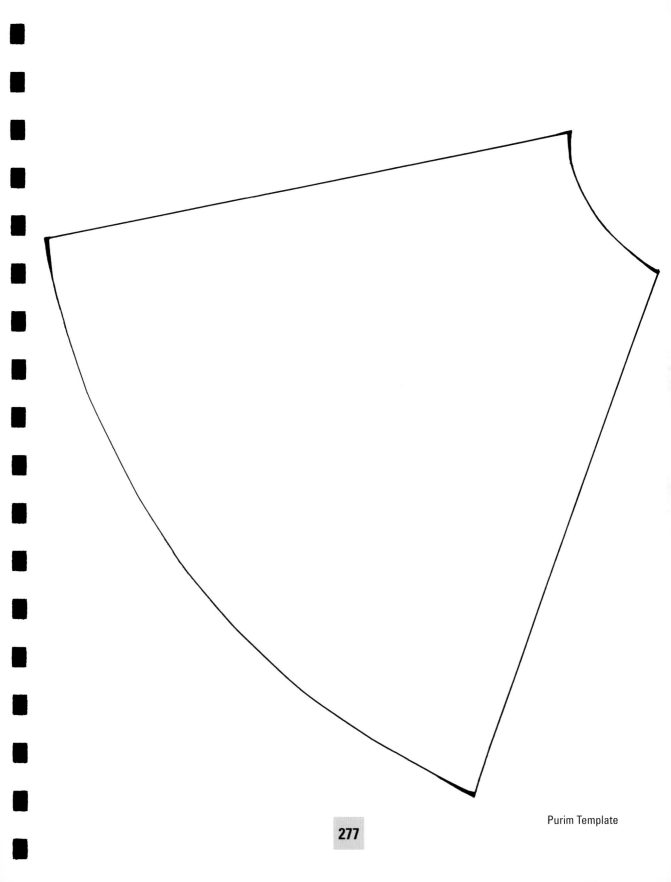

Purim Template

Purim Template

Passover Template

COUNTING the OMER

Shavuot — Day 50

49 48 47 46 45 44

43 42 41 40 39 38 37 36 35

34 33 LAG B'OMER 32 31 30 29 28 27 26

25 24 23 22 21 20 19 18 17 16 15 14 13

12 11 10 9 8 7 6 5 4 DAY 3 DAY 2 DAY 1 FIRST SEDER

Lag B'Omer Template

Yom Ha'Atzmaut Template

Appendix 2 - BLESSINGS

Index of Blessings

General Blessings

A. Blessing for washing hands (said before eating a meal – particularly one with bread)

B. HaMotzi – prayer for bread

C. Kiddush – prayer for wine

D. Eitz – prayer for fruit grown on trees

E. Adama – prayer for fruit or vegetables grown in the ground, on vines or on bushes

F. M'zonot – prayer for food made from grains that aren't bread (cookies, cakes, etc.)

G. Shehecheyanu – prayer said on certain holidays or when doing something new or eating something for the first time in the season or when wearing new clothes

H. Birkat HaMazon – prayer after a meal

Sabbath and Holiday Blessings

I. Nerot – Sabbath candles

J. Yom Tov – holiday candles

K. Eishet Chayil – blessing for the wife (Proverbs, chapter 31)

L. Banim – blessing over the children

M. B'samin – blessing over the spices (for Havdalah)

N. Eish – blessing for "Lights of the Fire" (for Havdalah)

O. Havdalah – blessing for separation of the Sabbath from the weekday

P. Shanah – prayer for apples and honey (for Rosh HaShanah)

Q. Sukkah – blessing for "Dwelling" in a Sukkah

R. Lulav – blessing for the Lulav and Etrog

S. Hanukkah – blessings for the Hanukkah candles

T. HaNerot Hallalu – additional Hanukkah blessings

Appendix – Blessings referred to in this book

Note:

1) In some cases, the following blessings have been simplified or abridged. These blessings have been marked with an asterisk (*). For the traditional longer versions, consult a standard *Siddur* (prayerbook).

2) In the interest of gender inclusive language, we have made slight adjustments in the English translations of the following blessings.

General Blessings

A. The blessing for washing hands (said before eating a meal – particularly one with bread)

בָּרוּךְ אַתָּה יְיָ אֱלֹהֵינוּ מֶלֶךְ הָעוֹלָם אֲשֶׁר קִדְּשָׁנוּ בְּמִצְוֹתָיו וְצִוָּנוּ עַל נְטִילַת יָדָיִם.

Baruch Ata Adonai, Eloheynu Melech ha-olam, asher kid'shanu b'mitzvotav v'tzivanu al n'tilat yadayim.

Blessed are You, Adonai our God, Ruler of the universe, who has made us holy with Your commandments and commanded us to wash our hands.

B. Hamotzi – blessing over the bread.

בָּרוּךְ אַתָּה יְיָ אֱלֹהֵינוּ מֶלֶךְ הָעוֹלָם הַמּוֹצִיא לֶחֶם מִן הָאָרֶץ.

Baruch Ata Adonai, Eloheynu Melech ha-olam, hamotzi lechem min ha-aretz.

Blessed are You, Adonai our God, Ruler of the universe, who brings forth bread from the earth.

C. Kiddush – prayer for wine.

בָּרוּךְ אַתָּה יְיָ אֱלֹהֵינוּ מֶלֶךְ הָעוֹלָם בּוֹרֵא פְּרִי הַגָּפֶן.

Baruch Ata Adonai, Eloheynu Melech ha-olam, boray pri hagafen.

Blessed are You, Adonai our God, Ruler of the universe, who creates the fruit of the vine.

D. Eitz – prayer for fruit grown on trees.

בָּרוּךְ אַתָּה יְיָ אֱלֹהֵינוּ מֶלֶךְ הָעוֹלָם בּוֹרֵא פְּרִי הָעֵץ.

Baruch Ata Adonai, Eloheynu Melech ha-olam, boray p'ri ha-eitz.

Blessed are You, Adonai our God, Ruler of the universe, who creates the fruit of the tree.

E. Adama – prayer for fruit or vegetables grown in the ground, on vines or on bushes.

בָּרוּךְ אַתָּה יְיָ אֱלֹהֵינוּ מֶלֶךְ הָעוֹלָם בּוֹרֵא פְּרִי הָאֲדָמָה.

Baruch Ata Adonai, Eloheynu Melech ha-olam, boray p'ri ha-adamah.

Blessed are You, Adonai our God, Ruler of the universe, who creates the fruit of the earth.

F. M'zonot – prayer for food made from grains that isn't bread (cookies, cakes, etc.)

בָּרוּךְ אַתָּה יְיָ אֱלֹהֵינוּ מֶלֶךְ הָעוֹלָם בּוֹרֵא מִינֵי מְזוֹנוֹת.

Baruch Ata Adonai, Eloheynu Melech ha-olam, boray minay m'zonot.

Blessed are You, Adonai our God, Ruler of the universe, who creates all sorts of food.

G. Shehecheyanu – prayer said on certain holidays or when doing something new or eating something for the first time in the season or when wearing new clothes.

בָּרוּךְ אַתָּה יְיָ אֱלֹהֵינוּ מֶלֶךְ הָעוֹלָם שֶׁהֶחֱיָנוּ וְקִיְּמָנוּ וְהִגִּיעָנוּ לַזְּמַן הַזֶּה.

Baruch Ata Adonai, Eloheynu Melech ha-olam, shehecheyanu, v'kiy'manu, v'higiyanu lazman hazeh.

Blessed are You, Adonai our God, Ruler of the universe, who has kept us alive, sustained us, and brought us to this season.

H. Birkat HaMazon – prayer after a meal*

בָּרוּךְ אַתָּה יְיָ הַזָּן אֶת הַכֹּל.

Baruch Ata Adonai, hazan et hakol.

Blessed are you Adonai, who sustains everything.

Shabbat and Holiday Blessings

I. Nerot – Sabbath candles.

בָּרוּךְ אַתָּה יְיָ אֱלֹהֵינוּ מֶלֶךְ הָעוֹלָם אֲשֶׁר קִדְּשָׁנוּ בְּמִצְוֹתָיו
וְצִוָּנוּ לְהַדְלִיק נֵר שֶׁל שַׁבָּת.

Baruch Ata Adonai Eloheynu Melech Ha-olam, asher kidshanu b'mitzvotav v'tzivanu l'hadlik ner shel Shabbat.

Blessed are You, Adonai our God, Ruler of the universe, who has made us holy with Your commandments and commanded us to light the Shabbat lights.

J. Yom Tov – holiday candles (If the holiday falls on Shabbat, add the parts in parenthesis.)

בָּרוּךְ אַתָּה יְיָ אֱלֹהֵינוּ מֶלֶךְ הָעוֹלָם אֲשֶׁר קִדְּשָׁנוּ בְּמִצְוֹתָיו
וְצִוָּנוּ לְהַדְלִיק נֵר שֶׁל [שַׁבָּת וְ] יוֹם טוֹב.

Baruch Ata Adonai Eloheynu Melech Ha-olam, asher kidshanu b'mitzvotav v'tzivanu l'hadlik ner shel (Shabbat v'-) yom tov.

Blessed are You, Adonai our God, Ruler of the universe, who has made us holy with Your commandments and commanded us to light the (Shabbat and) holiday lights.

K. Eshet Chayil – blessing for the wife (Proverbs, chapter 31)*

In the most traditional homes, the husband recites or chants this chapter praising the *Eshet Chayil* - the woman of valor. In many homes, everyone sings along including the wife.

L. Banim – blessing over the children

FOR BOYS:

יְשִׂמְךָ אֱלֹהִים כְּאֶפְרַיִם וְכִמְנַשֶּׁה.

Y'simcha Elohim k'Efrayim v'chi'M'nashe.

May God make you as Ephraim and Menasheh.

FOR GIRLS:

יְשִׂמֵךְ אֱלוֹהִים כְּשָׂרָה רִבְקָה רָחֵל וְלֵאָה.

Y'simeych Elohim k'Sara, Rivka, Rachel v'Leah.

May God make you as Sarah, Rebecca, Rachel and Leah.

FOR ALL CHILDREN:

יְבָרֶכְךָ יְיָ וְיִשְׁמְרֶךָ יָאֵר יְיָ פָּנָיו אֵלֶיךָ וִיחֻנֶּךָ יִשָּׂא יְיָ פָּנָיו
אֵלֶיךָ וְיָשֵׂם לְךָ שָׁלוֹם.

Y'varech'cha Adonai v'yishm'recha; Ya'er Adonai panav eylecha v'yichuneka; Yisa Adonai panav eylecha, v'yaseym l'cha shalom.

May Adonai bless you and keep you, May Adonai make His face shine upon you and be gracious to you, May Adonai turn His face to you and give you peace.

M. B'samin – blessing over the spices (for Havdalah)

בָּרוּךְ אַתָּה יְיָ אֱלֹהֵינוּ מֶלֶךְ הָעוֹלָם בּוֹרֵא מִינֵי בְשָׂמִים.

Baruch Ata Adonai, Eloheynu Melech Ha-Olam, borey miney b'samim.

Blessed are You, Adonai our God, Ruler of the universe who creates all kinds of spices.

N. Eish – blessing for lights of the fire (for Havdalah)

בָּרוּךְ אַתָּה יְיָ אֱלֹהֵינוּ מֶלֶךְ הָעוֹלָם בּוֹרֵא מְאוֹרֵי הָאֵשׁ.

Baruch Ata Adonai, Eloheynu Melech Ha-Olam, borey m'orey ha-eish.

Blessed are You, Adonai our God, Ruler of the universe, who creates the lights of the fire.

O. Havdalah – blessing for separation of the Sabbath from the weekday

בָּרוּךְ אַתָּה יְיָ אֱלֹהֵינוּ מֶלֶךְ הָעוֹלָם הַמַּבְדִּיל בֵּין קֹדֶשׁ לְחֹל.

Baruch Ata Adonai, Eloheynu Melech Ha-Olam, hamavdil beyn Kodesh l'chol.

Blessed are You, Adonai our God, Ruler of the universe who separates between the holy and the profane.

Note: A simple Havdalah ceremony would be lighting the multi-wicked Havdalah candle, saying the blessings over wine (C), Spices (M), fire (N) and separations (O). The traditional Havdalah ceremony includes several longer blessings and songs.

P. Shanah – prayer for apples and honey (for Rosh HaShanah)

יְהִי רָצוֹן מִלְפָנֶיךָ יְיָ אֱלֹהֵינוּ וֵאלֹהֵי אֲבוֹתֵינוּ
שֶׁתְּחַדֵּשׁ עָלֵינוּ שָׁנָה טוֹבָה וּמְתוּקָה.

Y'hi ratzon milfanecha Adonai Eloheynu vEylohey avoteynu she't'chadesh aleynu shana tova u'm'tukah.

May it be Your will oh Adonai our God and God of our ancestors, to renew for us a good and sweet year.

Q. Sukkah – blessing for "Dwelling" in a sukkah

בָּרוּךְ אַתָּה יְיָ אֱלֹהֵינוּ מֶלֶךְ הָעוֹלָם אֲשֶׁר קִדְּשָׁנוּ בְּמִצְוֹתָיו
וְצִוָּנוּ לֵישֵׁב בַּסֻּכָּה.

Baruch Ata Adonai Eloheynu Melech Ha-olam, asher kidshanu b'mitzvotav v'tzivanu leyshev ba-sukkah.

Blessed are You, Adonai our God, Ruler of the universe, who has made us holy with Your commandments and commanded us to dwell in a *Sukkah*.

R. Lulav – blessing for the lulav and etrog

בָּרוּךְ אַתָּה יְיָ אֱלֹהֵינוּ מֶלֶךְ הָעוֹלָם אֲשֶׁר קִדְּשָׁנוּ בְּמִצְוֹתָיו
וְצִוָּנוּ עַל נְטִילַת לוּלָב.

Baruch Ata Adonai, Eloheynu Melech Ha-olam, asher kidshanu b'mitzvotav v'tzivanu al n'tilat lulav.

Blessed are You, Adonai our God, Ruler of the universe, who has made us holy with Your commandments and commanded us to shake the lulav.

S. Hanukkah – blessings for the Hanukkah candles

FIRST BLESSING:

בָּרוּךְ אַתָּה יְיָ אֱלֹהֵינוּ מֶלֶךְ הָעוֹלָם אֲשֶׁר קִדְּשָׁנוּ בְּמִצְוֹתָיו וְצִוָּנוּ לְהַדְלִיק נֵר שֶׁל חֲנֻכָּה.

Baruch Ata Adonai Eloheynu Melech Ha-olam, asher kidshanu b'mitzvotav v'tzivanu l'hadlik ner shel Hanukkah.

Blessed are You, Adonai our God, Ruler of the universe, who has made us holy with Your commandments and commanded us to light the Hannukah lights.

SECOND BLESSING:

בָּרוּךְ אַתָּה יְיָ אֱלֹהֵינוּ מֶלֶךְ הָעוֹלָם שֶׁעָשָׂה נִסִּים לַאֲבוֹתֵינוּ בַּיָּמִים הָהֵם בַּזְּמַן הַזֶּה.

Baruch Ata Adonai Eloheynu Melech Ha-olam, sh'asa nissim la'avoteynu, bayamim hahem bazman hazeh.

Blessed are You, Adonai our God, Ruler of the universe, who has made us holy with Your commandments and commanded us who performed miracles for our ancestors in days of old, at this season.

T. HaNerot Hallalu – additional Hanukkah Blessings*

A longer blessing (HaNerot Hallalu/הַנֵּרוֹת הַלָּלוּ) and the song Ma'oz Tzur/מָעוֹז צוּר (Rock of Ages) are traditionally said after lighting the Chanukah candles.

Index

A

Abigael's Ponzu Sauce 232
Anise Honey Cake 255
APPETIZERS *(also see Dips and Spreads)*
    Baked Salami 195
    Fresh Tomato Tart 194
    Gefilte Fish 196
    Passover Sweet and Sour Meatballs 195
    Spinach and Mushroom Roll-Ups 198
    Sticky Chicken Wings 197
    Stuffed Bleu Cheese Mushrooms 199
APPLES
    Apple Crisp 260
    Apple Pudding 242
    Applesauce 246
    Chef Jeffrey Nathan's
        Fabulous Apple Cobbler 267
    Cornucopia Salad
        with Lime Vinaigrette 208
    Dried Fruit Charoset 248
    Jewish Apple Cake 251
    Matzos Apple Kugel 238
    Rum Glazed Tsimmes 242
APRICOTS
    Apricot Chicken
        with Cranberry Option 227
    Apricot Kugel 236
    Apricot Pineapple Filling 269
    Sweet Tsimmes 240
ARTICHOKES
    Artichoke Pizza 220
    Farmers Chop Suey 212
    Shabbat Salad 208
    Tomato and Artichoke Pasta 218
    Tuna Salad with a Twist 206
Asian Salad 233

ASPARAGUS

    Cream of Springtime Soup 217
    Marinated Asparagus 247
    Really Simple Fish 234
AVOCADOS
    Cornucopia Salad
        with Lime Vinaigrette 208
    Green Bean, Avocado
        & Tomato Salad 211

B

Baked Salami 195
BANANAS
    Banana Bread 200
    Banana Coffee Cake 258
    Israeli Charoset 248
BEANS AND PEAS
    Asian Salad 233
    Cholent: Beef or Kishka
        with Shabbat Eggs 224
    Couscous 248
    Curried Vegetable Stew 216
    Green Bean, Avocado &
        Tomato Salad 211
    Homemade Hummus 197
    Mediterranean Bean Salad 211
    Moroccan Couscous 249
    Oriental Cole Slaw 207
    Terrific Chili 227
    Vegetable Soup 215
    Vegetarian Southwestern Soup 214
BEEF
    Baked Salami 195
    Beef Cholent 224
    Beef Tenderloin 221
    Brisket 223

Chicken Fricassée with
    Meatballs and Knaidlach 229
Cholent: Beef or Kishka
    with Shabbat Eggs............................. 224
MATZO BRIE WITH SALAMI 218
    Passover Sweet and Sour Meatballs 195
    Steak Diane 221
    Stuffed Cabbage 226
    Sweet and Sour Brisket....................... 222
    Teriyaki London Broil 225
    Terrific Chili 227
Beet Borscht, Fannie's Fabulous.............. 217
Bittersweet Icing 253

BREADS
    Banana Bread 200
    Challah with a Twist 202
    Easy Passover Popovers 205
    Honey of a Challah 202
    Incredibly Easy Challah 201
    Italian Pizza Bread 204
    Monkey Bread Challah 203
    Onion Bread 203
    Onion Challah....................................... 202
    Passover Cherry Muffins 204
    Pizza Dough 203
    Pumpkin Bread..................................... 200
    Rainbow Challah 202
    Raisin or Nut Challah 202
    Rosemary and Coarse Salt Focaccia 205
    Zucchini Bread 201
Brisket 223

BROCCOLI
    Broccoli Cheese Soufflé 245
    Pasta Salad 210
Buttermilk Cinnamon Bars 261

C

CABBAGE
    Cabbage Soup....................................... 216
    Oriental Cole Slaw 207
    Stuffed Cabbage 226

Vegetable Soup 215
Caramel Brownies 264

CARROTS
    Carrot Cake with
        Cream Cheese Frosting.................... 257
    Carrot Kugel 239
    Matzo Meal Stuffing 235
    Mock Kishka 243
    Moroccan Couscous 249

CASSEROLES
    Apple Pudding 242
    Apricot Kugel 236
    Broccoli Cheese Soufflé 245
    Crustless Spinach Quiche 237
    Hot Fruit Compote 249
    Matzo Meal Stuffing 235
    Noodle Rice Casserole 239
    Parve Mushroom Kugel 235
    Passover Lasagna 219
    Passover Macaroni and Cheese 219
    Sour Cream Potatoes 243
    Squash Soufflé 238

CAULIFLOWER
    Curried Vegetable Stew 216
    Pasta Salad.. 210

CEREALS AND GRAIN (*also see Rice*)
    Apple Crisp 260
    Cholent: Beef or Kishka
        with Shabbat Eggs............................. 224
    Couscous... 248
    Honey Pecan Crusted Chicken 228
    Moroccan Couscous 249
    Mushroom Barley Soup 215
Challah with a Twist 202

CHEESE
    Passover Lasagna 219
    Passover Macaroni and Cheese 219
Chef Jeffrey Nathan's
    Fabulous Apple Cobbler...................... 267
Chef Jeffrey Nathan's Famous
    Nori Wrapped Salmon with Salad 232

CHERRIES

Dried Fruit Charoset 248
Hot Fruit Compote 249
Passover Cherry Muffins 204

CHICKEN

Apricot Chicken with
    Cranberry Option 227
Chicken Fricassée with
    Meatballs and Knaidlach 229
Chicken Marsala 228
Chicken Soup 213
Festive Chicken Salad 206
Honey Pecan Crusted Chicken 228
Low Fat Chopped Liver 192
Potato Chip Chicken Strips 230
Sticky Chicken Wings 197

CHOCOLATE (also see Desserts)

Bittersweet Icing 253
Caramel Brownies 264
Chocolate Farfel Nut Clusters 261
Holiday Chocolate Roll 254
"I Scream" Cake 252
Oreo Cheese Cake
    with Sour Cream Topping 250
Passover Brownies 265
Perfect Parve Chocolate Cake
    with Bittersweet Icing 253
Quick and Easy Flourless
    Chocolate Cake 252
Raspberry Meringue Kisses 263
Sari Balls 262
Cholent with Kishka 224
Cholent: Beef or Kishka
    with Shabbat Eggs 224

CONDIMENTS AND SAUCES

Abigael's Ponzu Sauce 232
Cucumber Dressing 193
Herbed Butter with
    Parmesan Cheese Sauce 241
Honey Mustard Sauce 230
Lime Vinaigrette 208
Sesame Lemon Sauce 241

Sweet and Sour Sauce 195
Tangy Dijon Sauce 241
Wasabi Rémoulade 232

CORN

Really Simple Fish 234
Vegetarian Southwestern Soup 214
Cornucopia Salad
    with Lime Vinaigrette 208
Couscous 248

CRAFTS AND ACTIVITIES

Afikoman Bags
    Felt Afikoman Bag 140
    Zipped Plastic Afikoman Bag 139
Book of Life Scrapbook 50
Burning Bush Table Centerpiece 143
Candlesticks
    Glitter Globe Candlesticks 12
    Salt Dough Candlesticks 14
    Soda Bottle Candlesticks 13
Challah Covers
    Collage Challah Cover 16
    Dye-Painted Challah Cover 17
Composing Your Own Prayers 51
Corrugated Crowns 117
Costumes
    Paper Bag Vests 115
    Pillowcase Dress 116
Decorated Tennis Shoes 52
Decorating the Sukkah
    Fruit and Vegetable Shapes 64
    Rosh HaShanah Card Collage 64
    Ushpizin Life Size Paper Figure 65
    Wind Socks 66
Decorations
    Add-a-Candle-Flame
        Refrigerator Stick Hanukkiah 82
    Handprint Hanukkiah Decoration 81
    Hanukkah Decoration Box 81
    Soda Bottle Wind Sock 103
    Spiral Paper Plate Mobile 104
Elijah's/Miriam's Cup 141
Foil-Tooled Mizrach 189

Games

    Idea 1: Three-legged Races 159

    Idea 2: Wheel Barrel Races 159

    Idea 3: Egg Races 160

Games Corner

    Go Plague! 135

    Passover Concentration 135

    Relay Races 136

Gift Ideas

    Jewelry Box 86

    Pencil Holder 88

    Picture Frame 87

Groggers

    Decorated Cans 118

    Paper Cup Shakers 119

Hanukkiah/Menorah

    Hanukkiah Drip Tray 80

    Layered Sand Hanukkiah/Menorah 79

    Striped Beeswax Candles 80

    Wooden Hanukkiah/Menorah 78

"Happy Birthday to the World"

    Banners 40

Harvest Ideas 68

Hats

    Newsprint Hat 157

    Visor Hat 157

Havdalah: Spice Boxes

    Fruit with Cloves 21

    "Stained-Glass" Spice Bottle 21

Homemade Seder Plate 138

Israel in Art

    "Jerusalem of Gold" 169

    "Jerusalem of Gold"

        Collage Picture 169

Israeli Independence Day Necklace 176

Israeli Marching Flags 175

Isreal in Art

    Clear Contact Paper

        Stained-Glass Window 172

    Fish Aquarium 173

    "Jerusalem of Gold" Wall Hanging 170

    Layered Sand Jars 171

Jeweled Kiddush Cup 15

Jewelry

    Dough Beads 120

    Rolled Paper Beads 121

Lag B'Omer Backpacks 158

Matzah Cover 142

Mishlo'ach Manot Baskets

    Mishlo'ach Manot Door Hanger 113

    Plastic Woven Baskets 112

    Woven Paper Cones 114

Nature Ideas

    Leaf Collecting 67

    Leafed Sukkah Table 67

    Melted Crayon Leaf Picture 68

    Nature Bracelet 67

    Nature Collages 67

    Nature Hike 67

Omer Counter 156

Party Ideas

    Cookie Decorating Contest 84

    Hanukkah Gift Game 85

Planters

    Ceramic-Tiled Pots 102

    Painted Pots 101

Puppets

    Hidden Puppets 122

    Stick Puppets 124

Rosh HaShanah Cards

    Apple Print Cards 35

    Sun Catcher Rosh HaShanah Cards 36

Rosh HaShanah Games Corner

    Magic Numbers Card Game 30

    Rosh HaShanah Tag 30

Rosh HaShanah Matching Game 37

Rosh HaShanah Table Setting Box 40

Salt Dough Map of Israel 174

Shabbat Candles

    Dipped Candles 11

    Wax Crystal Candles 10

Shabbat Tablecloths 18

Shavuot Parade 187

Shofars

    Party Horn Shofar 33

    Sewn Paper Plate Shofar 32

Sponge Painted Wrapping Paper 83
Stuffed Play Challah 34
Stuffed Torah 53
"Stuffed Torah" Cover 54
Tashlich Activities
    Rosh HaShanah Tactile Board 39
    Tashlich Walk 38
Tissue Flowers and Garland 188
Tree Projects
    Cardboard Tube Almond Trees 97
    Family Tree 98
    Tree Globes 100
Twisted Havdalah Candles 22
Tzedakah Boxes
    Fimo Clay Tzedakah Box 19
    Tissue Paper-Covered Tzedakah Box 20
Ways to Liven Up The Seder
    Crossing the Red Sea 146
    Frog Hats 148
    Kefias/Middle Eastern
      Head Coverings 145
    Parting of the Red Sea
      (Magic Trick) 145
    Plague Bags 144
    Tambourines 147
Cream Cheese Frosting 257
Cream of Springtime Soup 217
Creamed Herring 194
Crustless Spinach Quiche 237
Cucumber Dressing 193
Curried Vegetable Stew 216

D

DATES
    Dried Fruit Charoset 248
    Israeli Charoset 248
DESSERTS *(also see Chocolate)*
  Cakes
    Anise Honey Cake 255
    Banana Coffee Cake 258
    Carrot Cake with
      Cream Cheese Frosting 257

Holiday Chocolate Roll 254
"I Scream" Cake 252
Jewish Apple Cake.............................. 251
Oreo Cheese Cake with
    Sour Cream Topping 250
Passover Sponge Cake Madness 256
Perfect Parve Chocolate Cake
    with Bittersweet Icing 253
Quick and Easy
    Flourless Chocolate Cake 252
Candies
    Chocolate Farfel Nut Clusters 261
    Sari Balls 262
Cookies and Bars
    Buttermilk Cinnamon Bars 261
    Caramel Brownies 264
    Filled Cream Cheese Cookies 264
    Hamentaschen 268
      Apricot Pineapple Filling 268
      Poppy Seed Filling 268
      Prune Raspberry and
        Marmalade Filling 268
    Hanukkah Cookies 266
    Mandel Brot 263
    Passover Brownies 265
    Passover Caramel Pecan Squares 265
    Raspberry Meringue Kisses 263
    Rugelach 260
    Scrumptious Strudel 262
Desserts
    Apricot Pineapple Filling 269
    Chef Jeffrey Nathan's
      Fabulous Apple Cobbler 267
    Israeli Doughnuts (Sufganiyot) 267
    Poppy Seed Filling............................. 269
    Prune Raspberry and
      Marmalade Filling 269
Frostings and Icings
    Bittersweet Icing 253
    Cream Cheese Frosting 257
Frozen Desserts
    "I Scream" Cake 252
    Key Lime Pie...................................... 259

Pies
    Apple Crisp 260
    Key Lime Pie 259

DIPS AND SPREADS
    Creamed Herring 194
    Cucumber Dressing 193
    Easy Eggplant Dip 199
    Homemade Hummus 197
    Low Fat Chopped Liver 192
    Mock Chopped Liver 192
    Salmon Mousse
        with Cucumber Dressing 193
Dried Fruit Charoset 248

E

Easy Passover Popovers 205
Eggplant Dip, Easy 199
Eggs, Shabbat 225

F

Fannie's Fabulous Beet Borscht 217
Farmers Chop Suey 212
Festive Chicken Salad 206
Filled Cream Cheese Cookies 264

FISH
    Chef Jeffrey Nathan's Famous
        Nori Wrapped Salmon with Salad 232
    Creamed Herring 194
    Gefilte Fish 196
    Really Simple Fish 234
    Salmon Mousse with
        Cucumber Dressing 193
    Salmon with Brown
        Sugar and Mustard Glaze 233
    Sea Bass 234
    Tuna Salad with a Twist 206
Fresh Tomato Tart 194

G

Gazpacho 214
Gefilte Fish 196

Great Vegetable Side Sauces 241
Green Bean, Avocado & Tomato Salad 211

H

Hamantaschen 268
Hamentaschen 268
Hanukkah Cookies 266
Herbed Butter with
    Parmesan Cheese Sauce 241
Holiday Chocolate Roll 254
Homemade Hummus 197

HONEY
    Anise Honey Cake 255
    Honey Mustard Sauce 230
    Honey of a Challah 202
    Honey Pecan Crusted Chicken 228
Hot Fruit Compote 249

I

"I Scream" Cake 252
Incredibly Easy Challah 201
Israeli Charoset 248
Israeli Doughnuts (Sufganiyot) 267
Israeli Salad 207
Italian Pizza Bread 204

J

Jewish Apple Cake 251

K

Key Lime Pie 259

KIDS IN THE KITCHEN RECIPES
    Shabbat – Challah Surprise 6
    Rosh HaShannah –
        Creative Cake Cones 27
    Yom Kippur –
        Break-the-fast Goodies 46
    Sukkot – Graham Cracker Sukkah 60
    Hanukkah – Hanukkah Gelt 73

Tu Bishvat – Easy Bake
    Carob Crunch 93
Purim – Queen Esther
    Look-Alike Salad...............................109
Passover – Matzah Pizza 131
Lag B'Omer – Homemade
    Potato Chips 153
Yom Ha'Atzmaut – Pita Faces...............166
Shavuot – Yogurt Popsicles 183

KUGEL

Apricot Kugel 236
Carrot Kugel..239
Matzos Apple Kugel 238
Passover Matzos Farfel
    and Spinach Kugel 244
Puffy Noodle Kugel..............................237
Simple Crunchy, Crispy,
    Passover Potato Kugel 245

L

Lime Vinaigrette 208
Low Fat Chopped Liver 192

M

Mandel Brot 263
Marinated Asparagus 247
Matzo Brie Recipe 218
Matzo Brie with Salami 218
Matzo Meal Stuffing.............................235
Matzos Apple Kugel 238
Mediterranean Bean Salad....................211
Mock Chopped Liver 192
Mock Kishka 243
Monkey Bread Challah..........................203
Moroccan Couscous 249

MUSHROOMS

Mushroom Barley Soup 215
Parve Mushroom Kugel 235
Passover Matzos Farfel
    and Spinach Kugel 244
Ramen Noodle Salad 209

Simple Crunchy, Crispy,
    Passover Potato Kugel 245
Spinach and Mushroom Roll-Ups 198
Stuffed Bleu Cheese Mushrooms 199
Tuna Salad with a Twist 206

N

Noodle Rice Casserole 239

NUTS

Chocolate Farfel Nut Clusters 261
Israeli Charoset 248
Mock Chopped Liver 192
Passover Caramel Pecan Squares 265
Sari Balls 262
The Best Strawberry Salad....................209

O

Onion Bread 203
Onion Challah 202

ORANGES

Cornucopia Salad
    with Lime Vinaigrette 208
Hot Fruit Compote 249
Really Simple Fish 234
Tuna Salad with a Twist 206
Oreo Cheese Cake
    with Sour Cream Topping 250
Oriental Cole Slaw 207

P

Parve Mushroom Kugel 235

PASSOVER

Cabbage Soup.....................................216
Carrot Kugel..239
Chicken Soup 213
Chocolate Farfel Nut Clusters 261
Dried Fruit Charoset 248
Easy Eggplant Dip 199
Easy Passover Popovers 205
Gefilte Fish...196

Honey Pecan Crusted Chicken 228
Hot Fruit Compote 249
Israeli Charoset 248
Mandel Brot 263
Matzo Brie Recipe 218
Matzo Meal Stuffing 235
Matzos Apple Kugel 238
Passover Brownies 265
Passover Caramel Pecan Squares 265
Passover Cherry Muffins 204
Passover Lasagna 219
Passover Macaroni and Cheese 219
Passover Matzos Farfel
    and Spinach Kugel 244
Passover Sponge Cake Madness 256
Passover Sweet and Sour Meatballs 195
Quick and Easy
    Flourless Chocolate Cake 252
Simple Crunchy, Crispy,
    Passover Potato Kugel 245
Smoked Turkey Breast 230
Sticky Chicken Wings 197
World's Lightest,
    Fluffiest Matzah Balls 213

PASTA
Apricot Kugel 236
Noodle Rice Casserole 239
Oriental Cole Slaw 207
Parve Mushroom Kugel 235
Pasta Salad 210
Puffy Noodle Kugel 237
Ramen Noodle Salad 209
Tomato and Artichoke Pasta 218
Vegetable Soup 215
Perfect Parve Chocolate Cake
    with Bittersweet Icing 253

PINEAPPLE
Apricot Pineapple Filling 269
Carrot Cake with
    Cream Cheese Frosting 257
Sweet Tsimmes 240
Pizza Dough 203

Poppy Seed Filling 269
Potato Chip Chicken Strips 230

POTATOES
Cream of Springtime Soup 217
Matzo Meal Stuffing 235
Potato Latkes 246
Potato Salad 212
Simple Crunchy, Crispy,
    Passover Potato Kugel 245
Sour Cream Potatoes 243
Sweet Potato Latkes 240
Sweet Tsimmes 240

PRAYERS AND BLESSINGS .... starts on pg. 283

PRUNES
Dried Fruit Charoset 248
Prune Raspberry and
    Marmalade Filling 269
Pumpkin Bread 200
Sweet Tsimmes 240
Puffy Noodle Kugel 237
Pumpkin Bread 200

Q
Quick and Easy Flourless
    Chocolate Cake 252

R
Rainbow Challah 202
Raisin or Nut Challah 202
Ramen Noodle Salad 209
Raspberry Meringue Kisses 263

READ-ALOUD STORIES
Shabbat–The Rabbi and The Emperor 8
Rosh HaShannah – The Hidden Star 28
Yom Kippur – Jonah and
    The Big Fish 47
Sukkot – The Gourd's Journey 61
Hanukkah – The Miracle Moon 74
Tu Bishvat – Honi The Circlemaker 94
Purim – A Purim Rebus 110

Passover – The Passover Story 132
Lag B'Omer – A Fish Out of Water 154
Yom Ha'Atzmaut – Waking Up
   The Hebrew Language 167
Shavout – David's Wish 184
Really Simple Fish 234

RICE

Noodle Rice Casserole 239
Stuffed Cabbage 226
Rosemary and Coarse Salt Focaccia 205
Rugelach 260
Rum Glazed Tsimmes 242

S

SALADS

Asian Salad 233
Cornucopia Salad
   with Lime Vinaigrette 208
Farmers Chop Suey 212
Festive Chicken Salad 206
Green Bean, Avocado &
   Tomato Salad 211
Israeli Salad 207
Mediterranean Bean Salad 211
Oriental Cole Slaw 207
Pasta Salad 210
Potato Salad 212
Ramen Noodle Salad 209
Shabbat Salad 208
Sweet Potato Salad 210
The Best Strawberry Salad 209
Tuna Salad with a Twist 206
Salmon Mousse
   with Cucumber Dressing 193
Salmon with Brown Sugar
   and Mustard Glaze 233
Sari Balls 262
Scrumptious Strudel 262
Sea Bass 234
Sesame Lemon Sauce 241
Shabbat Eggs 225
Shabbat Salad 208

SIDE DISHES

Apple Pudding 242
Applesauce 246
Apricot Kugel 236
Broccoli Cheese Soufflé 245
Carrot Kugel 239
Couscous 248
Crustless Spinach Quiche 237
Dried Fruit Charoset 248
Great Vegetable Side Sauces 241
Hot Fruit Compote 249
Israeli Charoset 248
Marinated Asparagus 247
Matzo Meal Stuffing 235
Matzos Apple Kugel 238
Mock Kishka 243
Moroccan Couscous 249
Noodle Rice Casserole 239
Parve Mushroom Kugel 235
Passover Matzos Farfel
   and Spinach Kugel 244
Potato Latkes 246
Puffy Noodle Kugel 237
Rum Glazed Tsimmes 242
Simple Crunchy, Crispy,
   Passover Potato Kugel 245
Sour Cream Potatoes 243
Spaghetti Squash Primavera 247
Squash Soufflé 238
Sweet Potato Latkes 240
Sweet Tsimmes 240
Simple Crunchy, Crispy,
   Passover Potato Kugel 245
Smoked Turkey Breast 230

SOUPS

Cabbage Soup 216
Chicken Soup 213
Cream of Springtime Soup 217
Curried Vegetable Stew 216
Fannie's Fabulous Beet Borscht 217
Gazpacho 214
Mushroom Barley Soup 215

Vegetable Soup 215
Vegetarian Southwestern Soup 214
World's Lightest,
    Fluffiest Matzah Balls 213
Sour Cream Potatoes 243
Spaghetti Squash Primavera 247

SPINACH
    Crustless Spinach Quiche 237
    Italian Pizza Bread 204
    Parve Mushroom Kugel 235
    Passover Matzos Farfel
        and Spinach Kugel 244
    Spinach and Mushroom Roll-Ups 198
    Vegetable Soup 215

SQUASH (also see Zucchini)
    Curried Vegetable Stew 216
    Spaghetti Squash Primavera 247
    Squash Soufflé 238
Steak Diane 221
Sticky Chicken Wings 197
Strawberry Salad, The Best 209
Stuffed Bleu Cheese Mushrooms 199
Stuffed Cabbage 226
Stuffed Veal Breast 231
Sweet and Sour Brisket 222
Sweet and Sour Sauce 195

SWEET POTATOES
    Rum Glazed Tsimmes 242
    Sweet Potato Latkes 240
    Sweet Potato Salad 210
    Sweet Tsimmes 240

T

Tangy Dijon Sauce 241
Teriyaki London Broil 225
Terrific Chili 227

TEMPLATES .... starts on pg. 270
The Best Strawberry Salad 209

TOMATOES
    Fresh Tomato Tart 194
    Stuffed Cabbage 226
    Tomato and Artichoke Pasta 218
Tuna Salad with a Twist 206
Turkey Breast, Smoked 230

U

Unbelievable Blintzes 220

V

VEAL
    Stuffed Veal Breast 231
    Veal Daube 231
Vegetable Soup 215
Vegetarian Southwestern Soup 214

W

Wasabi Rémoulade 232
World's Lightest, Fluffiest Matzah Balls ... 213

Z

ZUCCHINI (also see Squash)
    Couscous...................................... 248
    Curried Vegetable Stew 216
    Zucchini Bread 201

Tastes of Jewish Tradition

% Jewish Community Center of Milwaukee

6255 North Santa Monica

Milwaukee, Wisconsin 53217

(414) 964-4444

Please send me:

Tastes of Jewish Traditions	@ $26.95 each	Quantity _____	$ _____
Postage & Handling for first book	@ $4.00		$ _____
Each additional book to same address	@ $2.00		$ _____
Sales Tax (Wisconsin Residents only add $1.50)	@ $1.50 each		$ _____
		Total Enclosed $	_____

Ship to:

Name _____ Address _____

City _____ State _____ Zip Code _____

Make checks payable to Jewish Community Center of Milwaukee

Charge to (circle one)   ❏ Visa   ❏ MasterCard

Signature _____

Account Number _____ Expiration Date _____

Thank you for your order.

Order on line @ www.jccmilwaukee.org

- -

Tastes of Jewish Tradition

% Jewish Community Center of Milwaukee

6255 North Santa Monica

Milwaukee, Wisconsin 53217

(414) 964-4444

Please send me:

Tastes of Jewish Traditions	@ $26.95 each	Quantity _____	$ _____
Postage & Handling for first book	@ $4.00		$ _____
Each additional book to same address	@ $2.00		$ _____
Sales Tax (Wisconsin Residents only add $1.50)	@ $1.50 each		$ _____
		Total Enclosed $	_____

Ship to:

Name _____ Address _____

City _____ State _____ Zip Code _____

Make checks payable to Jewish Community Center of Milwaukee

Charge to (circle one)   ❏ Visa   ❏ MasterCard

Signature _____

Account Number _____ Expiration Date _____

Thank you for your order.

Order on line @ www.jccmilwaukee.org

Tastes of Jewish Tradition

% Jewish Community Center of Milwaukee
6255 North Santa Monica
Milwaukee, Wisconsin 53217
(414) 964-4444

Please send me:

Tastes of Jewish Traditions	@ $26.95 each	Quantity _____	$ _____
Postage & Handling for first book	@ $4.00		$ _____
Each additional book to same address	@ $2.00		$ _____
Sales Tax (Wisconsin Residents only add $1.50)	@ $1.50 each		$ _____
		Total Enclosed	$ _____

Ship to:

Name _____ Address _____

City _____ State _____ Zip Code _____

Make checks payable to Jewish Community Center of Milwaukee

Charge to (circle one) ❑ Visa ❑ MasterCard

Signature _____

Account Number _____ Expiration Date _____

Thank you for your order.

Order on line @ www.jccmilwaukee.org

Tastes of Jewish Tradition

% Jewish Community Center of Milwaukee
6255 North Santa Monica
Milwaukee, Wisconsin 53217
(414) 964-4444

Please send me:

Tastes of Jewish Traditions	@ $26.95 each	Quantity _____	$ _____
Postage & Handling for first book	@ $4.00		$ _____
Each additional book to same address	@ $2.00		$ _____
Sales Tax (Wisconsin Residents only add $1.50)	@ $1.50 each		$ _____
		Total Enclosed	$ _____

Ship to:

Name _____ Address _____

City _____ State _____ Zip Code _____

Make checks payable to Jewish Community Center of Milwaukee

Charge to (circle one) ❑ Visa ❑ MasterCard

Signature _____

Account Number _____ Expiration Date _____

Thank you for your order.

Order on line @ www.jccmilwaukee.org